James Richard Joy

Rome and the Making of Modern Europe

James Richard Joy

Rome and the Making of Modern Europe

ISBN/EAN: 9783744773768

Printed in Europe, USA, Canada, Australia, Japan

Cover: Foto ©ninafisch / pixelio.de

More available books at **www.hansebooks.com**

Chautauqua Reading Circle Literature

ROME AND THE MAKING OF MODERN EUROPE

BY

JAMES RICHARD JOY, M.A.

FLOOD AND VINCENT
The Chautauqua-Century Press
MEADVILLE PENNA
150 FIFTH AVE. NEW YORK
1893

TO
MY WIFE

PREFACE.

In 1886-7 the author of this book prepared a primer of Roman history upon a plan devised by John H. Vincent. The volume, which was entitled *An Outline History of Rome*, was placed upon the Chautauqua reading course for the ensuing year, where it gave a considerable degree of satisfaction—perhaps quite as much as was to be expected of a sketch so brief and bony. The aim of the book had been to restrict the work to the significant events and important actors, sacrificing dramatic form and picturesque detail to the necessity of condensation.

The present work is an extension of the *Outline History*, so as to cover the historical period which bridges the gap between the Roman Empire and Modern Europe. The first six chapters are substantially a reprint of the former volume; the seventh has been rewritten; the three remaining chapters are new.

Acknowledgment should be made in this place to the large number of writers upon this period whose works have been freely consulted in the preparation of this book.

JAMES RICHARD JOY.

CONTENTS.

CHAPTER		PAGE
I.	Preliminary—Italy and the Italians—Rome and the Romans	9
II.	First Period—Rome under the Kings	30
III.	Second Period—The Roman Republic—I	52
IV.	Second Period (Continued)—The Roman Republic—II—The Punic Wars and Foreign Conquests	73
V.	Second Period (Continued)—The Roman Republic—III—The Civil Wars and the Fall of the Republic	100
VI.	Second Period (Continued)—The Roman Republic—III—From the Conspiracy of Catiline to the End of the Republic	131
VII.	Third Period—The Roman Empire from Augustus to Constantine	157
VIII.	Fourth Period—Fall of the Empire in the West—From Constantine to the First Carlovingian King of the Franks	198
IX.	Fifth Period—Europe in the Middle Ages—From the Coronation of Pipin to the Fall of Constantinople	238
X.	Conclusion — Modern Europe — From the Fall of Constantinople to the Present Time	282
	Index	303

ROME AND THE MAKING OF MODERN EUROPE.

CHAPTER I.

PRELIMINARY—ITALY AND THE ITALIANS—ROME AND THE ROMANS.

THE long, narrow peninsula of It′aly swings out from the body of Eu′rope into the Mediterra′nean Sea, tending to the eastward as it falls. Its contour on the map bears a singular and lively resemblance to a human leg and foot. The central mountain range suggests strength, and the tip of the toe, poised above the triangular island of Si′cily, suggests vigorous action. That strong peninsular limb, drawn back toward the east and ready to sweep forward toward the west, may fitly represent the Rome of history; restless, aggressive, mighty, disturbing the waters of the Mediterra′nean and sending heavy swells of war and conquest to every shore that guards the sea, and many a league beyond—to Par′thia on the Cas′pian and to Brit′ain in the Atlan′tic.

Position and contour of Italy.

The history which lies before us is not the history of this boot-shaped Ital′ian peninsula; it is the remarkable record of the rise and development of a single Ital′ian city from a position of insignificant weakness to the sovereignty, not only of It′aly, but of the world. Gre′cian history centers now in Spar′ta, now in

The history of a ruling city.

Thēbes, now in Ath′ens, now in Ma′cedon; but Ro′man history is the story of the acts and achievements of one city through twelve centuries of its growth, eminence, and decline. This single sovereign city was Rome.

The way to the study of Ro′man history lies through a knowledge of the geography of It′aly; for it is to this peninsula that Ro′man influence and authority were confined during the first five centuries of the city's existence.

It′aly is the central of the three peninsulas of southern Eu′rope, Spain lying to the west, and the Balkan′ peninsula, with Greece at its extremity, on the east. The Alps mountains, massive and lofty, cut it off from the continent, the two piers of their arch resting on the gulfs of Gen′oa and Ven′ice. On the east is the Adriat′ic, which the Ro′mans called the Upper Sea, in distinction from the Lower, or Tus′can Sea, which washed their western shores. The Iŏ′nian Sea, on the south, rolls between "the sole of the boot" and Greece, completing the natural boundaries. The extreme length of It′aly from Mount Blanc, in the northern highlands, to the southernmost point of Cala′bria, measures about seven hundred miles.

Geography of Italy.

Dimensions and area.

From the tip of the heel in Cala′bria to the tip of the toe at Rhē′gium it is two hundred miles as the crow flies. The breadth of the northern expansion is a little over three hundred miles. The ordinary width of the peninsula is about one hundred miles. The area of the country is somewhat less than one hundred thousand square miles, and is about twice that of the State of New York.

The Alps and the Ap′ennines are the only considerable mountain ranges. The former reach the height of fifteen thousand feet and present a difficult but not impassable barrier to foreign invasion. Where the Alps descend toward the sea at their southwestern end the

Mountains.

PRELIMINARY—ITALY AND ROME. 11

Ap′ennines have their beginning. This long and somewhat open chain at first trails eastward to the Adriat′ic and then turns sharply to the south, keeping the middle of the peninsula for a few hundred miles as a rocky midrib, and in the far south breaking up into a network of hills with intervening valleys. Besides these two main ranges there are a few famous volcanic summits, some wildly active, others long cold and silent. These are Æt′na, in Si′cily, and Mount Vul′tur, the Al′ban Hills, and Vesu′vius, on the mainland.

The Pā′dus, or Po—Vir′gil's "King of Rivers"—is the one large river of It′aly. With its tributaries—the Trĕ′bia, Ticī′nus, Ad′dua, and Min′cius—and the Ath′esis, it waters the great plain of Lom′bardy, as we call the flat district which lies between the Alps and the Ap′ennines. The other streams are small, and flow from the central watershed, eastward or westward, to the sea. The Adriat′ic receives the Ru′bicon, Metau′rus, Fren′to, and Au′fidus; the Mā′cra, Ar′nus, Ti′ber, Lī′ris, Voltur′nus, and Sil′arus flow into the Tus′can Sea.

<small>Rivers.</small>

Until late in the history of Rome the valley of the Po was not considered politically a part of It′aly, the northern boundary of which was not the Alps, but the Ap′ennine mountains and the water-courses Ma′cra and Ru′bicon. This extensive section, Northern, or Continental It′aly, as it is variously called, differed widely from the southern portion, or It′aly Proper, in physical features, population, and history. Northern It′aly included three distinct regions: Ligu′ria, on the west, skirting the Gulf of Gen′oa, Venē′tia, eastward, on the Gulf of Ven′ice, and between them Gal′lia Cisalpi′na,* or Hither Gaul, abound-

<small>Northern Italy: Divisions and cities.</small>

<small>* Gal′lia Cisalpi′na means "Gaul this side the Alps," or Hither Gaul, as distinguished from Gal′lia Transalpi′na, or Farther Gaul, corresponding roughly to the modern France. Cisal′pine Gaul was likewise called Gal′lia Toga′ta, because its people might wear the Ro′man robe or toga. The Transal′pine Gauls were *bracca′ti*—that is, "clad in breeches."</small>

ing in fertile fields, populous cities, and brave men. Among the towns of Northern It'aly were Augus'ta Taurino'rum and Gen'ua, in Ligu'ria; Pata'vium and Aquile'ja, in Vene'tia; and in Cisal'pine Gaul, Vercel'læ, Mediolā'nium, Tici'num, Cremo'na, Man'tua, Bono'nia, Placen'tia, Luc'ca, and Raven'na.

The country south of the Ru'bicon was It'aly Proper of the Ro'mans. It was made up of two general divisions, Central and Lower It'aly.

Central It'aly extended from the little rivers Ma'cra and Ru'bicon, on the north, to the Sil'arus and Fren'to, on the south, and from sea to sea. The central mountain range and tribal differences subdivided its territory into six districts. On the Tus'can seacoast were Etru'ria, La'tium and Campa'nia, and in the highlands were Um'bria, Picē'num, and Sam'nium, as well as the Sa'bine territory, sometimes reckoned as a seventh district.

Central Italy.

Etru'ria lay in the well-watered plain which was left by the Ap'ennines as they bowed toward the east. Its inhabitants, the Etrus'cans, were already an ancient race when Rome was founded. They had made progress in civilization and the arts, and their fleets were strong in the seas of the west. Lake Trasimē'nus was in their territory, as were the towns Volater'ræ, Arrē'tium, Clu'sium, Cæ're, and Ve'ii, long a rival of Rome.

Etruria.

Just south of Etru'ria, and almost midway of the peninsula, lay La'tium, a narrow strip of hill and plain between the Ti'ber and the Li'ris. Here, in a league of thirty communities, dwelt in very early times the Lat'ins. Here, also, were the Æ'qui, Her'nici, and Vol'sci, of slightly different blood and language. Prominent among the Lat'in towns were Al'ba Lon'ga, Ti'bur, Prænes'te, Mintur'næ, An'tium, Arpi'num, Fregel'læ, and pre-eminent

Latium.

among all the towns of La'tium, indeed, of all the world, Ro'ma (Rome).

Still farther south was Campā'nia, whose sunny skies and fertile hillsides early attracted colonists, and in the later days
Campania. of Ro'man luxury filled it with the costly villas of senators and knights. Here was Cu'mæ, where the Sib'yl had guarded her magic books; Ba'iæ, in whose waters emperors delighted to bathe; Cap'ua, whose pleasures made Han'nibal forget his oath; Misē'num, the headquarters of the imperial fleet; Neap'olis, on its famous bay; and near at hand Herculā'neum and Pompe'ii, under the threatening brow of Vesu'vius.

The district known as Um'bria extended from the Adriat'ic over the crown of the Ap'ennines to the borders of Etru'ria
Umbria and Picenum. and La'tium. The Ti'ber had its sources among these Um'brian hills, and within these borders were the towns of Arīm'inum, Spolē'tium, Nar'nia, and Sentī'num. Picē'num was a land of peace and plenty lying along the adjacent coast. Its people were of the Sam'nite stock, and near them lived the related Mar'si, Pælig'ni, and Frentā'ni. In the Pi'cene territory were Ancō'na, a Ro'man naval station, and As'culum, a fortress whose reduction long taxed the strength of Rome.

The Sam'nites occupied a range of the interior highlands and a seaboard strip on the Adriat'ic. They were hardy and
Samnium and the Sabines. frugal, like the early Ro'mans, and retained these simple virtues and the military spirit which sprang from them long after the Ro'man type had lost its best characteristics. The neighboring and kindred tribe of Sa'bines occupying the crest of the Ap'ennines northwest of La'tium, was one of the first to come in contact with the rising city, and the Sam'nites themselves were the most persistent enemies of Ro'man dominion in It'aly. Rea'te,

Amiter′num, and Cu′res were the best-known towns of the Sa′bine land. And Rome had more reason than have we to remember the names of the Sam′nite fortresses, Corfin′ium, Sul′mo, Boviā′num, Benevĕn′tum, and especially Cau′dium, the scene of a notable disaster.

Lower It′aly embraced all the peninsula south of the Sil′arus and Fren′to rivers. Its districts were four: Apū′lia, Calā′bria,
Lower Italy. Lucā′nia, and Brut′tium. So many colonies from Greece sprang up in the warm nooks of this lovely coast that the whole region received the name of Mag′na Græ′cia, or Great Greece. Apu′lia was a land of shepherds and herdsmen. Can′næ, a battlefield on the Au′fidus, was the most famous of its plains. Here, too, near the same river and below the silent crater of Mount Vul′tur, was Venŭ′sia, the birthplace of the poet Hor′ace. Calā′bria, the heel of It′aly, had both grazing lands and farmsteads. Two of its towns are prominent in history: Taren′tum, the Greek colony which vainly withstood the power of Rome, and Brundis′ium, (the modern Brin′disi) then as now a chief port of embarkation for travelers bound from It′aly to the O′rient. The broad Taren′tine Gulf rolled between Calā′bria and Brut′tium, "the toe," and Luca′nia, "the instep" of It′aly. In Luca′nia were numerous Greek towns—Pæs′tum, Metapon′tum, and Heraclē′a. Syb′aris, whose effeminating luxury contributed the word "sybarite" to our vocabulary, was in Brut′tium, as were Crō′ton, Lo′cri, and, at the very tiptoe, commanding the Sicil′ian straits, Rhĕ′gium.

At an early date there were no Ro′man islands, but the authority of Rome at length brought the neighboring Si′cily
Italian islands. (Trinā′cria), Sardin′ia, and Cor′sica within the Ital′ian domain, together with the islets and groups El′ba, Mal′ta, Cap′ri, Lip′aræ, and Ægŭ′sæ. The three larger islands furnished a share of the Ro′man

breadstuffs, and Si′cily, which had been settled by both Greeks and Carthagin′ians before the rise of Rome, had many thriving towns—Messa′na on the straits, Cat′ana at the foot of Æt′na, Agrigen′tum, Lilybæ′um, Drep′anum, Panor′mus—names which will occur again in the narrative, and Syr′acuse, a splendid capital for whose possession three empires made Si′cily their battleground.

The extent of the peninsula from north to south, and the large amount of high land included within its boundaries, secure to It′aly a great diversity of climate. Its northern boundary is on the parallel of Quebec′, in Can′ada, and the city of Rich′mond, in Virgin′ia, has the same latitude as its southern extremity; yet from several causes the differences of heat and cold are less than this comparison would suggest. For the high and massive mountain-walls modify the climate, and the surrounding seas temper and moisten the winds which blow to It′aly across their surface. In consequence the plains of upper It′aly enjoy a temperate and generally healthful climate. The Alps shut in the Po valley from the hard winters of Central Eu′rope; but chilling blasts sometimes swoop down from their icy summits to render summer days comfortless. The strip of seacoast between the Ap′ennines and the Gulf of Gen′oa—the modern Rivie′ra—is a winter paradise. Central It′aly—the It′aly of Rome and La′tium—is in the latitude of Boston, but its winters are mild and the hot season is not intolerable. Little snow falls except in the highlands, and the rivers seldom freeze. From Campa′nia southward the land enjoys almost perpetual summer. Magna Græ′cia is semitropical in its warmth and moisture, and Si′cily has a well-earned reputation for unclouded skies. The frequent references of the Lat′in poets to nipping frosts, snow-capped hills, and ice-bound rivers have prompted the question

Climate of Italy.

whether the climate of ancient It′aly was not more severe than that of the same districts in modern times; and it is now believed that the disappearance of the forests, which in antiquity covered a large part of the peninsula, has affected both the temperature and the amount of rainfall.

There have always been drawbacks from the pleasures of life in It′aly. From the days of the foundation of Rome the lowlands of La′tium and other regions have been haunted by malarial germs. The Ro′man Campagn′a was, and is, a plague-spot; the marsh lands of Etru′ria and the stagnant lagoons of Vene′tia poisoned the air at certain seasons of the year, and at times the Siroc′co, a burning wind from the Af′rican deserts, swept across the sea laden with fever and blight. But these were the only exceptions to the general beauty and comfort of the land. It was the "sunny It′aly"

Productions. that we know. The vine and olive have flourished and come to perfection on its hillsides since the early days when, as the Ro′mans thought, Sat′urn, the father of the gods, set them there. Besides the rich olive oil and delicate wines the land yielded the ruder staples—wheat, flax, and hemp. Orchard and forest fruits were abundant and various. The large fruit of the chestnut tree was an important feature of the yearly harvest, and lemons, oranges, figs, almonds, and dates were plentiful. The uplands were peculiarly adapted to the profitable raising of sheep and oxen, and agriculture or grazing was the natural industry of the Ital′ian.

The clear and brilliant atmosphere gives to the Ital′ian skies a richness of color which has always been the admiration of poets and the despair of painters. The omni-
Italy and Greece. present mountains and the never-distant sea lend to the landscape a living and ever-changing charm. The bays and inlets of the south, together with the tangle of the adjacent mountains, present a resemblance to the

Grecian landscape which could not have been lost upon the impressionable colonists who settled there from Eubœ'a, Meg'ara, and the Pel'oponnĕ'sus. Elsewhere the resemblance to Greece is noticeably wanting. The shores are low and regular. The mountains seldom approach the coast, and their general form is such that they do not form partition walls to shut up cities to themselves, like the Greek cantons, where every rock-walled valley was a sovereign state. It has been truthfully said that Greece and It'aly, though parallel, lay back to back; for the life and movement of the former were earliest and oftenest directed eastward from a score of harbor-towns by means of the Ægĕ'an islands—stepping-stones to the hospitable shores of A'sia. But on the side toward Greece It'aly had but two harbors, Anco'na and Brundis'ium. Rome, Gen'ua, and Neap'olis faced the setting sun, and the Ro'man armies had proved their prowess against Si'cily, Sardin'ia, and Car'thage before the first Ro'man trireme crossed the Io'nian Sea to plant the Ro'man standard on Hellen'ic soil.

The first inhabitants of It'aly of whom anything is known were the Iapyg'ians, who entered the peninsula from the north and retreated southward before successive waves of immigration. A few indecipherable inscriptions in their language remain; but in the Ro'man times they had ceased to be a nation of any strength or influence, having lost their individuality probably by blending it with the stronger Greek race which colonized their territory and reduced them to subjection. The Ital'ians who followed were of the same Ar'yan or In'do-Europĕ'an family as the Iapyg'ians. The Ar'yans are supposed to have lived before the dawn of history, perhaps in Eu'rope, perhaps on one of the great table-lands of Central A'sia. Thence from time to time, as their limits became too narrow for their necessities, colonies set out; not

The peopling of Italy.

Italians of Indo-European stock.

a few persons to found a town, but men, women, and children by the million to find homes and plant nations. These successive throbs of immigration were doubtless centuries apart, and these floods of people deluged both In'dia and Eu'rope. There is no literary record of these migrations. They took place before the days of writing, and no intelligible tradition has come down from those misty days. But the scientific comparison of the ancient languages has enabled scholars to group these nations in families and to calculate the bond of relationship between them. Thus it has been proved that the Ital'ians were closely related to the Hellēn'es or Greeks; that in their westward journeyings from the first home in Asia the two nations were in company long enough to acquire certain common traits of character, to practice similar customs, and in some cases to employ the same words to express their thoughts. A probable route of this supposed migration lay through A'sia Mi'nor, across the Bos'phorus, and through Thrāce. Here the Hellēn'es are thought to have turned southward to occupy their peninsula and to give it renown, while their former fellow-travelers moved on slowly toward the northwest, doubling the head of the Adriat'ic in the lapse of centuries and pouring down into the broad prairie-lands of the Po. The ages which had intervened since their separation from the Greeks had wrought changes in the Ital'ian character and language, and it was a stern, hardy, and unimaginative race that peopled It'aly, pushing the gentle Iapyg'ians before them.

There were marked differences among the Ital'ians themselves. Slight but essential variations in their use of the common language show plainly that the stock was divided. One part, composed of the Um'brians and Sam'nites, and hence called the Um'bro-Sabel'lian branch (including also Sa'bines and Os'cans), found

Branches of Italian stock.

its home among the mountains of Central and Southern It′aly, and spread thence to the Adriat′ic coast. The other branch,

Latins. the Lat′ins, dwelt in the hill-encircled plain on the east side of the peninsula south of the Ti′ber. It was, perhaps, less numerous than its congener of the adjacent highlands, but it was more fortunate in its location. For within its territory and of its people was Rome, whose citizens raised the Lat′in name and tongue to the first rank in It′aly.

Besides the retiring Iapyg′ians and the conquering Ital′ians, a third important race, the Etrus′can, had its home in It′aly,

Etruscans. coming whence and when is only to be conjectured. These people were probably Ar′yans, like their neighbors, but differently developed and leaving A′sia at another era. Their resemblance to the Greeks and Ital′ians was remote and indistinct. A credible theory is that they came into the peninsula by the land route and settled in the Po valley until expelled by stronger invaders. They then crossed the Ap′ennines and made their home in the district north of La′tium, between the Ti′ber and Ar′nus, which is still called Tus′cany, a reminiscence of their name. Here in early times they had a league of twelve strong communities, and it was their strength and superior civilization which placed the first serious check upon the power of Rome. They were ingenious metal workers, and their architects invented the arch. Etru′ria attained its prime about five centuries before Christ. It was then a naval power, and its fleets met those of Greece and Car′thage in equal combat. But the following century saw its decline, and by rapid degrees its territory and authority were acquired by Rome.

In the earliest historic times two other nations appeared in It′aly—the Gauls or Celts in the north, and the Greeks in the south. These Celts were an offshoot of the same

Ar′yan stock, and spread over Western Eu′rope before the advent of the German′ic tribes. The Gauls took full possession of the Po valley and gained for it the name of Cisal′pine Gaul. By degrees they lost their rudeness and, having adopted the Ro′man civilization, in the time of Cæ′sar they were admitted to the full dignities of Ro′man citizenship.

<small>Gauls in Italy.</small>

Unlike the four first-named peoples, Iapyg′ians, Ital′ians, Etrus′cans, and Celts, who entered It′aly through the Al′pine passes on the north, the Greeks came in at the south and by sea. Still, unlike the others, they came not as a migrating nation, but as a succession of colonies sent out to relieve the overflowing cities of Greece or as commercial enterprises. The date of their earliest settlements is in the vicinity of 1000 B. C., when some prehistoric commotion, possibly "the Tro′jan War," sent many a crew of mariners in quest of new adventures. The progress of colonization was most active in the eighth and seventh centuries before our era, and Greek cities sprang up thickly along the southern and western coasts as far north as Cū′mæ and the Bay of Na′ples. Temples, theaters, and schools arose wherever the Greeks found an abiding place, and the wealth and extravagant luxury of Mag′na Græ′cia were proverbial at a time when the name of Rome was unknown beyond its narrow circle of Lat′in villages. But the Greek cities, with the fatal political weakness of their race, preferred individual independence to union against a common enemy; and so it happened that, when the struggle for supremacy came, the culture and wealth of these elegant towns availed them nothing against the rude strength of the Ro′man commonwealth.

<small>Greeks.</small>

What, then, was Rome, and what manner of men were the Ro′mans that, one after the other, the several races of the peninsula bowed at her bidding? The remainder of this

PRELIMINARY—ITALY AND ROME.

volume will be an answer to this inquiry. But the answer will perhaps be clearer if the student will bear in mind the physical features of "the Eternal City" and the characteristics of the Ro'mans themselves.

Rome was on the west side of It'aly and about midway of its length. The city was built on a cluster of low hills in La'tium, on the left bank of the river Ti'ber, a few miles below its junction with the A'nio, and twenty-two miles from its mouth at Os'tia, on the Tus'can Sea. As it approaches the site of Rome the Ti'ber turns sharply toward the east, and then as sharply doubles back toward the west, thus describing a rude S. In the upper loop of the S is a broad plain on which the modern city, the capital of It'aly, is mainly built; but in the early times this was the parade-ground of the army, the muster-field of the populace, and was named the Cam'pus Mar'tius (Field of Mars), from the Ro'man god of war. Opposite the lower bend of the river are the seven hills of the ancient city. Almost on the bank are the Cap'itoline, Pal'atine, and Av'entine, and farther away, separated from these as by a hollow, like the palm of a mighty hand, rise four fingerlike eminences, the Cæ'lian, Es'quiline, Vim'inal, and Quir'inal. The sacred Cap'itoline bore the Arx, or citadel, and the splendid temple of Ju'piter. Up the slope of this hill moved the famous processions of victorious generals, and from the precipitous Tarpe'ian Rock on its water-side criminals were hurled to destruction. At the base of the hill was the Tullia'num, a dungeon in which, among other noted prisoners, St. Peter is said to have been confined. On the adjoining Pal'atine Hill were the colossal buildings which served the emperors Augus'tus and Nĕ'ro for a residence, and which have given the name palace (*palā'tium*) to any house fit for a king. Between this pile of palaces and the Av'entine—the

Topography of Rome.

The seven hills.

people's hill—was the Cir′cus Max′imus, where 200,000 persons might witness the sword-fights, races, and rough sports which constituted the Ro′man games. The low ground between these three hills and the river-bank was—and indeed is to this day—drained by an ancient arched sewer, the Cloā′ca Max′ima, and was assigned to the produce and cattle markets.

The principal market and meeting place of the city, however, was the Ro′man Fŏ′rum, which was situated at the base of the Cap′itoline Hill, in the hollow of that great thumbless Ro′man hand. The Fo′rum was, in fact, an open public square about 750 feet long by 250 broad. As a market place of the early city it naturally became the scene of public assembly for many important purposes. A space near one end, raised and cut off from the rest, was the ComI′tium, or official assembly-room of the citizens, and between this and the Fo′rum proper was the rostrum, or speaker's stand, from which the magistrates addressed the citizens or the populace. As the city grew in wealth and power this public square was adorned with noble buildings. On one or two sides the Fo′rum was lined with shops, but on the south was a row of law-courts and temples, among which the shrine of the goddess Ves′ta was the most notable. Past the Fo′rum ran the Vī′a Sa′cra (Sacred Street), by which the triumphal processions approached the Capitol. On the opposite of the square was the Cu′ria, or Senate Chamber. The world centered in Rome, and Rome centered in the Fo′rum, where, in the time of the empire, stood "the golden milestone," toward which all roads led and from which all distances in the realm were measured.

Roman Forum.

In this same hollow of the hills was the Subur′ra, the meanest and most crowded quarter of the city, and on its border, in bitter proximity, was the Cari′næ, the dwelling place of the richest and proudest of the citizens. In the

adjacent lowlands, but nearer the slope of the Es′quiline,
still stands the ruined Colossē′um, the remains of
the Flā′vian Amphithē′ater, from whose stone
benches 87,000 cruel Ro′mans have looked on
while Christian women were "butchered to make a Ro′man
holiday." The four outer hills seem to have been less thickly
settled than the others; but in the period of the city's
splendor they, too, were covered with magnificent baths and
public parks and gardens. Two hills, not to be included in
the famous seven, were situated on the right bank of the
Ti′ber. These are the Vat′ican, now occupied as the papal
residence, and the Janic′ulus, a Ro′man fortress. Modern
Rome has a population of 300,000. In the reign of the
Emperor Augus′tus it had 2,000,000 inhabitants.

The Colosseum of Flavius.

How did Rome become so populous and powerful? The
answer to this question does not appear at first sight. The
geographical situation possessed no pre-eminent
advantages, such as set apart Constantino′ple,
Alexan′dria, Lon′don, New York, Chica′go, and
San Francis′co for centers of trade and population. The
harbors of It′aly are at Ven′ice, Na′ples, Leg′horn, Gen′oa,
not on the bank of the Ti′ber; and Rome was the natural
market place of little La′tium only, by no means the largest or
most fertile division of the peninsula. It cannot be doubted,
therefore, that the wealth and commercial rank of Rome were
the consequences, and not the causes, of the city's political
supremacy. The elements of Rome's political strength are to
be sought in the character of her people.

Source of Rome's greatness.

During the long period covered by "the making of Rome"
the Ro′mans had six distinguishing national
traits: they were Rude, Superstitious, Proud,
Stern, and Steadfast, and possessed a real Genius
for Law and Government.

Six characteristics of Romans.

Rudeness and simplicity marked their manners and customs. Agriculture, war, politics, and little else, concerned the citizens. In refinement of thought and action, in art and literature, they were the late imitators of the Greeks, whose effeminacy they affected to despise, but whose graces they assiduously copied. Their national games were coarse and brutal. Chariot races, combats of men with wild beasts and with each other, were to the Ro'man what the competitions in athletics and in poetry, rhetoric, music, and the drama were to the Greek. The foreign conquests, which at length filled the city with public and private plunder, put an end to this age of simplicity. The frugality and the steady habits of the early Ro'man gave place to lavish extravagance and gross dissipation, which had a potent influence in the city's ultimate ruin.

<small>Roman rudeness.</small>

Ro'man superstition is shown in the religion of the state. Not until they had dipped into the fanciful mythology of the Greeks did the Ro'mans think of their gods as possessing human form and being subject to human passions. The divinities were many, and represented the powers of nature as well as the interests of the household and the nation. Ju'piter was the sky, and ruled over all gods and men. Ju'no, his feminine counterpart, was the guardian of motherhood. Ja'nus was god of light and beginnings. Miner'va was wise, Mars warlike, and Ves'ta the patron of the State. Besides Cē'res, Sat'urn, Tel'lus, Lī'ber, and others of almost equal rank, there were lesser divinities to attend to the varied activities of business and domestic life. Every person had his protecting genius, and in every Ro'man household the good spirits of the home (*la'res* and *pena'tes*) were the objects of daily offering and prayer. In the Roman mind religion was a contract, and worship was the human share in the bargain. The worshiper

<small>Roman superstition, religion, and mythology.</small>

gave vows, prayers, festivals, and fasts, and in return demanded as his right the favor of the gods. The State took
<small>Priesthoods.</small> charge of the religion, and supported a complex system of priestly associations (*collē'gia*) to superintend the religious observances. There were the white-capped Fla'mens, who officiated in the temples, and the six Ves'tal Virgins, who kept the eternal fire on the hearth of the State in the shrine of Ves'ta. Other associations were the Au'gurs, the Pontif'ices, Fetiā'les, etc. The Au'gurs consulted the will of the gods by observing the actions of certain sacred birds, the Pontif'ices interpreted the omens which the Au'gurs observed, and thus had great political power, since, by declaring the gods unpropitious, a public assembly might be dissolved, an election postponed, or the passage of an obnoxious law prevented. The Pon'tifex Max'imus—whose title is still borne by the Ro'man pope—was the head of the State religion. The Fetiā'les were the envoys or heralds of the State; they protected the sanctity of treaties and were the agents of the Senate in fixing boundaries and in declaring war. The Harus'pices, like the Au'gurs, consulted the gods, but in a stranger fashion. It was their function to seek for omens in the entrails of the sheep and oxen slaughtered for the sacrifices. They were Etrus'can soothsayers who came to Rome to ply their vocation and afterwards entered the service of the State. This religion, with its gloomy rites and with its superstitious faith in omens, sufficed for the days of unreasoning faith, but it had completely lost its hold upon the thinking classes before the advent of Christianity.

The Pride of a Ro'man noble or patrician was colossal. The
<small>Roman pride.</small> internal history of the State through the first four centuries revolves about the resistance of a few patrician families to any encroachment upon their monopoly of religious and political power. The com-

mons or plebeians were not legally citizens, and it was the fixed policy of the patricians that they should not be. No plebeian might hold office, and the intermarriage of the two orders brought disgrace and social degradation to the patrician, whether man or woman. At last the barrier fell, and the class pride gave way to the common pride in citizenship, which the consolidated Ro′mans guarded as jealously from the Ital′ians and provincials as the patricians had fortified it against the plebs.

To his Rude manners, his Superstitious mind, and his Haughty demeanor the Ro′man added a Sternness of spirit which at times deserves no better name than cruelty. Their history abounds in anecdotes of magistrates who sentence their sons to death, of generals who devote themselves to death to save their armies, of noble youths who throw away their lives to propitiate the offended gods, or who hold their right hands in the flames to prove to an alien king that torture has no terrors for a Ro′man. "Callousness to human suffering was a Ro′man virtue," and the pages of history are red with Ro′man slaughterings.

Roman sternness.

"As faithful as a Ro′man sentinel" is the world's highest tribute to fidelity, and, in truth, the Pompe′ian soldier who was pelted to death at his post by the fiery hail of Vesu′vius grandly typifies the Steadfastness of the Ro′man character. It may have been the outcome of the stern discipline which the father in the family, the consul in the city, and the general in the army consistently enforced, or it may have been an inborn virtue; but this splendid trait stands out in every relation of their common life and at every turn of their history. In politics, under the name of "conservatism," it was this faculty of standing by settled principles which made the Ro′man constitution so slow

Roman steadfastness.

in its development and so stable in its strength ; and in war it was this same firmness of purpose which enabled the single city to maintain itself against Greek, Celt′ic, Carthagin′ian, and Teuton′ic invasions, and, without the aid of conspicuous generals or remarkable statesmen, to drive the invaders out of It′aly, pursue them to their homes, and vanquish them.

Couple with this pertinacity of the Ro′mans their exquisite Political Faculty and seek no farther for the sources of the Ro′man power. This faculty is expressed in their respect for law and their correct understanding and application of the principles of justice ; it is pre-eminently exhibited in the skill with which they adapted the constitution to the changing conditions imposed by the extension of the Ro′man realm. These changes did not take place in popular convulsions, rending the State, but came through long periods of agitation, and finally as the result of compromise. Finally the whole civilized world formed a single well-welded State, and the Ro′man law became the basis of Europe′an jurisprudence.

Roman political genius.

From this description of the land and the people we pass on to their history.

ANALYSIS OF CHAPTER I.

Preliminary: The peninsula and the city, 9.*
I. *Geography of Italy*, 10–17:
    Dimensions and area, 10.
    Physical features; mountains, 10, rivers, 11.
      Political Divisions, 11-14:
        Northern Italy, 11 ;
          Venetia, Liguria, Cisalpine Gaul, 11.
        Central Italy, 12-14:
          Etruria, 12 ; Latium, 12 ; Campania, 13 ; Umbria, 13.
          Picenum, 13 ; Samnium, 13 ; Sabine Land, 13.
        Lower Italy, 14 :

---

* The numbers refer to the pages of this volume.

            Apulia, Calabria, Lucania, Bruttium, 14.
     Islands, 14.
     Climate and productions, 15, 16.
     Contrast with Greece, 16.
II. *People of Italy*, 17-20:
     Iapygians, 17.
     Italians, 17-19:
           Umbro-Sabellians, 18; Latins, 19.
     Etruscans, 19.
     Gauls or Celts, 19.
     Greeks, 20.
III. *Topography of Rome*, 21-23:
     The Seven Hills, 21.
     The Roman Forum, 22.
     Districts and buildings, 22, 23.
IV. *Six Elements of Roman Character*, 23-27:
     Rudeness, 24.
     Superstition, 24:
           Religion and priesthoods, 24, 25.
     Pride, 25.
     Sternness, 26.
     Steadfastness, 26.
     Political genius, 27.

REVIEW EXERCISE.

Italy and the Italians—Rome and the Romans.

1. How does the Italian peninsula typify Rome?
2. What distinguishes Roman history from that of other states?
3. State the dimensions and area of Italy.
4. Name two mountain ranges, and two famous volcanoes.
5. Name three important Italian rivers.
6. What does the name "Gallia Cisalpina" signify?
7. Name the states of Northern Italy, and one city in each.
8. Name the states of Central Italy, and one city in each.
9. Name the Lower Italian states and one important city or locality in each.
10. In what part of Italy was Rome?
11. Name three Italian islands.
12. What are the characteristics of the climate of Italy?
13. What are the chief natural productions of Italy?
14. How did Italy and Greece lie "back to back"?
15. What name is given to the earliest people of Italy?

16. To what family of nations did the Italians belong?
17. Who were the Latins?
18. Who were the Etruscans?
19. What portion of Italy was settled by the Celts?
20. What and where was Magna Græcia?
21. Locate Rome, and name and place its hills.
22. Describe the Roman Forum.
23. Where must the secret of Roman greatness be sought?
24. Name the six leading traits of Roman character.
25. Give a brief account of the Roman religion.

CHAPTER II.

FIRST PERIOD.

Rome Under the Kings. (244 Years.) 753–509 B. C.

Difficulties of tracing ancient history. Whoever attempts to trace the history of an ancient State must come to a point in the remote past of which no written records survive. Yet the student of Ro′man history finds a detailed account of what are professedly the acts of the people of the ancient city from the very day of its foundation. The record which confronts us is one which the Ro′mans themselves made and believed. Their later historians used it with little doubt of its authenticity. Their poets looked to it for material with which to adorn their patriotic verse. Even modern scholars seem to have accepted its statements as substantial truth until a little more than a century ago. The doubts which were then first quietly suggested were put forward in more positive form by the Ger′man historian, Nie′buhr (1776–1831), who proved, to the satisfaction of himself and many others, that the common account of the beginnings of Rome was rather poetry than history, and rested only upon a slight basis of truth. Recent investigation has modified Nie′buhr's conclusions, and the substance of modern belief is

The modern theory. this: That the history of Rome previous to the fourth century before Christ is a fabric in which certain main outlines are true, while the masses of detail which make up the narrative are either greatly exaggerated or entirely imaginary. The argument for the rejection of the greater part of the story as it stands is unanswerable. It is rich in incredible marvels and miracles, its chronology is involved and inconsistent, and it relates as facts certain undoubted fables borrowed from the legends of other Ar'yan nations—or, rather, common to all of that family of nations. Yet the sub-stratum of truth which underlies this quicksand of invention forbids the historian to disregard it. The legends will be given here at such length as the limits of the volume permit, and with the understanding that they are not offered as genuine history. The fanciful narrative will be followed by the reconstructed story.

The legends ran in this wise:

After the Greeks, under Agamem'non, had taken the city of Troy, in A'sia Mi'nor,—eleven hundred years before the Christian era—Æne'as, the son of Pri'am, the Tro'jan king, escaped, with many companions, and came by sea to the western coast of It'aly, where he founded Lavin'ium, on the shore of La'tium. For three hundred years this Tro'jan line of kings ruled the La'tian or "Lat'in" tribes, having their royal seat at Al'ba Lon'ga, the "long white" city on the Al'ban Mount. In time two sons, Nu'mitor and Amū'lius, were born to Sil'vius Pro'cas, king of the Al'bans. The latter usurped his brother's throne and consecrated his brother's daughter, Rhē'a Sil'via, a vestal virgin, in order to extirpate the line of Nū'mitor. But when, by the war god Mars, the vestal became the mother of two sons, their cruel uncle had the babes thrown into the Ti'ber. The river was swollen with the spring floods and the boys floated ashore unharmed, and lodged in the branches of a figtree on the inundated meadow at the foot of a hill called Palati'nus. A she-wolf took pity on them and nourished them with her whelps. In these strange surroundings the

The Legendary History. Trojans at Alba Longa.

twins were discovered by a shepherd of those regions, who adopted them out of pity. The boys were named Rom′ulus and Rĕ′mus, and lived among the herdsmen until they reached manhood, when, having discovered their origin, they killed their wicked uncle, and re-established their grandfather, Nu′mitor, on the Al′ban throne. But the young princes had ambitions of their own, and, soon collecting a little colony, they founded a new city on the Pal′atine Hill which Rom′ulus, favored by the gods, called from his own name, Rome. April 21, 753 B. C., was the accepted date of this momentous act. The slighted Re′mus showed his derision of the puny defenses of his brother's city by leaping over its walls; whereat Rom′ulus, in his anger, slew him, declaring that a similar fate awaited all future assailants of the city. On the neighboring Cap′itoline Hill Rom′ulus opened an "asylum" or refuge for the oppressed and discontented people of the surrounding country; and as wives were wanting for the new settlers the Sa′bines of the neighboring town of Cu′res were bidden to a religious festival at Rome; the Ro′man brigands seized the Sa′bine women while the husbands and brothers were witnessing the games. In the war which followed a Ro′man girl, Tarpe′ia, betrayed the city in return for "what the Sa′bine soldiers wore on their arms." But when she had let the Sa′bines inside the capitol they crushed the traitress with their heavy shields; for these also did they wear on their arms as well as the heavy bangles of gold which had tempted the maiden. Thanks to the intervention of the Sa′bine women, this war ended in the union of the two tribes, and until his death the Sa′bine chief reigned jointly with the Ro′man.

After this Rom′ulus framed a constitution for the state. A number of families were set apart to be the "patri′cians," or nobles, to distinguish them from the "plebe′ians," or commons, who, though dwelling in the city, had no political power. The patricians were divided into three tribes—Ram′nes, Ti′ties, and Lu′ceres—each tribe being composed of ten wards or *cu′riæ*. From the wisest patricians one hundred were chosen to form an advisatory council, or Senate, to assist the king when called upon for their opinion, and from the younger nobles was levied the first legion—an army of 3,000 foot and 300 horse. When the new constitution had been put in working order the gods caught up Rom′ulus from the sight of the people, but his name was revered, and he was worshiped as a divinity ever afterwards under the name of Quirī′nus, on the Quir′inal Hill.

Constitution of Romulus.

The throne was vacant for a year before the Senate selected a worthy successor to the founder of the city. The choice fell upon a Sa′bine named Nŭ′ma Pompĭl′ius, whose consort, the nymph Egĕ′ria, aided him in his especial work of teaching the people the principles of morals and religion. He erected a temple to Ves′ta, the goddess of the home, and trained his subjects to be peaceful and pious. During the forty-three years of his reign the city was prosperous and happy.

Second King, Numa Pompilius.

Tul′lus Hostil′ius, the third king, was a great warrior. It was in his time that Rome began her conquests. The first struggle was with the mother city, Al′ba Lon′ga. In this war three Ro′man and three Al′ban brothers, the Hora′tii and the Curia′tii, fought as champions for their respective armies, and by a notorious stratagem the Ro′mans won after two of the Hora′tii had already fallen. In the end Al′ba was taken and burned, Rome succeeding to the older city's commanding place among the Lat′in towns. The warrior-king was rendered impious by his

Third King, Tullus Hostilius.

victories, and, although he fought stoutly for Rome against both the Etrus'cans and the Sa'bines, the offended gods destroyed him by a thunderbolt in the thirty-third year of his reign.

The fourth monarch in the line was An'cus Mar'tius, the descendant and disciple of the holy Nu'ma. He was both brave and good. Under him the gods were reverenced and the boundaries of the city were enlarged.

Fourth King, Ancus Martius.

He extended its authority still farther among the Lat'in towns, and fortified the Janic'ulum Hill on the right bank of the Ti'ber as a stronghold against Etrus'can attack. The houses of the city spread over the Av'entine, now that his victories brought so many new residents to Rome, and to its mouth the Ti'ber became a Ro'man river.

Of the first four rulers of the city two had been of Ro'man, two of Sa'bine blood. The fifth king was Etrus'can. Lû'cumo, a man whose Greek father had migrated from Cor'inth to the Etrus'can town of Tarquin'ii, removed to Rome in the days of An'cus Mar'tius

Fifth King, Tarquinius Priscus.

with Tan'aquil, his able wife. Prophetic intimations of coming glory were not wanting, and, Romanizing his foreign name to Lu'cius Tarquin'ius, the newcomer took hold of public affairs with an energy and wisdom which won the approval of the king. An'cus made the foreigner the guardian of his young sons, and at their royal father's death the Senate preferred the guardian to his wards and put the scepter in the hands of this Lu'cius Tarquin'ius, known in history as Tarquin'ius Pris'cus, or "Tar'quin the Ancient." He showed himself a worthy follower of An'cus. His prowess in battle overcame the Etrus'cans, who sent to him the golden crown, the scepter, the purple robe, the ivory chair, and the *fas'ces*, which remained forever the emblems of Ro'man authority. To adapt the old constitution to the needs of the new metropolis the king doubled the number of senators and of the patrician tribes, and to make the city worthy of its rank he established annual games in the Cir′cus Max′imus, set apart the Fo′rum for a public market and meeting place, built the massive stone sewer, the Cloä′ca Max′ima, which still drains the low ground between the hills, and commenced the erection of a temple of Ju′piter on the Cap′itoline. Here the workmen dug up a human skull (*ca′put*), which was interpreted to mean that this spot was to be the capital of the world. Some of the ancient shrines were torn down to clear a space for the new temple; but the gods of Youth and of Boundaries resisted all attempts to remove them, and their chapels were left undisturbed, in token that the city should continually renew its vigorous youth and its boundaries should remain inviolate.

Tarquin′ius was an able ruler, but the sons of An′cus could not forget that his influence with the Senate had cost them the throne to which they had a fancied claim. Moreover, as the king waxed old they perceived that Ser′vius Tul′lius, the son of a slave-girl of the palace, had found favor in his sight. In their jealous rage they had the aged king assassinated; but before they could profit by their crime Tan′aquil, the sagacious queen dowager, had thwarted their plans. She addressed the people from the palace-steps, telling them that her husband had been attacked and dangerously wounded, and that Ser′vius Tul′lius had the royal warrant to conduct the business of the kingdom until the monarch's recovery. Although coming to the throne in this irregular manner Ser′vius gradually won to himself the support of both citizens and Senate. He was a statesmanlike ruler, and, apart from his campaigns against the Etrus′cans, his labors were those of peace. In his time a wall was built inclosing the seven famous hills. But it is as a

Sixth King, Servius Tullius.

political reformer that this king is best remembered. His lowly birth seems to have given him sympathy with the plebeians, for it was by his constitution that they were first admitted to any share, however slight, in the government or defense of the city. Ser'vius abolished the three patrician tribes and redivided all the people, gentle and simple, into four tribes. Furthermore, and far more memorable, was his organization of the people into "classes" and "centuries" for military and political purposes. Admission to these classes depended upon the amount of property which an individual possessed, and was entirely independent of blood nobility. The wealthiest young men were chosen for cavalry duty, and were called *eq'uites* (horsemen, or knights). When the people were called together to vote upon any public matter, such as a declaration of war, they assembled in accordance with this military order, and their gathering was called the *Comi'tia Centuria'ta*, the Assembly of the Centuries. This assembly, existing side by side with the Senate, was for many hundred years the popular branch of the Ro'man legislature.

<small>Reforms of Servius.</small>

Tarquin'ius Pris'cus had left two sons, the gentle Ar'uns and the haughty Lu'cius. To these men King Ser'vius married the two Tul'lias, his daughters, who were as diversely tempered as their husbands. The matchmaking was wretchedly done, and eventually Lu'cius put to death his wife and brother and wedded his sister-in-law, a woman after his own heart. The pair then compassed the death of the good king, and it is said that the ruthless Tul'lia, hastening to hail her husband by his new title, drove her chariot over the corpse of the gray-haired king, her father, as it lay in the public street.

Lu'cius was the second of the Tar'quins and the last of the kings. Super'bus, "the Haughty," was the name he bore, and merited. For he walked not in the righteous statutes of his predecessor, but disregarded equally the old laws, the advice of the Senate, and the reformed, or "Ser'vian," constitution. He enjoyed absolute sway, like the tyrants who were in power in Greece at the same period, and by his wars he placed Rome indisputably at the head of the league of Lat'in towns. With the spoils of his victories the city was adorned and the magic books of the Cumæ'an Sib'yl were purchased after a famous haggle. The king's successes hardened him in his iniquity, and the story runs that in his old age he sent his two sons and a nephew, Bru'tus, to Del'phi in Greece to consult the oracle of Apol'lo, the god. Bru'tus was considered stupid, but he secretly made a rich gift to the priestess and rightly interpreted her response to the question which the envoys put to the oracle regarding the next ruler of the city. "He shall rule who first shall kiss his mother," was the simple answer, and while the two Tar'quins were hastening homeward and drawing lots for the privilege the dull Bru'tus stumbled and pressed his lips to Mother Earth. Afterwards the king's wild son, Sex'tus Tar'quin, dishonored Lucre'tia, the wife of his cousin. Then the injured husband, with Bru'tus and other patriots, aroused the people to rid themselves of the tyrant and his kin. So the Ro'mans shut the gates against the monarch and vowed to have no more kings, forever, but in their stead to elect each year two con'suls, or colleagues, of equal authority, to rule in war and peace. A long war followed. The Tar'quins hatched conspiracies within the walls and instigated foreign invasions. Bru'tus, whom the citizens had made one of the first consuls, adjudged his own son to death for complicity in one of these plots. The people now banished the Tar'quin family, root and branch, and took their corn land, the Cam'pus Mar'tius, for a muster field for the troops. Next the exiles sought Etrus'can support, and the two cities, Tarquin'ii and Ve'ii, aided them. The patriot Bru'tus fell in the great battle which the Ro'mans fought near the wood of Ar'sia. Lars Por'sena, the Etrus'can king of Clu'sium, befriended the Tar'quins. He marched on Rome with an army, drove the defenders within the walls, and "would have sacked the town" had not Hora'tius Co'cles, with two more to help him, held the foe in play while the wooden bridge, which furnished the only approach to the city, was hewn down. Still Por'sena besieged the city. Mu'cius Scæ'vola, a Ro'man youth, failed in an attempt to kill the king in his tent. Scæ'vola was seized and condemned to torture; but to show his contempt of the sentence he thrust his right arm into the flame of an altar and held it steadily there until the hand was burned off. The king marveled at this exhibition of firmness and pardoned the boy. Then there was peace with the Ro'mans, and the Tar'quins had to turn from Por'sena to the Lat'in towns for succor. The final contest was so desperate that the Ro'mans dared not risk the divided leadership of two consuls. In the place of the two equal magistrates they appointed a single temporary commander-in-chief, or dictator, who had all the power of the old kings, but who held office for only six months at the longest. The first dictator, Mar'cus Valē'rius Public'ola, fell in with the Lat'ins near the shore of Lake Regil'lus, and beat them in a bloody battle, the good gods, Cas'tor and Pol'lux, coming to lead the Ro'man legions just at the critical moment when their ranks had begun to waver before the mad charge of the last of the Tar'quins. This ended the struggle of the dynasty. The royal outlaw died at Cū'mæ, and for five hundred years consuls were the chief magistrates of Rome.

So ends the legendary story of the kings.

ROME UNDER THE KINGS.

The historian has but a prosy substitute to offer for the interesting fables which were so long accepted as the veritable annals of these early times. And it must be remembered, furthermore, that he is guided by no explicit records, and must state probabilities where the wished-for facts are wanting. So, not forgetting the fascinating stories of the Tro′jans, and Al′ba, and Rom′ulus, let us seek the sober truth.

Absence of records.

Reference has already been made to the Ital′ian race as the main division of the inhabitants of the peninsula, and it has been related that the western branch of this stock—the Lat′ins—coming earlier or with greater power, took for their abode the hill-studded plain surrounded by the Ti′ber river, the Ap′ennine mountains, and the Vol′scian hills, which here jut out along the Tus′can sea. It may have been a thousand years before Christ that this occupation took place, perhaps at the same time that Sol′omon was ruling at Jeru′salem and "Ho′mer" composing his Il′iad in the Greek cities of A′sia Mi′nor. These Lat′ins were of a clannish spirit, and agriculture was their only occupation. Thus the descendants of a common ancestor lived together as a clan, and several clans tilling adjacent tracts combined for mutual advantage in a larger political body, or canton. Such a cantonal community would center about a village in some spot easily capable of defense. To this citadel, for which a hill would furnish the most eligible site, the settlers would retire for safety in case of danger. There were hostile tribes in the immediate neighborhood, not only the dreaded Etrus′cans, but rough Sa′bines and Sam′nites from the mountain districts, and nearer yet the Æ′qui, Her′nici, and Vol′sci. The common peril perhaps—facilitated by a community of race, to which both language and religion bore witness—led

The earliest history.

The Alban league of Latin cantons.

the Lat'in cantons to form a league. Good evidence points to such a league of thirty members, the head of which was Al'ba Lon'ga, itself a canton-center on the Al'ban mount, and probably the earliest Lat'in settlement in La'tium. Here the Lat'ins celebrated the annual festival of their race.

One member of this league was Rome, the center of its own canton. When and by whom the city was really founded is now unknown. Strong probability there is that three independent communities had their citadels on as many of the original hills of the city—the earliest on the Pal'atine, the others on the Cap'itoline and Quir'inal—and that with characteristic political sagacity the people of the three hill-communities combined to form a single stronger city-state, called Rome, in which the original parts preserved their identity for many generations in the three tribes of Ro'man citizens—Ram'nes, Ti'ties, and Lu'ceres. There is some evidence to show that at least one of these uniting cantons was of Sa'bine race, thus accounting for the legends of a Sa'bine union in the reign of Rom'ulus. This triple city, which by its later expansion added four other eminences to the original three, had now an advantage over the surrounding towns. Three clustered hills were better than one; a river town had more resources than a rural village; a frontier post must be jealously defended, and a rude people could reap only gain from frequent contact with a more polished nation. So the Ro'mans on the Ti'ber diversified their industries, adding trade with the river region to the staple Lat'in occupation of farming and sheep-raising. The other Lat'ins could not object if Rome fortified herself stoutly against the Etrus'cans, who were the foes of all; and from her constant intercourse with these civilized foreigners the Ro'mans grew in grace and in knowledge of the arts

Rome, a hill canton.

The three-hilled city.

Its advantages.

of war and peace. Thus we may believe that Rome became a border fortress and agricultural center, with some claim to local commercial importance. But it would be a mistake to suppose that Rome was rich and powerful in the times of the kings. Her wars were waged and her victories were gained with isolated towns, and the name of the city was hardly known outside the little circle of the league. Indeed, it is scarcely probable that her entire possessions at the time of the expulsion of the kings—about five centuries before Christ—comprised more than a strip of territory a few miles in width extending from the city to the sea along the left bank of the Ti'ber. Her influence, however, was somewhat wider than her boundaries, for by this time (509 B. C.) Al'ba Lon'ga had been destroyed and her leading place in the Lat'in league usurped by Rome. The Lat'in towns retained their independence and Rome was not in any sense their ruler, except of a few which she had taken in war; but hers was now the weighty voice in the general councils of the league, and she presided at the national festival. At the close of this period, therefore, Rome had not yet achieved the mastery even of her nearest neighbors, although she had taken the first steps in that direction.

President of Latin league.

The government of Rome in the regal period is worthy of careful attention. Not all those who dwelt in the city were its legal citizens. The free population was composed of two distinct classes or orders: patricians and plebeians. The patrician order monopolized all political power and privilege. All offices of the State, all military commands (indeed, all military service), all priestly and pontifical positions, and all participation in the debates or voting of the public assemblies was restricted to these favored beings. The patricians ("fathers," or "children of the

Roman government in the regal period.

Patricians and plebeians.

fathers,") were probably descended from the first settlers of these hills, and it was to them alone that the triple tribal classification into Ram'nes, Tī'ties, and Lu'ceres applied. These three patrician tribes (*tri'bus*), or communities, were organized by families or households, ten families making up one clan, or *gĕns*, ten clans one ward, or *cu'ria*, ten wards one community, or *tri'bus*, although this decimal division was not strictly carried out. These three tribes formed the whole political body. In theory they were the only citizens, and it was of them alone that the term *pop'ulus Roma'nus*, "Ro'man people," was correctly used.

Patrician organization.

At the outset the patricians (and their slaves) were probably the only inhabitants, as well as the only citizens, of Rome; but as the city grew in power it gained in population. Lat'ins were brought to Rome from conquered towns; other Lat'ins were attracted to Rome for safety or for the commercial facilities which began to exist there; and these men and their descendants made up the second Ro'man order, the plebeians—the word *plebs* meaning the "masses," the multitude, or the "commons." Some plebeians were directly dependent upon the great patrician families, receiving support from them and making return in service—a condition not considered degrading, and certainly very far from slavery. These were called clients (*clien'tes*), and their patrician lords were their patrons (*patrō'ni*). But by far the more numerous class were dependent upon no particular patrician. They enjoyed the protection of the whole citizen body and were free from any serious burdens of service or of taxation. They seem to have had large liberties in the city. They might buy and sell, and, if they could, get gain; they and their property were defended by the walls which the patricians had built, and their homes were guarded by the armies of the State,

Status of the plebeians.

in which only patricians might serve. But politically they were not reckoned in the account at all. They were barred by law and custom from public career of any kind; there was no office which a plebeian might hold in the government, the army, or the Church, and he had not even the right to vote at the election of his patrician ruler. There was a great gulf fixed between the two orders which no man might pass. Wealth furnished no means of bridging the chasm. Birth alone, or the interposing favor of the king, determined his status. The intermarriage of the orders was illegal, and dragged the highborn party (man or woman) to the level of the plebeian. The absence of political rights was, in itself, hard enough to bear, but the arrogance and insolence of the aristocrats rendered intolerable the lot of a high-spirited commoner. It is important to understand the position of these two orders, for the internal history of the Ro′man State for many years turns upon the patrician resistance to the plebeian demand for admission to political and social equality.

Apart from, and far beneath both orders, stood the Ro′man slaves. Slavery existed in the city in very early times, and its victims continued to increase in numbers with the extension of wealth and extravagance. The number was small at first but in the times of the later republic and the empire all countries contributed their quota. Prisoners of war were naturally enslaved, and as Rome needed more servants than her conquests yielded she purchased them in the slave markets of the East. Negro slaves were comparatively rare, but rough Gauls and Thrā′cians herded with polished Greeks and Asiat′ics in the Ro′man slave pens, and Syr′ians were chained with Egyp′tians at the oars of Ro′man triremes, and with them pruned the vines on Campā′nian plantations. The slave owner had power of life and death over his chattels, and oftentimes the condition of the Ro′man

Roman slavery.

slave was horrible in the extreme, although a clement master would spare his human property.

The legends doubtless say truly that the earliest government was a monarchy, varying somewhat in its character in the two or three centuries of its existence and coming to a close in the remarkable aristocratic republic known as the Ro′man Commonwealth.

Governmental machinery.

The organization of the patrician order and its exclusive political powers have already been noticed, and it is now time to inquire how this power was exercised. In the first place, the whole citizen-body (namely, the patricians), which was the source of authority in the State, held meetings from time to time called the *Comi′tia Curiā′ta*, or Assembly of the Cu′ries. Theoretically this assembly had high powers: (1) to elect the king; (2) to confer on the king the *impe′rium*; (3) to decide on declarations of war, appeals, adoptions, etc., but in later practice it performed but a few duties in its own name. The most important assembly was really the Senate. The senators, at first one hundred, later three hundred in number, were the elders of the patrician order. Their experience in life fitted them especially for dealing with public questions, and it was upon them, therefore, rather than upon the Comi′tia Curia′ta, that the principal legislative duties devolved. The patricians who composed the Senate were the picked men of the curies; so that the Senate may be looked upon as a highly competent executive committee of the former assembly. The Senate, to which plebeians became eligible under the Republic, continued to be a leading feature of the Ro′man constitution through all its changes, and in its prime it represented in a high degree the energy and conservatism of the people, and was probably the most dignified and able legislative body that the world has known. From its

Comitia Curiata.

Senate.

subordinate position as a royal council it came to wield a power of its own, and in the splendid days of the republic the force and intellect which ruled the city, directed war, and organized the whole known world into provinces, was the Ro′man Senate.*

At the head of the patricians was the king (*rex*). He was the head of every department of the government. With the advice, should he require it, but not necessarily with the consent, of the Senate he published his edicts, which were the laws. Representing the citizen body much as the father of a Ro′man family represented his household, he acted as high priest and the head of the State religion. Either in his own person or through deputies he presided in the law-courts, and in him rested the supreme command of the army. In all but one important particular his sway was absolute, viz. : his power was derived from, and at his decease returned to, the people—not to his son, nor to any man of his selection. His term of office was for life, and he had no authoritative voice in the choice of his successor. When a king died the Senators in turn acted as vice-kings (*in′ter-re′ges*) until they could agree upon a new sovereign. The patrician whom the Senate selected had to receive the approval or ordination of the Comi′tia Curia′ta, and that body only could confer upon him the *impe′rium*—the right to rule in the city and the command of the army in the field.

The king.

The succession.

Such seems to have been the primitive monarchical government of Rome—two orders dwelling within the same city limits : a ruling order, conducting the business of government through the Comi′tia, and the Senate, and indirectly through one of its own number elevated

Summary.

---

* The official title of the Ro′man Commonwealth was always SENA′TUS POP′ULUS′QUE ROMA′NUS, "the Senate and the Ro′man people." The abbreviated form of the Lat′in being S. P. Q. R.

to almost absolute power as king; the other order composed of freemen, destitute of active political rights.

Every fresh advance of Rome swelled the number of the plebeians. Their order gained by every successful war and by every new trader who settled in the city. The patrician order relied only upon natural causes for its growth, and even this increase was retarded by the compulsory military service which subjected the patricians alone to the ravages of frequent campaigns. Excluded by law from camp and court and temple, the ambitious plebeian plunged into trade and agriculture. Ro′man energy and Ro′man brains were not a patrician monopoly, and there gradually arose among the plebeians a set of men whose achievements in private life encouraged them to ask a share in public affairs. Moreover, it was no easy matter for the small patrician order to bear all the weight of war. From these two causes sprang the reform in the government which has been attributed to King Ser′vius Tul′lius, and which is called the Ser′vian Constitution. In order to divide the patrician military burden with the plebeians, and at the same time to admit the latter in a certain limited sense to an equality with the former, this memorable reform in the composition of the army was introduced. The three historic tribes were abolished and all the Ro′man freeholders who dwelt within the walls were included in four new tribes, according to the region or city ward in which they lived. A census or numbering and valuation of the tribesmen was then taken, and from it a new muster-roll for the army was drawn up. All male property-holders between the ages of seventeen and sixty were divided into five "classes." The first class comprised those who owned at least twenty *ju′gera* of tilled land. These men must present themselves fully armed, and they

Growth and ambition of plebeian order.

The reform of Servius Tullius.

The classes.

were divided into eighty "centuries" (hundreds, or companies) one half of them liable for field duty, the other half, composed of older men, being assigned to service as a reserve. The second class comprised twenty centuries similarly divided. Only fifteen *ju'gera* of land was the standard of admission to this class, and its members were not compelled to furnish a full suit of armor. Membership in the third, fourth, and fifth classes was assigned on a similar scale; but the fifth class numbered thirty centuries. These 170 centuries made up the infantry of the new army. The cavalry was recruited by levying twelve new centuries of the wealthiest young men, both patricians and plebeians, and adding these to the six patrician centuries of horse which had served in the old army. These rich knights (*eq'uites*) cut a considerable figure in the later history of the city, the equestrian order being always the representatives of the great capitalists. Five centuries of engineers, musicians, etc., made up the full number of 193.

In the new army, then, the two orders stood for the first time side by side. Both were taxed for its support, both were subjected to its hardships, both shared its glories. The plebeian, although still far removed from the right to hold political office, was at last recognized as of some account in the State. In the army he might even rise to the rank of centurion or military tribune, and exercise authority, petty though it was, over such patricians of slender income as chanced to form the rank and file.

<small>A military reform.</small>

This military organization of Ser′vius Tul′lius was the source of the first political rights which the plebeians obtained; for to this army, composed of both orders, the king submitted proposals concerning war. There was no debate, probably no formal voting; but in some rude way, by shout or by clash of shield and spear,

<small>Beginnings of plebeian power.</small>

the people made known their approval or dissent. It was this Ser'vian muster of the people by centuries which developed into the Comi'tia Centuria'ta of republican times, the powerful citizen body which elected most of the magistrates and possessed high legislative authority. Under the kings, however, this assembly was probably devoid of political power beyond the slight degree which has just been referred to, the Senate of elders and the Assembly of the Curies (Comi'tia Curia'ta), both thoroughly patrician, being still the recognized legislative bodies.

The first essential change in the form of government sprang not from plebeian oppression, but from the ambition of the kings. The student of the legends must have noticed a strain of violence and despotism running through the stories of the later kings. The monarch is no longer the revered judge and priest of the people, but has become a military leader. The throne no longer descends peacefully to the patrician whom the Senate nominates and whom the curies and the gods approve. The monarch contrives that the succession shall remain in his own family or descend to a man of his selection. The Tar'quins are foreigners, Etrus'cans, and they introduce foreign customs, outlandish symbols of royalty, and seem to have ruled over Etru'ria as well as Rome. From these and other indications it is concluded that at one time Rome succumbed to the many attacks of its enemies north of the Ti'ber and was forced to accept a foreign ruler. These Tar'quins, the Etrus'can kings of Rome, disregarded Senate and patrician assemblies and ruled as despots. Their absolute power and their military skill placed Rome at the head of the Lat'in towns, but bred dissatisfaction and revolution. The Tar'quins resembled the tyrants who were at the same time lording it over the cities of Greece, adorning them

The decline and fall of the kings.

The tyranny of the Tarquins.

with splendors of architecture but depriving them of their liberties. This military despotism ended in revolt. Lucre'tia's dishonor and the patriotism of Bru'tus may be fictions, but the fact is indubitable that the citizens at length drove out the kings and put elective consuls in their place.

The causes of the overthrow of the kings are in plain sight. The monarch had gained his despotic power at the expense of the patricians. The plebeians had nothing to lose. The patricians had been the State. King and Senate were of their own number and governed in their interest. A usurping foreign king, who disregarded the advice of the Senate and treated the curies with contempt, was intolerable to their order. The arrogance of Tarquin'ius Super'bus hastened the crisis. The kings were expelled after a long war which weakened the city and degraded it from its leadership in La'tium. But the persistence with which the people maintained the struggle against the Tar'quins and their Lat'in and Etrus'can allies is evidence of the sincerity of their hatred. In after times the very name of king (*rex*) was accursed in the city, and there was no surer way of crushing a public man than to spread the report that he aimed to make himself king. The republic which succeeded the monarchy lasted for nearly five hundred years and passed through many changes. Within that time many men strove to seize the chief power in the State, but no man dared to wear the crown. Even Cæ'sar, who put an end to the republic and was the virtual sovereign of an empire, refused the regal title, in deference, doubtless, to this persistent hatred.

Why monarchy fell.

No more kings.

In another chapter we shall see how the patricians endeavored to secure for themselves the sovereignty in the republic.

ANALYSIS OF CHAPTER II.

Preliminary: Difficulties of ancient history, 30.
I. *Legendary History*, 31-38:
    The Trojans in Italy, 31.
    Founding of Rome, 31.
    The seven kings, 32-38:
        1. Romulus, 32, 33.
            Early constitution, 33.
        2. Numa Pompilius, 33.
        3. Tullus Hostilius, 33.
        4. Ancus Martius, 34.
        5. Tarquinius Priscus, 34, 35.
        6. Servius Tullius, 35, 36.
            Servian reforms, 36.
        7. Tarquinius Superbus, 36-38:
            End of monarchy, 37, 38.
II. *The Probable History*, 39-49:
    The Latin cantons, 39.
    Founding of Rome, 40.
    Rome, the head of Latium, 41.
    Rome under the kings, 41-49:
        Social and political orders, 41-43:
            Patricians, 41.
            Plebeians, 42.
            Slaves, 43.
        Government, 44, 45:
            Comitia Curiata, 44.
            Senate, 44.
            King, 45.
        Rise of plebeians, 46-48:
            Servian Reforms, 46.
            Classes, 46, 47.
            Comitia Centuriata, 48.
        The fall of the kings, 48, 49.

REVIEW EXERCISE.

First Period. Rome Under the Kings, 753-509 B. C.

1. What is the modern view of early Roman history?
2. What is the legend of the founding of Rome?
3. Give the main features of the constitution of Romulus.
4. Name the seven kings of Rome.
5. For what is the reign of Servius Tullius famous?

6. What was the character of the second Tarquin?
7. Tell the story of Brutus and the liberation.
8. In what year and with what battle did the monarchy end?
9. Describe the "cantonal" system of the early Latins.
10. What was the first Latin settlement in Latium?
11. How did Rome probably begin?
12. What were the advantages of its site?
13. What were the territories and influence of Rome in 509 B. C.?
14. Who were the patricians and what were their privileges?
15. Describe the status of the plebeians.
16. What were the composition and power of the Comitia Curiata?
17. What were the composition and functions of the Senate?
18. What was the position of the king?
19. How was the king's successor chosen?
20. What contributed to the growth of the plebeian order?
21. What did the Servian reforms aim to effect?
22. How did the Comitia Centuriata take its rise?
23. What made the monarchy unpopular?
24. To what Greek rulers may the Tarquins be compared?
25. How were the kings regarded in later times?

CHAPTER III.

SECOND PERIOD.

The Roman Republic. (478 Years.) 509-31 B. C.

The traditional date of the expulsion of the Ro′man kings is 509 B. C., and it is an accepted fact that the empire was established in the year 31 B. C. Throughout the intervening period of four hundred and seventy-eight years Rome was a republic.

Duration of the Republic. 509-31 B. C.

The history of these times may be divided for convenience into three parts; namely,

I. 509-264 B. C.—The Rise of the Plebeians in the City and the Rise of Rome in It′aly.

II. 264-133 B. C.—The Pū′nic Wars and Foreign Conquests.

III. 133-31 B. C.—The Civil Wars. Conquests Abroad. The Fall of the Republic.

These three divisions will be considered in turn, and it will be shown how the republican city consolidated its own elements of strength, united It′aly with Ro′man cement, crushed its civilized rivals—Car′thage, Cor′inth, A′sia—repelled German invasion, conquered the Gauls in their own lands, and then, in full possession of wealth and power extraordinary, fell upon times of corruption and civil disorder which ended in the overthrow of the republic by Ju′lius Cæ′sar, who founded a personal monarchy to maintain the conquests which the commonwealth had made.

Part I. *509-264 B. C.*
THE RISE OF THE PLEBEIANS IN THE CITY AND THE RISE OF ROME IN ITALY.

The earliest historians of Rome, the so-called annalists, Fa′bius Pic′tor and Cincius Alimentus, wrote about 200 B. C., and the modern student is dependent upon accounts written from three to five centuries after the occurrence of the events which they narrate.

Scanty materials for accurate history.

Consequently the early chapters of the republic are almost as rich in fanciful legends as were the stories of the kings. The chief sources from which the Ro′man writers made up their narratives were the annals kept on a whited board (*album*) by the pontifex maximus, the lists of holidays, the laws and treaties preserved on metal tablets in the temples, and the private records of the patrician families, who treasured with jealous pride the names of their ancestors who had held high office in the State.

In the histories of Liv′y (d. 59 B. C.) and Dionys′ius (30 B. C.) this framework of fact is so lavishly upholstered with legendary material that it is often difficult to detect the truth. Many of the legends have become familiar in literature, and for that reason some of them will be repeated here, with due warning to the reader.

Legends.

The period before us has two aspects. At one and the same time two changes were taking place in the Ro′man State. Within the city her people, patrician and plebeian, gentle and common, were fighting face to face for political equality. Without the walls patricians and plebeians were fighting shoulder to shoulder to extend the authority of the city over the Ital′ian peninsula. In following the two lines of development the scenes will shift more than once.

Two irrepressible conflicts.

The Ro′man monarchy had been originally aristocratic.

The elective king was a patrician—that is, of "noble" blood;
his council, the Senate, was exclusively patrician;
he was the pope of the patrician priesthood and
the general of the patrician army. The plebeians
dwelt in the city, but had no part nor lot in
public affairs. When the Etrus'can monarchs—the Tar'quins
of the legends—made themselves absolute rulers the Ro'man
patricians, angry at their loss of influence, headed a revolution
and drove out the kings forever. The government which
they set up was as thoroughly patrician as its founders dared
to make it. The chief magistracy was bestowed upon two
patrician consuls of equal authority, who held office for a
single year. The king's religious duties went to a patrician
"king of the sacrifices" (*rex sacro'rum*), and much of the
judicial and financial authority fell to two *quaes'tors*, also
patricians. In case of extreme peril the Senate might commission a *dicta'tor*, who was in fact absolute king for the six
months to which his authority was limited. This officer
appointed his own lieutenant (*magis'ter eq'uitum*, or "master
of the horse"), and—until 356 B. C.,—was chosen, like the
other magistrates, from the patrician order.

The monarchy becomes an aristocratic republic.

The Senate of the earlier period was little changed by the
revolution. But its numbers fell off in the wars with the
banished kings, and the new consuls filled up the
ranks with men from the rich families. It is believed that there were plebeians among the families
thus ennobled, though it is uncertain whether the plebeian
senators came at once into the full senatorial dignity and privilege, indeed it is urged that the official title of the Senate,
pa'tres (et) conscrip'ti, implies the presence of patricians and
members enrolled from the plebeian body.

Plebeian recruits in the Senate.

In the monarchical system there had been but one assembly
of the citizens—the patrician Comi'tia Curia'ta—based on the

triple tribal division into Ram′nes, Ti′ties, and Lu′ceres. In
the republic this assembly survived, but its power
The citizen assemblies. sank with the rise of the plebeians until it came
to deal only with exclusively patrician matters.
Besides this ancient Assembly of the Curies two other comitia,
or assemblies, grew until they usurped its powers and overshadowed its importance. The elder of these was
Comitia Centuriata. the Comi′tia Centuria′ta, or Assembly of the
Centuries. The organization of the landowning
Ro′mans of both orders for military purposes took place under
the kings. It was the substance of the reform of "Ser′vius
Tul′lius." In essence it enlarged the body of Ro′man citizens
by admitting to service in the army and to petty military
office the landowning plebeians. The centuries, or hundreds,
were at first purely military groups, and had no other voice in
affairs of State than the simplest expression of opinion upon
the question of declaring war. In itself this was little; in its
possibilities of expansion it was much; for it was the first
recognition of the political existence of the plebeians. The
distribution of the citizens in the centuries and the methods
of voting gave the rich men a preponderating influence in
this body, so that, although the centuries included both
orders, the wealthy patrician aristocracy controlled its action.
The military Comi′tia Centuria′ta of Ser′vius became the
great popular assembly of the republic. The right of electing
the higher magistrates was transferred from the curies to the
centuries, and the course of appeal from the consul's death
sentence was similarly altered. It was, perhaps, a little later
that the Assembly of the Centuries actually gained the right
of accepting or rejecting the bills proposed to them by the
consul. This right, early secured, made this mixed assembly
a lawmaking body, or legislature; but it differed from most
modern lawmaking bodies in its composition. It was not a

representative body; its members were not elected; every man represented himself alone, and in theory the Assembly of the Centuries included every Ro'man landowner, the only distinctions being those of property.

In addition to the old patrician Assembly of the Curies and the newly enfranchised Assembly of the Centuries, there originated somewhat later a third and (perhaps, though this is doubtful), purely plebeian body, the Assembly of the Tribes, or Comi'tia Tribu'ta. These tribes were not the three ancient aristocratic divisions, but were rather districts of the city and its suburbs, at first twenty in number, later twenty-one, and finally thirty-five. How this assembly began is doubtful, but it rose with the rise of the plebeians, who at least preponderated in its membership, until it became co-equal with the Assembly of the Centuries, and ultimately the chief legislative body.

Comitia Tributa.

The patricians had been the chief gainers from the expulsion of the kings. They had secured patrician magistrates and generals, a patrician senate and priesthood, and patrician ascendency in the Assembly of the Centuries; even the admission of the plebeians to the army was a gain for the aristocrats. The long struggle with the exiled Tar'quins, which the legendary story embellishes with the great deeds of Hora'tius, Por'sena, and Sccæ'vola, and which closed with the memorable victory at Lake Regil'lus, brought sore distress to the common soldiers of the lower "classes." They were the owners of small farms, which suffered from the absence of their proprietors in the wars. The soldier served without pay. Debt was inevitable. The Ro'man law gave the debtor to his creditor as a slave. The booty of successful war went to the State, and the patricians had the use of its fruits. Public land (*a'ger pub'licus*) acquired by conquest was leased to the patrician landholders,

Sufferings of plebeians.

but the rents were carelessly collected, and the patrician to whom the lands were assigned often clung to his holding as if it were his by grant or purchase. Great estates grew up, tilled by slave labor, and the small farmers, between debt and military service, were driven to despair and revolt.

In 494 B. C. the plebeians of the Roman army, returning from a successful campaign, encamped on a height at the junction of the Ti′ber and A′nio rivers, and declared their independence. They determined to rid themselves of patrician oppression by abandoning Rome and founding a plebeian city on the site of their encampment. Their numbers and spirit were a menace to Rome, and the aristocrats were forced to a compromise. The seceders re-entered Rome, but they marched in as victors. By the so-called "sacred law" their debts were forgiven, their revolt went unpunished, and they received—what they had never had before—magistrates of their own. Plebeians were not admitted to any of the existing offices, but Tribunes of the Commons (*tribu′ni ple′bis*), at first only two, like the consuls, afterwards five, and after 457 B. C., ten, were constituted to preside at plebeian meetings and to champion the rights of the commons at all times and places except in the army. The tribunes were elected by the plebeians themselves, in what assembly at first is doubtful, but after 471 B. C. in the Comi′tia Tribu′ta. They had the right of *vē′to* ("I forbid") upon the acts of all magistrates and assemblies. They could not be legally prosecuted during their year of office, and their houses were a legal refuge for plebeians charged with crime. The rights of veto and of protection were enormous concessions on the patrician side, and from this time the contest of the orders was hotly waged. Plebeian *œ′diles* were elected to assist the tribunes and supervise the markets. The hill

"First Secession of the Plebs." 494 B. C.

Tribunes of the People.

where the plebeians had encamped was afterwards known and honored by that order as the Sacred Mount (*mŏns sā'cer*), and the whole episode is called "The First Secession of the Plebs."

Amid the disorders of the revolution and the secession Rome lost her place at the head of La'tium. The legends indicate that the Etrus'cans were for a time victorious over the Ro'mans, and after their retreat the various tribes of La'tium were at war with their former leader. The Lat'ins and the Ro'mans combined against the neighboring Sa'bines, Æ'qui, Vol'sci, and Etrus'cans, and almost every year had its campaign. Incessant wars again impoverished the plebeians; and it is said that in a year of famine (491 B. C.) Coriolā'nus, consul at Rome, sought to induce the plebeians to give up the tribunate in return for free grants of grain from the State. For this and for contempt of court he was banished, and, joining the Vol'sci, afterwards led them against Rome, and would have taken it had he not yielded to the tearful entreaties of his Ro'man wife and mother. To separate her enemies, the Vol'sci and Æ'qui, Rome allied herself to the Her'nici (486 B. C.), thus contributing much to the re-establishment of her former strength.

Petty wars. Coriolanus. 491-486 B. C.

Notwithstanding the concessions of the Sacred Law the condition of the poorer people of Rome was rendered worse and worse by the continual wars. Much military duty, with no pay and scanty harvests, drove the farmers into bankruptcy, which was sheer ruin. The public lands continued in the possession of the patricians or the equally greedy plebeian capitalists. Slaves increased in numbers and in value and the dignity of free labor declined. In 486 B. C. Spu'rius Cas'sius, consul, proposed a land-law, or "Agrarian law" (Lat. *a'ger:* land), the first of many by which it was sought to curb the greed of the wealthy

Agrarian troubles. Death of Spurius Cassius. 486 B.C.

Ro'mans. This bill provided that all public lands should be surveyed and a portion of them be leased for the profit of the State. The remainder should be distributed freely among needy citizens of both orders and among the Lat'in allies. The last clause aroused the jealousy and pride of the Ro'mans. They would admit no Lat'in to a share in Ro'man privileges. The cry was raised that the consul was thus purchasing popularity, scheming to make himself king, and the wise man who had generously prescribed the only remedy for the ills of the city was denounced as a traitor, condemned, and executed. So the plebeians gained nothing.

Still there was discord in the city. One patrician family—the Fa'bii—went into exile to shun the strife, and

<small>Strife of the two orders. Plebeian encroachments. 480–448 B. C.</small> met death at the brook Crĕm'era at the hands of the Etrus'cans (477 B. C.). Four years later a tribune was murdered, in spite of his inviolability, because he had used his legal power against two patrician consuls. In 471 B. C. the Publil'ian law confirmed the right of the plebeians to elect their magistrates in the Comi'tia Tribū'ta, which was either exclu-

<small>Publilian law. 471 B.C.</small> sively plebeian or under plebeian control. Thus for fifty years the lower order held what it had gained. But its position was insecure. The laws were made for and by the patricians, and in most cases interpreted by

<small>462 B. C.</small> patrican magistrates. In 462 B. C. the Tribune Terentil'ius demanded that the body of unwritten law be revised by a commission, reduced to its simplest form, and published so that it might be known and read of all men. The patricians succeeded in postponing this reform for a decade. To pacify the plebeians they increased the number of tribunes to ten, and divided the unoccupied grounds on the Av'entine Hill among the poorer families. But the demand was only deferred, and in 451 B. C. it was granted. The

patricians gave up their consuls and the plebeians their tribunes, and the consular power was given for the space of one year to a committee of ten, the Decem′virs (*de′cem vi′ri*,

The Decem-
virs. 451-450
B. C.
ten men), chosen from the patricians. A second board of Decem′virs, this time including three plebeians, was elected for the year 450 B. C. The Decem′virs formulated a code of twelve laws, which were accepted by the people, and then published on brass tablets,

"Laws of the Twelve Tables."
which were posted in the city square. These Laws of the Twelve Tables were not new legislation, but their principles served to fix the hitherto doubtful or arbitrary decisions of the patrician magistrates, and were thus of great benefit.

The work of the Decem′virs was done, but the enjoyment of power was too sweet to be freely put aside; accordingly

Appius Claudius. Second secession of Plebs. 449-448 B. C.
they continued in office in 449 B. C., and with Ap′pius Clau′dius at their head ruled as tyrants. The legends tell of their foul murder of Lu′cius Dentā′tus, the bravest soldier of Rome, and of the attempted abduction of the fair Virgin′ia by Ap′pius. These outrages led the plebeians to retire to the Sacred Mount, the scene of their former victory. The second secession was equally profitable. The moderate aristocrats effected an arrangement for the re-establishment of consuls and tribunes. The Decem′virs abdicated and died in prison or in exile,

Valerio-Horatian laws. 448 B. C.
and the plebeians returned to Rome (448 B. C.), where the Vale′rio-Hora′tian laws still further fortified their position. This legislation (1) indorsed the Laws of the Twelve Tables; (2) compelled every magistrate to allow a condemned man to appeal to the Assembly of the Centuries; (3) allowed the tribunes to inflict fines; (4) established two additional patrician quæstors as treasurers of the military funds; (5) allowed the tribune

to witness the proceedings of the Senate and interpose his veto; (6) reasserted the inviolability of the tribunes, invoking a curse on their assailants.

Success emboldened the plebeians. They knew their value to the city's prosperity, and their demands grew in number and audacity. In 445 B. C. the law of Canule′ius bridged the gulf between the orders by legalizing the marriage of patricians and plebeians.

Intermarriage legalized. 445 B. C.

The same tribune proposed, three quarters of a century in advance of his time, that the consulate be opened to all citizens. This was denied; but the patricians devised a makeshift by which the assembly might decide in any year to elect six military tribunes (*tribu′ni mil′itum*), with consular power, in place of the two patrician consuls. To this new tribunate both orders were eligible.

Military tribunes. 444 B. C.

Thus the aristocracy were compelled to grant in reality what they attempted to deny. They would not admit their rivals to the consulate; but they would not exclude them from the consular tribunate, which had almost equal power. To save their dignity still farther the patricians established a new office of their own. Hitherto the consuls had taken the census of the citizens—an enrollment which determined the standing of the individual in the Assembly of the Centuries and in the Senate. To withhold the control of the Senate from the possibly plebeian influence of the consular tribunes the censorship was created (444 B. C.). Two *cen′sors*, both patricians, were chosen by the centuries, and clothed with power to take the census of polls and property every five years, and compile the lists of citizens, senators, and knights. They had the responsible supervision of the State revenues and expenditures, and were charged with the oversight of public morals.

Censors. 444 B. C.

In 421 B. C. the office of *quæs′tor*, hitherto patrician, was first opened to the plebeians. This was significant of the end, for it was the first of the higher magistracies for which they were made eligible. Three of them had been decemvirs and others had gained consular rank as military tribunes, but they had been debarred the ancient honors, which the quæstorship now opened to them.

Plebeian quæstors. 421 B. C.

From 405 to 396 B. C. Rome was engaged in a duel with Ve′ii, a strong town of southern Etru′ria. The war was as fruitful of prodigies as the famous siege of Troy by the Greeks, and the Ro′mans, who were eventually successful under the leadership of Camil′lus, told wonderful stories of their own heroic deeds. It was in this prolonged campaign that the citizen soldiery of Rome first received pay, the army remaining in the field all winter. The fall of Ve′ii was a heavy blow to Etrus′can prosperity, but her countrymen could neither lend aid to the city nor avenge its destruction, for their land was threatened by an invasion from the north. The Gauls, a Celt′ic tribe, had long before entered the valley of the Po and driven the Etrus′cans into the limits in which we first find them. Hither the Gauls pursued them, and the aid which Ro′man envoys gave to the men of Clu′sium provoked the barbarians to declare war on Rome itself.

War with Veii. Exploits of Camillus. 405–396 B. C.

The annals relate that the Gauls routed the Ro′man army on the brook Al′lia, a few miles from Rome, 390 B. C. The citizens fled, only a few remaining to guard the Cap′itoline temples. The Gauls burned the city, murdered the steadfast senators, and, had it not been for the cackling of Ju′no's geese, would have surprised and sacked the citadel. It is believed that "Bren′nus," the Gaul′ish chief, was bribed to abandon the siege; but tradition has it that Camil′lus, "the second founder of Rome," sur-

Rome taken by the Gauls. 390 B. C.

prised and defeated the besiegers. Then the citizens returned after considering the question of abandoning the ruins and planting a new Rome at Ve'ii. The Gauls proceeded southward, and in the following years often threatened, but never re-took, the city. At last they settled in the Po valley and adopted the Ro'man civilization.

The long war with the people of Ve'ii and the disastrous inroads of the plundering Gauls increased the miseries of the poorer citizens and hastened the means of relief.

Internal distractions. Mælius, 439 B. C. Manlius. 384 B. C. The debt and destitution of the plebeian poor had already touched many hearts in both orders. In 439 B. C. Spu'rius Mæ'lius, a rich plebeian, was killed by Aha'la, a high officer, for distributing grain to the needy. The patricians accused him of courting popularity for ambitious ends. In 384 B. C., Man'lius, who had kept the Cap'itoline against the Gauls, was thrown from its cliffs as a punishment for paying the debts of bankrupt plebeians. The patricians said he wanted to be king and was stealing the hearts of the people. But isolated executions could not suppress the popular cry for equal political rights and equal justice in regard to the public lands. In 376 B. C. the popular demand took form in the propositions of the tribunes, Licin'ius and Sex'tius, which in 367 B. C. were accepted by the assembly and became the famous Licin'ian laws.

It was enacted: (1) That the office of consular military tribune should be abolished, and that at least one of the two annually elected consuls must be a plebeian; (2)

The Licinian laws. 367 B. C. that plebeians should be admitted to priesthoods of a certain class. These two laws equalized the political status of the two orders and realized one of the objects for which the plebeians had battled since 509 B. C. Furthermore (3) it was enacted that no one should occupy more than a certain share of the common pasture-lands or till more than three hundred acres of the State domain; (4) that freemen, as well as slaves, must be employed on every estate; and (5) that interest already paid on debts should be deducted from the principal.

The patricians made futile attempts to nullify this legislation. As they had established the censorship to keep certain privileges away from the plebeian military tribunes, they now (366 B. C.) created a new office, the prætorship. The *præ'tor*, who must be a patrician, was to act as consul in the absence of those magistrates, and was at all times to act as a judge in the highest court of the city. Two curule ædiles, also patricians, were likewise appointed to manage the Ro'man games and public markets. But these offices did not long remain the exclusive property of the old aristocracy. One after another they were yielded to the commons. The Licin'ian law, of 367 B. C. legalized plebeian consuls; in 356 B. C. the dictatorship was opened to plebeians; in 351 B. C. the restrictions were removed from the censorship; in 339 B. C. the Publil'ian law ordered that one of the censors must be a plebeian; in 337 B. C. the commons were made eligible to the prætorship; in 300 B. C. the Ogul'nian law admitted plebeians to office in the priestly colleges of the augurs and pontifices; and in 287 B. C. the Horten'sian law, brought about by the Third Secession of the Plebs, established the decrees of the plebeian Assembly of Tribes (*Comi'tia Tribu'ta*), as of equal authority with the laws passed by the whole body of citizens in the Assembly of the Centuries (*Comi'tia Centuria'ta*).

The Licin'ian law, with its sequels, the Publil'ian, Ogul'nian, and Horten'sian laws, broke down the bar which had divided the Ro′man orders. The distinction still survived in the pride of the patrician families, but politically the orders were equal. All the honors of State and religion were open to the plebeians; the resolutions of their assembly were the laws of the State; their consuls led the armies; their senators sat and voted with the representatives of the ancient houses. The enormous changes which this chapter summarizes were two hundred years in consummation. Considered in the aggregate they represent a complete revolution in the Ro′man constitution. It is the spectacle of a subject class extorting not only liberty for itself but privilege and power from its superiors, and acquiring an equal share in the government. Similar results have been achieved in other countries and in modern times, notably in France at the beginning of the present century, but the Ro′mans alone possessed that political faculty which secured this revolution without anarchy. The struggle for the equalization of the orders was fiercely contested, but it was fought in legal forms, not with fire and sword, and the many years that preceded its consummation were so many years of education in those qualities of self-control which enabled the new Rome to master the world.

The revolution complete but gradual.

While the constitution of the city-state was in this stage of its development Rome was engaged in a series of wars which resulted in the conquest of the entire peninsula. She had no longer to fight for her existence. Her supremacy in La′tium was again recognized as it had been in the times of the kings, and she made leagues of equality with the Lat′ins and Her′nicans. Until the wandering Gauls settled themselves finally and quietly upon the plains of Lom′bardy their forays brought them into frequent contact with the Ro′mans, but after the time of Camil′lus they never again approached

The Roman conquest of Italy. 375–275 B.C.

the walls of the city. With the repulse of the Gauls, and the submission of the Lat′in and Her′nican towns, three rival nationalities under Rome remained in the peninsula. In closest contact were the Etrus′cans, weakened by the loss of Ve′ii and suffering from Gaul′ish raids. East and south of Rome were the Ital′ians of whom the Sam′nites, rude farmers though they were, were the leading division; related to the Sam′nites were the Vol′sci and Æ′qui, whose lands adjoined the Lat′ins. The third people were the Greeks of the south; by this time luxurious, cultured, and indolent, abounding in material resources but deficient in patriotism, and cursed by the political incapacity of their race. Before 265 B. C. Rome had mastered all three races—Etrus′can, Ital′ian, and Greek.

Three hostile races.

Etru′ria was in disorder, and its cities fell one by one until the entire southern section of the country, with the cities of Tarquin′ii, Cæ′re, and Fale′rii, was subject to Rome (351 B. C.). It was, perhaps, this success which led Car′thage, the Af′rican city which was then one of the great powers of the world, to sign its first treaty with the victor (348 B. C.).

Subjection of Etruria. 351 B. C.

Rome's next campaigns (350–345 B. C.) were against the Vol′scians and their kindred Ital′ians on the south, and resulted in a further extension of Ro′man power. It was for these wars that the old military formation was reorganized. The heavy infantry of the legion (regiment) was divided into thirty man′iples (battalions) of two centuries (companies) each. These fought in triple line of battle, the first two rows being armed with sword and spear, the third with long lances. The legion numbered 300 horse and 4,200 foot, of whom 3,000 were heavy armed troops.

Campaigns against the Italians, 350-345 B. C. Military reforms.

The Ro′man state, which had suffered much from Gaul and Tus′can, was now surely in the ascendant in central It′aly.

Its powerful alliance was sought by distant tribes. A treaty of this sort precipitated the inevitable and obstinate struggle with the Sam′nites. Two truces divide the conflict into the three Sam′nite wars. The first was of little importance. Beginning in 343 B. C. with an alliance between Rome and Cap′ua, it lasted till 341 B. C., when the Sam′nites were distracted by a Greek attack in their rear and the Ro′mans by a revolt of the Lat′ins. In the settlement Rome annexed the pleasant city of Cap′ua.

Samnite wars.

First Samnite war. 343-341 B. C.

The Lat′in war (340-338 B. C.) was the protest of the Lat′in towns against Ro′man exclusiveness. Ro′mans and Lat′ins had fought side by side as allies, but Rome had claimed the spoils of the victory. The city was prospering and growing in power and wealth, and the Lat′ins demanded a share in its government. They saw the first triumphs of the plebeians, and they raised a cry for equal recognition in the affairs of the city. But it was a fundamental doctrine of the Ro′man republic to restrict as far as possible the rights of citizenship to actual inhabitants of the city. The war resulted in the complete victory of the Ro′mans; the Lat′in league was dissolved. Its cities made separate treaties with Rome and were cut off from direct intercourse with each other. Ro′man garrison towns (colonies) were planted among them and the ancient Lat′in State was at an end.

Latin war. 340-338 B. C.

In 326 B. C. the second Sam′nite war began. It lasted, with varying fortunes, until 305 B. C., and involved nearly all the nations of the peninsula. The mountaineers were led by the Sam′nite, Ga′vius Pon′tius, who (321 B. C.) entrapped both the consular armies in the pass near Cau′dium, known as the "Cau′dine Forks," and compelled the consuls to accept humiliating terms, which the Senate rejected. The Etrus′cans took sides with the Sam′-

Second Samnite war. 326-305 B. C.

nites (in 312 B. C.), but were beaten at the Vadimo'nian Lake (310 B. C.). Gradually the Samnites were deprived of their allies, and in 305 B. C. their capital, Bovia'num, surrendered to the Ro'mans. Peace was made on equal terms.

Although the Ro'mans held the advantage in these wars their stubborn foe was by no means subjugated. Rome occupied the seven years which elapsed before the third outbreak in strengthening her own position. In La'tium she forced the subject tribes to accept a form of citizenship which was like that of the plebeians two centuries earlier. They were citizens without suffrage—that is, they served in Ro'man armies and paid taxes to Rome, but could not vote in the city assemblies (*comi'tia*) nor hold Ro'man office. Throughout the conquered territory that peculiar institution, the Ro'man colony (*colo'nia*), was planted. Lands near the conquered towns were assigned to Ro'man citizens, soldiers, usually, who removed thither with their wives and children. These colonists retained their full rights as citizens of Rome, and when in the mother city might vote in the assemblies. In their new homes they were not only garrisons, but centers of Ro'man influence of every sort, contributing to the extension of the Lat'in language and Ro'man law, by which the races of the peninsula were brought into union and their differences worn away. To facilitate communication between the scattered colonies, and to furnish means for the rapid transportation of troops, the Senate authorized the construction of an elaborate system of military roads. These magnificent highways perfectly graded, drained, and paved, some of which still remain in use, were extended as fast as the conquests permitted. Before the third Sam'nite war a large part of that "queen of roads," the Ap'pian Way (*Vi'a Ap'pia*), which was to connect Rome and Brundis'ium, was

How Rome held her conquests.

Colonies.

Roads.

built, and two northern roads, the Flamin'ian and Vale'rian, were constructed into the heart of the Sam'nite mountains.

The mountaineers perceived the hostile significance of these operations, and formed alliances with the Etrus'cans and Gauls of the north and the southern Ital'ians, preparatory to a decisive struggle against Rome.

Third Samnite war. 298-290 B. C.

The third Sam'nite war lasted from 298 B. C. to 290 B. C., and the Ro'mans won by striking the members of the league in turn before they could combine. In the great battle of Senti'num the Gauls and Sam'nites were defeated by the Ro'man consuls. The allies fell away, but the Sam'nites held out five years longer, until 290 B. C. They secured honorable terms of peace, but were so weakened that they were no longer an obstacle to the supremacy of Rome in the Ital'ian peninsula.

The Ro'man conquests were rapidly secured by strong colonies and fine roads. Ro'man influences had now reached southern It'aly, and a three-years' war, with an alliance of Ital'ian tribes (285-282 B. C.), ended in the partial destruction of the Gaul'ish Sen'ones and the establishment of Ro'man garrisons in several of the Greek cities of that section. Taren'tum, a proud and wealthy city of this neighborhood, jealous of the Ro'man advance, attacked a Ro'man fleet and invited war (282 B. C.). Pyr'rhus, the King of Epi'rus, crossed the Adriatic with war elephants and a great army to aid the Taren'tines. The Ro'mans refused to yield, though dismayed by the strange force which confronted them. Their army was beaten at Heracle'a (280 B. C.), and again at As'culum (279 B. C.). Still the result was indecisive. The Ro'man allies joined Pyr'rhus, but the Ro'mans resisted heroically and inflicted tremendous losses. "Another such victory," said Pyr'rhus, "and I am undone." Affairs in Sic'ily

The subjection of the south.

War with Tarentum. 282-272 B. C. Invasion of Pyrrhus.

demanded the presence of the king, and on his return he found the Ro'man position greatly strengthened. In the battle of Beneven'tum (275 B. C.) he was utterly defeated.

Italy conquered. 264 B. C. Pyr'rhus then left Mag'na Græ'cia at the mercy of Rome. Taren'tum surrendered (272 B. C.), and the Sam'nites and other tribes who had broken their treaties were severely punished. By the year 264 B. C. all It'aly, from the Ru'bicon to the Straits of Messi'na and the Io'nian Sea, was subject to the seven-hilled city.

In this united It'aly the citizens of Rome were the governing body. Their local senate and assemblies made the laws

The government of Italy. and through their magistrates attended to their execution. Outside of Rome there were three general classes of communities—the colonies, whose citizens were still full citizens of Rome; the municipalities (*municip'ia*), whose citizens, like the early plebeians, bore the burdens of Ro'man citizenship, the taxes and liability to military service, but could neither vote at Rome nor hold a Ro'man office; and the allies, or *so'cii*, who were bound to Rome by treaties upon various terms of dependence.

The first stage of the Ro'man Republic began with the expulsion of the kings, 509 B. C., and ended with the unification

Summary. 509-264 B. C. of It'aly, 264 B. C. The political character of the people was now formed, their military organization improved, and their triumph over Pyr'rhus and the Greeks encouraged them for the impending contest with Car'thage for the supremacy of the Mediterra'nean Sea.

ANALYSIS OF CHAPTER III.

General view and divisions of republican history, 52.
Two great conflicts of the first part, 53.

I. *The Rise of the Plebeians,* 53–65:

The aristocratic monarchy becomes an aristocratic republic, 54.
> The magistrates, 54.
> The Senate, 54.
> The citizen assemblies (*comitia*), 54, 56.
> Oppression of the plebeians, 56.
> Tribunes of the people, 57.

Petty wars in Latium, 58.
Agrarian troubles, 58.
Plebeian encroachments, 59-61.
> Publilian law, 59.
> Decemvirs and " Laws of Twelve Tables," 60.
> Second Secession and Valerio-Horatian Laws, 60.
> Intermarriage and military tribunes, 61.
> Quæstorship opened to plebeians, 61.

War with Veii, 62.
Rome taken by the Gauls, 62.
Fresh plebeian advances, 63-65:
> The Licinian Laws (plebeian consuls), 63, 64.
> Restrictions removed from higher offices, 64.
> The revolution complete but gradual, 65.

II. *The Roman Conquest of Italy*, 65-70:
Roman enemies in the peninsula, 65, 66.
Subjection of Etruria, 66.
Campaigns against the Italians, 66.
The three Samnite wars, 67, 69.
The Roman bonds—colonies and roads, 68.
Subjection of the South (Pyrrhus), 69, 70.
Government of Roman Italy.

REVIEW EXERCISE.

Second Period. The Roman Republic. Part I. 509-264 B. C.

1. How long did the Roman republic last?
2. Into what three parts may the history of the republic be divided?
3. What were the authorities of the early historians?
4. What two great conflicts engaged the Romans?
5. Into what was the Roman monarchy transformed?
6. What magistrates received the royal authority?
7. What changes took place in the Senate?
8. What was the great popular assembly of the republic?
9. What third comitia (assembly) attained eminence?

10. Which class profited most by the expulsion of the kings?
11. What were the grievances of the plebeians?
12. Give an account of the "First Secession of the Plebs."
13. How did the tribunes originate and what were their powers?
14. What enemies had the young republic? Tell the story of Coriolanus.
15. Give some evidence of agrarian distress.
16. What did the Publilian law confirm?
17. For what were the Decemvirs appointed?
18. Of what benefit were the "Laws of the Twelve Tables"?
19. What caused the Second Plebeian Secession and what was its effect?
20. Name six points of the Valerio-Horatian laws.
21. When was the intermarriage of the orders legalized?
22. For what was the censorship established?
23. Describe the invasion of the Gauls.
24. What did the famous Licinian laws secure?
25. In what years did plebeians become eligible to the several higher offices?
26. What did the Third Secession of the Plebs accomplish?
27. What distinguished the political revolution?
28. What nations did Rome conquer in Italy?
29. Describe the three Samnite wars.
30. How did Rome hold her conquests?
31. Describe the war with Tarentum. How did Rome govern Italy?

CHAPTER IV.

SECOND PERIOD (Continued).

THE ROMAN REPUBLIC.

Part II. (*264–133 B. C.*)

THE PUNIC WARS AND FOREIGN CONQUESTS.

AT THE beginning of the second stage of the republic Rome was confronted by her first foreign rival, Car′thage. Tyre and Si′don, the famous coast cities of Ca′naan or Phœnī′cia, planted their trading colonies at many points on the Mediterra′nean before 1000 B. C. There are distinct traces of Phœnī′cian influence in Greece, and the Bible bears witness to the boldness of their commercial enterprise. Among the Phœnī′cian—in Roman language "Pu′nic"—settlements in the western seas Car′thage easily gained and held the first rank. Its situation, near that of the modern city of Tu′nis, was a highly advantageous point for trading, and the Tyr′ians who settled there made the most of their opportunity. Phœnī′cia itself was suffering from the oppression of the Assyr′ian conquerors and many of its best citizens emigrated to this new Tyre in the far west. Car′thage became the center of a commercial empire; her fleets covered the Western Mediterra′nean and visited Brit′ain, and her own trading colonies abounded in Si′cily, Sardin′ia, and Spain, as well as along the Af′rican coast. The city demanded tribute from every dependency

Phœnicians found Carthage. 814 B. C. (?)

and filled the ranks of her armies with mercenary troops paid from her full coffers. Only the generals were Carthagin'ians, and the love of country which animated the Ro'man citizen soldier was unknown among the Lib'yans and Numid'ians who fought in the pay of the Af'rican city. Car'thage was governed by an oligarchy of wealthy merchants who lived in oriental luxury. There was no prosperous middle class of citizens, the whole State being made up of capitalists, of landless freemen, and of slaves, myriads of whom cultivated the plantations and handled the goods of the merchant princes.

Power of Carthage.

A comparison between Rome and Car'thage at the outbreak of the war is favorable to the former. Rome was far poorer in money and material resources, and far less advanced in the arts of civilization, but she had the support of united It'aly, whose people were related to each other and bound to herself by the expectation of some share in the glory and profits of her greatness. Car'thage had enormous wealth and was invincible on the sea; but her land army was composed of hired aliens or impressed subjects, not of freemen, and her dependencies hated her as a monopolist of trade and a greedy collector of tribute.

Rome and Carthage compared.

The duel between Rome and Car'thage began in Si'cily, and in this wise: A band of ruffians from Mag'na Græ'cia, calling themselves "Sons of Mars" (Mam'ertines) seized the important citadel of Messa'na, in Si'cily, the key of the straits, and held it against the assaults of Hi'ero II., king of the Greek city Syr'acuse, who sought to dislodge them. In their extremity they asked aid of the Ro'mans, who had as yet no foothold in the island, and of the Carthagin'ians, who had more than a score of colonies there and who had long disputed possession of Si'cily with the strong Greek power which centered at Syr'acuse. The

Outbreak of hostilities.

conservative Ro'man Senate hesitated to send an army out of It'aly, and Car'thage, by prompt action, got possession of the town before the consul's army crossed the straits. But the Ro'mans ultimately drove out the Carthagin'ian garrison and occupied Messa'na for themselves. Car'thage thereupon declared war (264 B. C.). Rome had the advantage during the first eight years of the contest. King Hi'ero attached himself to her, and their united forces made short work of the interior towns. Agrigen'tum, also, was taken after a long siege; but there the Ro'man conquests were stayed. The strong coast fortresses were safe from her land attacks, and Rome had no navy worthy of the name. The Senate resolved to supply the deficiency; indeed, a fleet was necessary not only for offensive purposes, but to protect the defenseless Ital'ian harbors. A Carthagin'ian five-decker (*quīn'querēme*), beached on the Lat'in coast, supplied a model, and in 260 B. C. the energy of the Ro'mans equipped a fleet of one hundred and twenty large vessels of war. To offset their rude seamanship they crowded the bows of their galleys with fighting men and provided grappling-irons and boarding bridges by which their soldiers might come to close combat with the Carthagin'ian marines. This was an innovation in sea-fighting, for the Greeks, the pioneers in this art, had employed few marines, relying mainly upon maneuvers and ramming strokes of their armored prows. The device worked admirably, however, and Cā'ius Duīl'ius won Rome's first naval battle with their aid, in this same year, 260 B. C., off My'læ, near Messa'na. The fleet seized several towns on the shores of Si'cily and Cor'sica; but Panor'mus, Drep'anum, and Lilybæ'um resisted stoutly, and Hamīl'car, the Carthagin'ian general in Si'cily, even won back some of the inland cities. In order to stop this desultory warfare the Ro'man

First Punic war. 264-241 B. C.

First Roman war-fleet. 260 B. C.

Senate fitted out a fleet of three hundred and thirty ships for an attack upon Car'thage itself. A Pu'nic fleet of equal numbers was beaten at Ec'nŏmus, and (256 B. C.) the Ro'mans landed a few miles from the great city. Overconfidence induced them to send back a portion of the ships and soldiers, leaving the Consul Mar'cus Atil'lius Reg'ulus in command. The city would have fallen had the consul "pushed things;" but his terms of surrender were too exacting, and before he was ready to strike reinforcements had arrived. Hamĭl'car hastened from Si'cily with his veterans, and Greek infantry and Numĭd'ian horsemen were hired in multitudes. Xanthip'pus came from Spar'ta, that nursery of warriors, to superintend the military operations. The Spar'tan cut the Ro'man legions to pieces with his cavalry and elephants, and took the consul captive (255 B. C.). The fleet which the Ro'mans sent to bring off the remnant of the army was shattered in a storm.

Defeat of Regulus. 255 B. C.

There is an interesting Ro'man story, which we should like to believe, that Reg'ulus was sent to Rome with a Carthagin'ian embassy to treat for peace. It was supposed that the captive noble would use his great influence for a cessation of hostilities and his own release. But the proud and patriotic Ro'man begged the senators to prosecute the war with all their might and so avenge the disgrace of his defeat. Then he went back voluntarily to his dungeon in Car'thage, and his captors avenged their disappointment by tormenting him to death (250 B. C.).

Story of Regulus.

The Af'rican campaign, then, ended in failure, and Si'cily again became the scene of war. Panor'mus capitulated to Rome (254 B. C.). Storms had again wrecked a Ro'man fleet (255 B. C.) and the enormous expense and insubstantial gains of naval warfare had disgusted the Senate. On the land success was rare. In 251 B. C. the Consul Metel'lus defeated

Has'drubal near Panor'mus, but two years later the Carthagin'ians destroyed the remnant of the Ro'man sea force.

Hamilcar Barca. Active operations now languished; but Hamil'car, surnamed Bar'ca, "The Lightning," from his fierce and unexpected strokes, maintained himself in Si'cily, harassing the consuls and playing havoc with the allies of Rome and Syr'acuse. The Ro'man merchants, whose trade had declined in consequence of the exhausting war, raised a naval fund among themselves and presented it to the State. The Consul Lutā'tius Cat'ulus was assigned to the command of the new fleet, which won the decisive battle of the Ægu'san Islands (241 B. C.). This closed the first Pu'nic war. The treaty of peace awarded to Rome all the Carthagin'ian possessions in Si'cily and a war indemnity amounting to $4,000,000 to be paid within ten years.

Close of first Punic war. 241 B. C.

Neither Rome nor Car'thage was idle in the twenty-three years which elapsed between the first and second Pu'nic wars. Rome's first care was to strengthen her defenses. It'aly proper was already bound to her. She now (241 B. C.) organized her Sicil'ian conquest into a province—the first of her outlying possessions which were to include the whole Mediterranean world. Sardin'ia, also, was won over from Car'thage, and combined with Cor'sica to form a second province (231 B. C.). The organization of the provincial government was carried out by the general who had conquered it, assisted by a senatorial commission, the existing law of the land being disturbed as little as possible. Affairs in the west being satisfactorily composed, the Senate—now a body of great wisdom and executive force—turned its attention to the east and north. The Illyr'ian pirates, whose haunts were among the inlets and islets of the eastern border of the Adriat'ic, and who had harassed the commerce

First Roman province. 241 B. C.

of It′aly and preyed upon the coast cities of Greece, were thoroughly chastised between the years 229 B. C. and 219 B. C. The Greek towns, relieved from their fears, admitted their Ro′man liberators to share their national games and religious rites. It was a dangerous and greedy guest that they had bidden to their feast.

Rome crosses Adriatic.

Another invasion by the restless Gauls from the Po valley aroused the Ro′mans to the necessity of subjugating these turbulent northern neighbors. They were beaten (225 B. C.) in the battle of Tel′amon, and driven back from Etru′ria into Cisal′pine Gaul. Here the Ro′mans planted important colonies—Placen′tia, Cremo′na, Muti′na—and extended the Flamin′ian military road to this region. These measures were scarcely completed when the Carthagin′ians precipitated the second Pu′nic war.

Subjugation of Cisalpine Gaul. 225 B. C.

After her first encounter with Rome Car′thage had come under the influence of a great man. Hamil′car Bar′ca, the dashing leader who had delayed the Ro′man conquest of Si′cily, was keen enough to see that there was an inevitable conflict of interest between the two great cities. Car′thage had lost Si′cily, and he accepted the bitter fact, endeavoring to build up another and richer province in the west, to offset the loss, and to afford resources upon which to draw in time of need. The Carthagin′ians granted him an army and dictatorial power, and with these he crossed over to Spain (238 B. C.). By his skill as a general and his ability as a statesman he established a strong Spanish state, dependent upon Car′thage and yielding a valuable revenue from its mines. When he fell in battle (228 B. C.) his son-in-law, Has′drubal, continued the work. Rome took alarm and fixed the river Ibē′rus (modern E′bro) as the eastward limit of Carthagin′ian conquest; but no aggres-

Hamilcar in Spain.

sive action was taken until Has'drubal was too strong to be put down. When an assassin's dagger ended his life (220 B. C.), the command of the Carthagin'ians in Spain fell into most efficient hands.

When Hamil'car Bar'ca left Car'thage on his Spanish errand he called to the altar of his country's gods his eldest son, Han'nibal, a boy of nine years, and made him swear a solemn oath to cherish undying hatred toward Rome. This boy served with his father and brother-in-law in the western campaigns, and became the pet and pride of the soldiers. He was twenty-eight years old when Has'drubal died, and the army hailed him as its leader. He perceived that the moment for which his father had been working in patience was now at hand. The Span'ish province was firmly established, and its revenues not only paid the expense of government and conquest, but yielded a surplus to the treasury of the mother city. The army which had accomplished this work was not the usual mercenary medley which fought for Car'thage. Its men had been hardened by long campaigns, inspirited by repeated successes under Hamil'car and Has'drubal; they were well-paid and well-fed veterans, devoted to their leader and their profession and fired with his own lofty enthusiasm. Han'nibal himself was the central figure of the war. He was one of the greatest commanders in history, and his talent far transcended that of a mere leader of troops. He was a statesman of foresight and energy, and until he died Rome trembled at the whisper of his name.

Hannibal's oath.

Character of Hannibal.

To break the peace Han'nibal sacked Sagun'tum, a border town under Ro'man protection, and disregarded the limits which Rome had fixed for the extension of Carthagin'ian power in Europe. The envoys of the Senate demanded the surrender of Han'nibal for

Second Punic war. 218-202 B. C.

this alleged breach of faith. Car'thage refused, and war was declared, 218 B. C.

<small>Hannibal's plan of campaign.</small> The second Pu'nic war was not, like the first, a succession of desultory and, for the most part futile, campaigns, but was conducted by Han'nibal upon a carefully elaborated plan. He saw that the strength of Rome rested in her allies—that united It'aly was his real foe. To deprive the city of its allies would be its ruin. The prospect for the success of such a policy seemed bright. The Cisal'pine Gauls were still in angry mood from their recent chastisement and from the erection of the military colonies on their lands in the Po valley. There were still living Sam'nites and Etrus'cans who could remember when their countries were free from the Ro'man yoke, and who still sighed for their lost liberty. The Greek towns of southern It'aly could feel but slight concern for the city which had conquered them only fifty years before. These considerations determined Han'nibal's plan of attack. He would enter northern It'aly with all speed, call the disaffected Gauls to his standard, and then march southward in the guise of a liberator, seducing Etrus'cans, Sam'nites and Greeks from their Ro'man allegiance. Having shorn Rome of her allies he would crush her legions with his veteran troops. We shall see how closely this design was followed and with what success.

<small>Hannibal crosses the Alps. 218 B. C.</small> Having made provision for the defense of Spain and Af'rica, Han'nibal set out in the spring of 218 B. C. on his famous march. He chose the land route to It'aly, his road crossing southeastern Spain, the Pyr'enees Mountains, southern Gaul (France), and thence over the Al'pine barrier to the valley of the Po. He had 90,000 infantry, 12,000 cavalry, and 37 elephants; but when he reached the river Rhône the force had been reduced

by hardships and detachments for garrison duty to 50,000 infantry and 9,000 cavalry, the flower of an army which had been seasoned by twenty years of fighting. The cautious Ro'man general, Pub'lius Cornē'lius Sci'pio, was out-maneuvered, and the Carthagin'ian army crossed the Rhône in safety and made its way to the Alps unmolested. It was September. The half barbarous mountaineers were hostile and the autumn snows had begun to fall; but Han'nibal pressed on undismayed over the Little St. Bernard' pass, and with the loss of half his foot soldiers and one third of his mounted men descended to the plains of the upper Po in Cisal'pine Gaul.

The Ro'mans were taken by surprise. The two consular armies, which had been sent, the one to Spain, the other to Af'rica, were recalled in all haste. The Gauls fulfilled Han'nibal's expectations by crowding to his headquarters and enlisting for the war. By the time the northern army under Pub'lius Sci'pio was ready to face him his troops were rested and half Cisal'pine Gaul was at his back. The two armies met (218 B. C.) in the battle of Ticī'nus, to the discomfiture of the Ro'mans; although the masterly retreat of the wounded Sci'pio across the Po checked Han'nibal's immediate progress. But the advantage was lost by the other consul, Semprŏ'nius, who was enticed into the battle of Trĕ'bia (218 B. C.), which resulted in the defeat of the Ro'mans and the complete submission of the Cisal'pine Gauls.

Conquest of Cisalpine Gaul. 218 B. C.

The fortified Ro'man colonies, however, did not yield, and Han'nibal, who could not stop for sieges, must needs leave these dangerous posts behind him. Adhering to his plans he lingered in the north only to the end of winter, and then hastened southward over the Ap'ennines to Etru'ria and It'aly proper. His coming was heralded by the Ital'ian captives whom he had taken at Trĕ'bia and Ticī'nus and released with honors to scatter the news of his approach. He proclaimed himself the liberator of the Ital′ian towns, and treated them with distinguished consideration. But his Ro′man captives were punished with cruel severity. Thus he sought to impress upon the people that his quarrel was with Rome alone, and that the Ital′ians might find security and honor in alliance with him against a common foe.

Policy of Hannibal.

The Carthagin′ians sickened in great numbers from the malaria of the Etrus′can swamps, and Han′nibal lost an eye from a disease contracted there. But the Ro′mans, cursed with incompetent leaders, offered no opposition until these ills were over and the enemy reached firm ground again. Then the new consul, who had stayed in camp in the east at Arrē′tium while the enemy were laboring down the other border of the peninsula, gave tardy chase. The Ro′mans came up with the Carthagin′ians in a defile near Lake Trasimē′nus and plunged headlong into a snare which Han′nibal had laid. Fifteen thousand Ro′mans fell and half as many were taken prisoners in this disaster, which was too one-sided to be called a battle (217 B. C.). Rome stood aghast. All Etru′ria was lost; Han′nibal might march to the Ti′ber unopposed; still there was no demand for peace. On the contrary Rome gathered all her strength to resist the shock. Quin′tus Fa′bius Max′imus was appointed dictator and a new army of defense was levied.

Battle of Lake Trasimenus. 217 B. C.

Some have wondered that Han′nibal did not follow up his success at Lake Trasimē′nus with an attack on Rome. But his plan was wiser. The cavalry which won his battles could not take a walled city, and his army was not prepared for a long siege in the heart of a hostile country. So he turned eastward to

Hannibal in Central Italy.

gather forage and plunder in Um′bria and Picē′num, and to drill and discipline the masses of raw Gaul′ish volunteers who flocked to his camps.

The dictator Fa′bius had learned a lesson from the three defeats of his predecessors. He had not the cavalry nor the skill to defeat the invader in battle; but he hoped to frustrate his plans without fighting. Han′nibal had been in It′aly two years, but, excepting the Gauls, hardly a single ally of Rome had deserted what surely must have looked like a losing cause. The Ro′man political system and the colonial "patches of Rome" throughout the peninsula held the subject countries to their fealty. Han′nibal's schemes depended upon breaking this allegiance, and the longer he remained in It′aly without doing so the weaker his position became. So Fa′bius followed the invader instead of facing him. The eager Ro′man mob denounced him as *cunctā′tor* ("Loiterer"), and clamored against him at the news of Han′nibal's raids in the rich Campa′nian farm lands. His dictatorship expired without a decisive engagement, and two consuls, the hare-brained Var′ro and the cautious Paul′us, were elected for the year 216 B. C. The defect of the Ro′man consular system hastened the catastrophe. The two generals had equal authority, and to avoid conflicting orders on the battlefield it was agreed that each should be supreme on alternate days. The army, with its alternating commanders, was posted in Apū′lia watching Han′nibal. The impetuous Var′ro, tired of "Fa′bian" tactics, gave battle in the open plain of Can′næ, on the little river Au′fidus—a singularly injudicious choice. The level ground was perfectly adapted for the evolutions of the Af′rican horse. The legions fought with their usual stubborn energy, but they were out-generaled, surrounded, their lines broken, their soldiers slaughtered.

Margin notes: Q. Fabius, "cunctator." — Roman defeat at Cannæ. 216 B. C.

Seventy thousand Ro'mans fell victims to Var'ro's headstrong folly.

That the government of Rome survived the shock of such a disaster was prophetic of the outcome of the war. Cap'ua, the second city of It'aly, now joined Han'nibal. The Sam'nites and Luca'nians broke their treaty pledges, and sent reinforcements to the invader. But the great body of the Ital'ians clung to Rome. Scarcely a colony wavered. Han'nibal had struck his heaviest blow; he could not hope to surpass his successes at Trĕ'bia, Trasimĕ'nus, and Can'næ; yet the political unity of It'aly was unbroken.

Stability of Rome.

At this period Rome indeed deserved the confidence of her allies. There was no suggestion of defeat in the proud spirit of the Senate. No time was wasted in lamentation for the dead, still less in proposals of peace; but every freeman of military age was impressed for the war, and even slaves were armed. Fa'bius, Grac'chus, and Marcel'lus led the new levies and prosecuted the war in It'aly. In Spain the brothers Pub'lius and Cnĕ'ius Scip'io engaged young Has'drubal, and prevented him from aiding his brother, Han'nibal. Car'thage sent scanty reinforcements to It'aly. Phil'ip, king of Macedo'nia, promised much; but Rome took care that he should perform little. Hieron'ymus of Syr'acuse lent but feeble co-operation. Han'nibal's cause declined steadily after Can'næ. The cohesion of the Ro'man state, the revived energy of Senate and citizens, delayed the consummation of his plans; and for him delay meant decay. In 215 B. C. he lost his first battle at No'la. The Ro'mans kept Phil'ip occupied by the indecisive first Macedo'nian war (215-206 B. C.), and Marcel'lus punished Hieron'ymus of SI'cily by the war which ended in the siege and capture of Syr'acuse (212 B. C.).

Energy of the Senate.

From 212 B. C. to 207 B. C. Han'nibal remained comparatively inactive. He captured and lost individual cities, but made no real progress toward the realization of his project. In the year 210 B. C., Pub'lius Corne'lius Scip'io, a son of the old consul, went to Spain to crush the Carthagin'ians there. He was fortunate, but Has'drubal eluded him, 208 B. C., and hastened across the Alps with reinforcements for his brother. The consuls of 207 B. C. were Liv'ius and Ne'ro. The former was in the north of It'aly with an army ; the latter, in the south, was dogging Han'nibal's track, and endeavoring to prevent a junction of the two sons of Hamil'car Bar'ca. By a forced march Ne'ro joined Liv'ius on the Metau'rus, defeated and destroyed the auxiliaries under Has'drubal, and returned to his position in front of Han'nibal before that general was aware of his brother's arrival in It'aly. The loss of the Span'ish reinforcements was disheartening ; Han'nibal retired to Brut'tium and abandoned aggressive operations.

Operations in Italy. 212-207 B. C.—Scipio.

Rome now became the attacking party. The young Scip'io returned from Spain in 206 B. C. He had utterly subdued the kingdom which Han'nibal's father had established there. In 205 B. C. he was made consul, and prepared "to carry the war into Af'rica," as the best means of dislodging the enemy from It'aly. With the enthusiastic support of the Senate he assumed control of the military operations. One army covered the movements of Ma'go, Hamil'car's youngest son, who had landed in northern It'aly ; but the greater armament sailed for Car'thage (204 B. C.). The next year Han'nibal was recalled to Af'rica to defend the capital, but the resources of the state were already exhausted. Scip'io defeated him at Za'ma (202 B. C.) and ended the war.

Carrying the war into Africa. 204 B. C.

Zama. 202 B. C.

Car'thage bought peace dearly. She gave up all claim to

her former dominions outside of Af′rica, transferred the tributary kingdom of Numid′ia to Massinis′sa, an ally of Rome, destroyed her war fleet, and bound herself to pay an annual tribute. The Ro′mans greeted Scip′io with extraordinary honors, and gave him the name "Africă′nus" ("the man of Af′rica"), in commemoration of his triumph.

Humiliation of Carthage.

The close of the war left Rome with many things to do. Those Greek and Ital′ian cities that had sided with Han′nibal she disgraced and humiliated by deprivation of lands and political rights. Pleasant Cap′ua, the second city of It′aly, was made desolate. The Cisal′pine Gauls were resubjugated and fettered by means of roads and colonies (200-191 B. C.). In Spain there were constant wars, but the country was parceled into two Ro′man provinces under the government of prætors.

Pacification of Roman domain.

The dethronement of Car′thage made Rome the leading power in the Mediterra′nean, and her relations with eastern nations soon involved her in wars which widely extended her conquests beyond the Adriăt′ic.

Eastern wars.

Many circumstances prepared the way for an easy conquest of the East. Civilization was at the flood in the countries at the eastern end of the Mediterra′nean, but power was at a low ebb. Macedŏ′nia, Greece, Syr′ia, and Egypt were the most important divisions. Their condition at the close of the war with Han′nibal will explain their subsequent history. Macedo′nia was a country of Eu′rope skirting the northern shore of the Æge′an Sea. Under two kings, Phil′ip (339-336 B. C.) and Alexan′der the Great (336-323 B. C.), it had risen from obscurity to the mastery of Greece, A′sia, and Af′rica. At Alexan′der's untimely death the empire was divided among a number of his generals, some of whom were capable rulers,

The East after Alexander.

Macedonia.

who built up the prosperous kingdoms of the Ptol'emies in E'gypt, of the Seleu'cidæ in Syr'ia, of Per'gamon and Bithyn'ia in A'sia Mi'nor, and in Macedo'nia, the old home territory. The three last-named were among the weaker divisions, and Macedo'nia, especially, soon lost its leading place. Greece had been the first conquest of Alexan'der's father, Phil'ip, and had exhausted itself in efforts to regain its freedom. The cities of Greece bound themselves loosely together in two leagues, the Ætō'lian and the Achæ'an—notable as the earliest known experiments in federal government—with the object of expelling Macedo'nian garrisons from their citadels. But these leagues were engaged in almost continual disputes with each other, and, despite their patriotic aims, really contributed to the downfall of the nation by dividing and consuming its strength and so inviting foreign interference.

Greece.

The kingdom of Syr'ia was for a time the most powerful segment of Alexan'der's empire. It comprised the eastern half of A'sia Mi'nor and the whole of Per'sia. At the close of the second Pu'nic war its ruler, Anti'ochus the Great (224-187 B. C.), was in his prime. He had added many provinces to his dominions, had adorned his capital, An'tioch, on the Oron'tes, with every magnificence, and had decked his court with all that lavish splendor which had formerly distinguished the households of Dari'us and Xer'xes. Like those Per'sian conquerors, Anti'ochus assumed the title of "King of Kings," or "The Great King," and exacted slavish submission from his people. It was with declining Macedo'nia, distressed Greece, and luxurious Syr'ia that Rome came in contact near the close of the third century before Christ. Egypt was her later prey.

Syria under Antiochus.

The statesmanship of Han'nibal had prompted him to form a league of all the Mediterra'nean nations in opposition to

Rome, and one of his most promising alliances had been with Phil′ip V., king of Mac′edon, whom the success at Can′næ (216 B. C.) won to the Carthagin′ian side. But the exertions of Rome nullified the king's intentions. The Senate sent a small force into Greece and involved the Æto′lian League in war with Phil′ip. This first Macedo′nian war (215-206 B. C.), while not in itself decisive, served Rome's purpose, for it held one enemy in check and enabled the hard-pressed Senate to concentrate all its forces against Han′nibal, its mortal foe. The close of this war did not alter the independent relations of Rome and Mac′edon. Phil′ip was left free, but his use of his liberty soon involved him in a second war. He was a bold, restless spirit, endowed with real genius, but cursed with periods of weakness and inaction. Before the battle of Zā′ma he re-opened his alliance with Car′thage, and after the peace he attacked the Greek cities which the Illyr′ian pirate-hunting expeditions had inclined toward friendship with Rome. On these grounds the Senate decided to renew the war (200 B. C.). The two Greek leagues joined the Ro′mans and drove the Macedo′nians out of Central Greece. Phil′ip made a stand in Thes′saly, but was routed at Cynosceph′alæ (197 B. C.) by the Consul Ti′tus Quin′tius Flamini′nus. The terms of peace included the practical disarmament of the Macedo′nians. Their treasury was emptied by a heavy war tribute, their land and naval forces were cut down to insignificance, and their foreign affairs were yielded to Ro′man direction.

First Macedonian war. 215-206 B. C.

Second Macedonian war. 200-197 B. C.

Cynosceph-alæ. 197 B. C.

The part which the Greeks had taken in these campaigns deserved the friendship of the Ro′mans, and one of the first acts of the victorious Flamini′nus was to declare the independence of the Greek cities. This was done at the national festival of the Isth′mian games (197 B. C.) amid great rejoicings, which were, perhaps, uncalled for; for this " in-dependence " which was so freely bestowed really meant nothing more than relief from Macedo′nian supremacy, and real dependence upon Rome. The cities were left to themselves; the Achæ′an League was, perhaps, encouraged; but the Ro′mans took care that no foreign influence except their own should dominate the Greek cantons and that no Greek confederacy should acquire a dangerous degree of power.

"Independence" of Greek states. 197 B. C.

After the disaster at Zä′ma, Han′nibal, whom the magnanimity of Scip′io had spared, devoted himself to the rehabilitation of his country. He penetrated to the defects of its political system with the same piercing vision which had directed his campaigns and had detected the weaknesses of his enemies. Although defeated, he was a popular hero, and wielded a power in Car′-thage which Rome wisely feared. His opponents in the former city accused him before the Ro′man Senate, and that body was willing enough to stay his reforms and banish their author. Han′nibal escaped with his life. The oath which his boyish lips had sworn in the presence of his glorious father upon the solemn Phœni′cian altars he had religiously cherished. His hatred of Rome was undying, and when his own city closed her gates against him and his efforts to re-organize her resources were thwarted, he clung to his single purpose, the destruction of Rome. The court of Anti′-ochus the Great was his natural refuge (194 B. C.). He won the favor of the Great King, who had not yet come in conflict with the conquering city of the West. Han′nibal engaged the king in his projects of revenge. Together they planned an anti-Ro′man coalition of Greeks and Asiat′ics. Rome deemed the monarch's reception of Han′nibal and his negotia-

Hannibal after Zama.

tions with the "independent" Greeks a sufficient ground for hostilities, and her so-called "War with Anti′ochus" began in 192 B. C.

The war opened with a Syr′ian invasion of Greece (192 B. C.); but the Greek cities, with Mac′edon and Per′gamon, helped the Ro′mans to scatter the king's army. In 190 B. C. Ro′man and Rho′dian fleets defeated Han′nibal's armada at the Eurym′edon. The Ro′man forces in A′sia Mi′nor were commanded by the Consul Lu′cius Scip′io, assisted by his brother, the victor of Zā′ma; they ended the war by the battle of Magnē′sia (190 B. C.). Anti′ochus gave up his possessions in Eu′rope and the western part of his Asiat′ic provinces, and paid a war indemnity. Han′nibal escaped, but the hatred of Rome followed him to the Bithyn′ian court, and in 183 B. C. he took his own great life by a draught of poison. Scip′io Africa′nus, his conqueror, died at about the same time, an exile by choice from his native city, where his later years had been clouded by disappointment and by real or fancied neglect.

War with Antiochus. 192-190 B. C.

Death of Hannibal. 183 B. C.

Macedo′nia was the next state to adopt the plans of Han′nibal for a combination against the menace of Rome. The new king, Per′seus, restored to some extent the prosperity of his own realm, gained the fickle favor of the Greek cities, and conceived other alliances, which, however, were still incomplete in 172 B. C., when Rome resolved upon war. For three years the incompetent consuls accomplished little or nothing; but in 168 B. C. Lu′cius Æmil′ius Pau′lus, a patrician of the best sort, brought his energy and ability to the conduct of the war. His legions shattered the Macedo′nian phalanx at Pyd′na (168 B. C.), and with that battle broke the power which, at the death of Alexan′der, a

Third Macedonian war. 172-168 B. C.

Pydna. 168 B. C.

century and a half earlier, had overshadowed all the East.
The independence of Greece, Mac′edon, and Illyr′ia was taken
away, and there was now no civilized court about the Mediter-
ra′nean in Eu′rope, A′sia, or Af′rica where the authority
of the Ro′man Senate was not recognized and obeyed. There
were still semi-dependent kings in A′sia Mi′nor and E′gypt,
but they only awaited their doom. No monarch ventured
to oppose his will to that of the Ro′man Senate.

Car′thage was still a city of mercantile prosperity and
wealth. Her days of empire were ended, but nothing could
close her markets or her harbors. Something
"Delenda est Carthago." of her old pride yet remained, and her citizens
were galled by the encroachments of Massinis′sa,
whom Rome had established on her borders as king of Nu-
mid′ia. Rome supported this Af′rican in his appropriations of
Carthagin′ian territory and refused either to send out an army
or to allow Car′thage the means of defending herself. Without
troops, without a fleet, without a leader, the desperate city
took up arms against the king, and the Senate, led by the
censor, Mar′cus Por′cius Cä′to, who made reiterated demands
for the destruction of Car′thage ("*Delen′da est Cartha′go*"),
interpreted this as an act of war against Rome. This third
Pu′nic war began in 149 B. C., with the Ro′man
Third Punic war, 149-146 B. C. invasion of Af′rica. Car′thage yielded and was
disarmed ; but when the Ro′mans ordered the
citizens to pull down their walls and houses, and desert the
old harbor town for a new site ten miles inland, the Phœni′-
cian spirit flamed out fiercely as it had done in the days
of Reg′ulus. The gates were closed against the Ro′mans,
weapons were contrived in haste, a fleet was built, and the
defense maintained at terrible sacrifice. In 147 B. C. Pub′lius
Cornē′lius Scip′io Æmiliä′nus, the son of Æmil′ius Pau′lus
and the adopted heir of the great Scip′io, took charge of

the besiegers. His lines cut Car'thage off from land communication and he choked the harbor mouth with a wall of stone. Pestilence and famine weakened the defenders, and in the spring of 146 B. C. the Ro'mans scaled the ramparts. The citizens contested the possession of every house and street, but fire and sword overcame them after six days of bloody combat. The walls and buildings were leveled and a curse was laid upon the ashes of the city. A part of its territory was annexed to Numid'ia, Rome's subject kingdom, and the remnant was made the province of Af'rica, with U'tica as its capital. The name of Carthage no longer existed on the map of the world.

Destruction of Carthage. 146 B. C.

While Rome was wreaking this terrible vengeance upon her sole western rival, the liberties of Greece and Mac'edon were expiring. After the fourth Macedo'nian war (148–146 B. C.) Macedo'nia became a province of Rome. The constant strife among the Greek States induced Rome to crush them into submission. Lu'cius Mum'mius defeated the Achæ'ans at Leucope'tra (146 B. C.), and in the same year obeyed the command of the Senate to destroy the city of Cor'inth, at that time the metropolis of Gre'cian art, commerce, and civilization.

Fourth Macedonian war. 148–146 B. C.

Corinth destroyed. 146 B. C.

The Celt'ic tribes of northern Spain did not take kindly to Ro'man dominion, and the Lusita'nians, dwelling in the region now known as Por'tugal, made serious inroads on the Ro'man provinces. Viriā'thus, the Lusita'nian leader, was one of the ablest warriors that Rome ever encountered. With no advantages, save familiarity with the country in which he fought, this leader of half-civilized hordes held out for ten years (148–139 B. C.) against the best armies which could be sent to defeat him. The Ro'man governors were powerless to

Wars in Spain. Viriathus. 148–139 B. C.

crush him and had recourse to perfidy. In 139 B. C. they procured his assassination, much to their relief, and soon brought his followers to terms. The Celtibē'rians in northern Spain were basely treated by the provincial prætors, and retaliated by a fierce war, in which they inflicted heavy losses before they had to yield.

To this same period belongs the Numan'tine war. Numan'tia, a town among the mountains of eastern Spain,

Numantine war. 137-133 B. C. held out for four years single-handed against the Ro'man generals. The armies which had terrified the world could do nothing against these free people. The incompetence and faithlessness of the generals prolonged the war beyond all endurance. In 134 B. C. Scip'io Æmiliā'nus, who had commanded in the third Pu'nic war, was sent to Spain. For many months the heroic Numan'tines withstood even his energy and determination. At last, worn out by their exertions, weakened by famine and disease, they set fire to their houses and died defiantly as the Ro'mans broke into the town (133 B. C.).

These obstinate Span'ish wars and the heroic defence of Numan'tia are not to be ignored because of their small place

Demoralization of State. in history; they have a peculiar significance, and suggest important inquiries in regard to the condition of Rome at this time. The successful stands of Viriā'thus, of the Celtibē'rians, and of Numan'tia, are surprising, coming, as they do, at the time when Rome had shown herself incomparable in arms against civilized peoples. The power which withstood the assaults of Han'nibal was baffled by a tribe of savage mountaineers! Car'thage and Cor'inth, the "Lon'don" and the "Par'is" of that age, were destroyed, but their conqueror seems to have met her match ten years later at Numan'tia! It is true that a change had taken place at Rome. A transformation, outwardly for the better, but demoralizing within, was passing over the Commonwealth. It began at the close of the second Pu′nic war. The tribute money exacted from Car′thage and from the subject kingdoms of the East was the original source of the corruption. The provinces which the Senate erected from time to time out of its conquests were ruled by Ro′man prætors, later by pro-consuls, who took advantage of their brief terms of office to plunder their territories. The taxes of the provinces were farmed by Ro′man speculators, who paid the State a round sum for the right to collect the taxes and then extorted from the poor provincials money enough to yield them an enormous profit. These tax-farmers were usually men of the "equestrian order" (*eq′uites*), and their subordinates in the provinces were the hated *publicani* ("publicans").

Corruption.

From the conquests in Greece and A′sia the Ro′mans gained new ideas of luxury which sorted ill with their ancient simplicity. The art treasures of Ath′ens and Cor′inth were shipped to Rome to adorn the city. The theater of Greece was copied and the corrupt comedies of the Greek stage were adapted to the coarse language and ideas of Rome. The Greek language, already the language of Ro′man books, became the language of polite society. The sons of rich men went to Ath′ens to perfect their education, and Greek teachers established themselves in Rome. The Ro′mans began to spend more money on their homes, on personal adornment, and especially on their pleasures. It was an undoubted fact that the ancient strength of character which had been the pride of the race was relaxing under the strain of foreign influence and increasing wealth.

Influx of Greek ideas and manners.

Still another germ of disease in the State was slavery. This had existed from the most remote ages; but with the extension of foreign conquest it increased beyond all former limits.

<small>Slavery.</small> Slaves by the hundred thousand were imported from Greece and A′sia, and every form of domestic and agricultural labor was wrested from freemen and imposed upon slaves. The cruelty of the Ro′man had not declined with the decay of his firmness, and the lot of the plantation-hand consequently had few ameliorations. It was a short life of utter misery. This slave-system was a two-edged sword cutting into the life of the republic: it maintained a population of several millions of men who were ready to seize the slightest opportunity to break away from their masters and begin the most terrible of insurrections, and it destroyed the dignity of free labor. The free agriculturists could not compete with the chain-gangs, and the result was that the landless class in It′aly, deprived of the means of support, flocked to the capital, forming a needy populace with which the government had to reckon at every turn.

Until this period of our history our information concerning Ro′man men of note has been so confused and so intermingled with fictitious tales that it has scarcely been worth the repetition. But from the era of the Pu′nic wars until the last days of Rome there is a generally trustworthy record, increasing in copiousness with every decade and abounding in the names and exploits of individual Ro′mans.

Cā′to, "the Censor," who is not to be mistaken for Cā′to "the younger" of a century later, was a type of the ancient <small>Marcus Porcius Cato.</small> Ro′man. He was born in 234 B. C., and lived a large part of his life in the country, where he owned and tilled a farm. From the rural assemblies and from service in the army he turned to Rome and engaged in politics as a reformer. His popularity, especially with the country voters, who flocked to the elections when he was a candidate, gained for him the highest offices in the city and important military commands.

Ca'to set himself against the flood of new ideas which swept in upon It'aly after communication was opened with Greece. He revered the old Ro'man gods and respected the ancient Ro'man ideals of manliness, simplicity, and frugality. As censor his power was exerted to counteract extravagance and atheism and to strengthen the constitution on the old basis. As a statesman he saw the evils of the new *régime*, and sought to avoid them by restoring the old. He had not the constructive ability to remodel the constitution to suit the altered needs of the State, and could only insist upon reviving its outgrown principles and combating what was firmly established.

Pub'lius Corne'lius Scip'io Africa'nus was a man of other manners. His family, the Corne'lii, were patricians of ancient lineage and boundless pride. The dark days of the war with Han'nibal found the young Scip'io distinguished among the city youth for his beauty, eloquence, and heroic conduct in his father's army. The dearth of great commanders at Rome, the failure of Han'nibal's plan of conquest, and the final resolve of Rome to end the war at any cost were his opportunity. By no means the equal of his opponent in genius, he nevertheless defeated him at Zā'ma and gained almost divine honors at Rome. After the wars in Af'rica and A'sia, Scip'io Africā'nus lived on a scale of luxury which called forth the condemnation of the stern old Ca'to and led to Scip'io's withdrawal from Rome. He died in his voluntary exile about 185 B. C.

Publius Cornelius Scipio Africanus.

Scip'io Æmilia'nus, the son of the brave Æmil'ius Pau'lus and the adopted heir of the great Scip'io, was a worthy member of both families. As a soldier he won the title of "Africa'nus Minor" by the capture and destruction of Car'thage, and of "Numan'ticus" by the reduction of the Span'ish town. Into both these campaigns he entered with the old Ro'man energy, after his weakling predecessors had frittered away years and legions. His tastes were cultivated, and in Rome he sought out Greek teachers and studied the works of the Gre'cian sages. Æmilia'nus tried to stay the misfortunes which threatened the State; but his talents as a statesman were exceeded by his good intentions, and bore but little fruit.

<small>Scipio Æmilianus.</small>

The outline of the second stage of the republican history has included nearly every country on the shore of the Mediterra'nean. The single Ital'ian city which first achieved the supremacy of the peninsula has now become the leading power in the civilized world and threatens to become its sovereign. Car'thage, Sic'ily, Macedo'nia, Greece, Spain—have sunk to the condition of Ro'man provinces. In a third section of this period we shall consider how the Ro'man system of government endured the enormous strain of this responsibility.

<small>Summary of second stage.</small>

ANALYSIS OF CHAPTER IV.

1. *Conquests in the West*, 73-86:
    First Punic war, 73-77:
        Carthage and Rome, 73, 74.
        Outbreak of war, 74.
        First Roman navy, 75.
        Defeat of Regulus, 76.
        End of war, 77.
    Organization and extension, 77-78:
        First Roman provinces, 77.
        Illyrian expeditions, 77.
        Subjection of Cisalpine Gaul, 78.
    Second Punic, or Hannibalian, war, 78-86:
        Carthaginian domain in Spain, 78.
        Character and policy of Hannibal, 79-80.

The invasion of Italy, 80.
Conquest of Cisalpine Gaul, 81.
Hannibal in Central Italy, 82.
The Fabian policy, 83.
The disaster at Cannæ, 83.
Stability of the Roman state, 84.
Capture of Syracuse, 84.
Scipio " carries the war into Africa," 85.
End of the war, results, 85, 86.
Pacification of Italy, 86.

II. *Conquests in the East*, 86-92:
The East after Alexander's death, 86, 87.
First and Second Macedonian wars, 88.
The " Independence " of Greece, 89.
Hannibal after Zama, 89, 90.
War with Antiochus, 90.
Third Macedonian war, 90.
Third Punic war, 91, 92.
Fourth Macedonian war, 92.
Destruction of Carthage and Corinth, 92.

III. *Signs of Weakness in the Roman Republic*, 92-95:
Inglorious wars with barbarians, 92, 93:
   With Viriathus, 92.
   With Celtiberians, 93.
   With Numantines, 93.
Official corruption, 94.
Influx of Greek ideas, 94.
Degradation of free labor, 94.

IV. *Eminent Men of the Time*, 95-97:
Marcus Porcius Cato, 95.
Publius Cornelius Scipio Africanus, 96.
Scipio Æmilianus, 96, 97.

REVIEW EXERCISE.

Second Period. The Roman Republic. Part II.
264-133 B. C.

1. When, where, and by whom was Carthage founded?
2. Compare the strength of Rome and Carthage at the outbreak of the first Punic war.
3. What precipitated the first Punic war?
4. How was the first Roman sea fight won?

5. Tell the history and legend of Regulus.
6. What Carthaginian general distinguished himself in Sicily?
7. What battle closed the first Punic war and what were the terms of peace?
8. What were the earliest Roman provinces?
9. What did Rome accomplish in the interval between the first and second Punic wars?
10. How did Carthage make amends for the loss of Sicily?
11. What was the origin and character of Hannibal?
12. What precipitated the second Punic war?
13. How did Hannibal propose to break the power of Rome?
14. Describe Hannibal's route of invasion.
15. Describe the conquest of Cisalpine Gaul.
16. What victory did Hannibal win in 217 B. C. and why did he not advance on Rome?
17. By what policy did the dictator Fabius win his nickname?
18. What disaster befell the Romans in 216 B. C.?
19. How did the Senate display its energy?
20. When, where, and by whom was the second Punic war terminated?
21. What terms were imposed on Carthage?
22. What punishment was inflicted on the Italians?
23. Describe the condition of the East after Alexander.
24. Describe the first Macedonian war; the second.
25. What did the declaration of Flamininus to the Greeks signify?
26. Describe the career of Hannibal after Zama.
27. Narrate the principal events of the war with Antiochus.
28. What war practically established Roman supremacy in the East?
29. Narrate the events and results of the third Punic war.
30. What two famous cities were destroyed in 146 B. C.?
31. What wars engaged Rome in the Spanish peninsula?
32. What influence did the foreign conquests have upon the Romans?
33. How did the extension of slavery weaken the Roman state?
34. What did Cato "the Censor" endeavor to do?
35. What manner of men were the Scipios?
36. What did Rome accomplish in the second stage of the republic?

CHAPTER V.

SECOND PERIOD (Continued).

THE ROMAN REPUBLIC.

Part III. (*133–31 B. C.*)

THE CIVIL WARS AND THE FALL OF THE REPUBLIC.

THE concluding century of the Ro′man republic introduces us to new phases and is crowded with memorable events; and remarkable men—among them two, at least, of the world's greatest—jostle each other on the crowded stage.

In considering the results of the extension of Ro′man dominion we were reminded of the evil influences which had thus been introduced into the once sober city. In the present chapter we must note the working out of these vicious principles in their many forms. We shall see their effect upon society and upon government both at home and in Rome's relations with foreign states; we shall examine the numerous attempts at reform and their successive failures, and we shall see how the imperial mind of Ju′lius Cæ′sar seized the crumbling constitution, arrested its fall, and, by instituting a strong central government under an absolute monarch, preserved for half a thousand years the vast domain which it had taken the republic half a thousand years to win.

War and conquest fill nearly every page of the record of Rome for the one hundred and fifty years between the passage of the Horten'sian law (287 B. C.) and the outbreak of the land, or agrarian troubles, in the times of the Grac'chi, 133 B. C. That famous law had opened every avenue of political distinction to the plebeians, and leveled the old social wall of patrician privilege. This led to a change in the officeholding class in the city. About the year 180 B. C. it was enacted that no man should hold one of the higher (or *curule*) magistracies who had not served ten years in the army. A minimum age was also fixed as a qualification for these positions. For ædile this was thirty-seven years, for prætor forty, for consul forty-three. It became customary also for the ædile to relieve the State of the burdensome expense of the national games by bearing it himself. This custom practically excluded poor men from the first step toward the consulship. Where it failed to exclude them it often did worse. Their ambition led them to borrow the enormous sums which the ædile's display rendered necessary. This plunged the office-seeker into debt, out of which there was but one escape. The prætors and the consuls, at the expiration of their year of office, were assigned to the government of the provinces into which the foreign conquests had been organized. In the plunder of his province the debt-ridden magistrate sought relief. The corruption of the provincial governments was incredible. The courts were controlled by the Ro'man governor, and too often his judgment was for sale to the highest bidder. Tribunals were established in Rome for the purpose of trying the persons accused of bribery and corruption in the provinces, so extensive did these practices become; but the evil outstripped all the devices which were contrived to check it.

The Senate was largely recruited from the ex-consuls and ex-prætors, and thus became the repository of wealthy office-seekers and of needy and ambitious adventurers. The

Assembly of the Centuries (Comǐ'tia Centuriā'ta) which elected all high officers, had also suffered a change by which the first classes (see page 36) lost their right of influencing the election by casting the first vote. Men who owned no land were also enrolled among the centuries, so that this once conservative assembly was transformed into a democratic body in which wealth and family conferred no special privilege.

Changes in Senate and Comitia.

The restrictions upon officeholding, together with the system of slave labor and the changes in the comǐ'tia, caused a redivision of Ro'man society. There was the officeholding class, enormously wealthy or abysmally insolvent, and bent upon compelling a fortune out of the State. These men, mostly senators, gained the party name of "the best men," or "aristocrats," (*optimā'tes*) and they formed a body very difficult of access. A man who pushed his way to the Senate by sheer force of talent as a general or orator was called a "*nŏ'vus hŏ'mo*" (new-man, upstart), as the first man of his family to hold high office, and was slighted and snubbed by his proud colleagues.

The party of the "Optimates."

The class of small farmers, who are the strength of any nation by reason of their intelligence, frugality, and conservatism, had disappeared from Ro'man society. The corn-kings and cattle-kings of the peninsula, with their boundless cattle-ranges and sheep-pastures, had crowded them to the wall. The slave system, importing its human victims by thousands and working them to an early death, destroyed the competition of free labor and left the Ital'ian freeman no resource. Such as possessed the cherished rights of Ro'man citizenship went to live at the capital, and, becoming tainted with the miasma of corruption which infected the official classes, made their citizenship yield them support. The offices of state were for sale to the man

The popular party. "Populares."

who should bid highest for the favor of the populace. The second class in the decaying republic were these people, the *popula'res*, or "people's party," who exercised a voting power which their character rendered dangerous. Demagogues instigated them against the optimates, and hurried them into projects of socialism and anarchy. Rich candidates courted their favor by open bribes, or by the more subtle method of distributing free bread and celebrating free festivals of costly grandeur.

Between the populares and the optimates—the popular party and the senatorial party, as we shall hereafter call them— was a third party, or rather faction, whose weight was thrown on one side or the other of the scale, as its selfish interests dictated. This was the equestrian order (the *eq'uites*, or knights of the Ser'vian constitution). These men were capitalists from whom the senatorial party drew its recruits; but many of the knights were of plebeian origin, and not being the social equals of the senators, were made to feel their inferiority in a way which frequently drove them into popular alliance against the aristocracy. Besides these factions within the city there were thousands of men in It'aly who had fought in the Ro'man armies and believed themselves worthy of citizenship. These Ital'ians had a just claim to a share in the government, and Rome was at length forced to recognize it after a bitter war.

<small>The equestrian order, "knights."</small>

<small>The Italians.</small>

At the outset of the third period of the republic we have these elements of danger: A venal Senate, a distressed and discordant citizen-body, and a noncitizen population clamoring for recognition.

<small>Elements of danger.</small>

Two brothers, Tibē'rius Grac'chus and Cā'ius Grac'chus, brought the civil strife to a head, and forfeited their lives by their efforts for reform. Tibē'rius Semprō'nius Grac'chus, the elder brother, was but a young man when he entered public life. His ancestry was of the oldest and best. Cornē′lia, his mother, was the daughter of Pub′lius Scip′io, the conqueror of Han′nibal, and her two boys, Tibē′rius and Cā′ius, were the famous "jewels" which she had displayed to the boasting wife of a Ro′man millionaire. Scip′io Æmiliā′nus, his cousin and brother-in-law, was the leader of the senatorial party; Ap′pius Clau′dius, his father-in-law, was a patrician of the best type; but, cutting loose from all the traditions of his family, the young Tibē′rius, generous, impulsive, brave, and beloved, cast his lot with the poor.

The Gracchi.

The Tribunes of the People were established in the first days of the republic to guard the infant rights of the plebeians. With the equalization of the orders the ground of their existence vanished, but the office remained and tribunes were chosen every year by the plebeian tribes. These officers found a new field for action in this era of party strife. They no longer served the interests of one class, but utilized their high prerogatives as their principles prompted or their interests paid. Thus we shall see the board of tribunes divided against itself, some serving the Senate, others obeying the populace. The tribune's power of veto and his influence in the assemblies made him the approved instrument of political agitation, as we shall clearly see.

The Tribunes.

Tibē′rius Grac′chus was elected tribune of the Ro′man people for the year 133 B. C. and immediately proposed his measures of reform. The young tribune—he was scarcely thirty—was versed in law and history, and he knew that when, in former times (367 B. C.) Rome had been subject to similar evils the tribune Licin′ius had passed a law which had somewhat abated the misery. Rome was overcrowded with idle citizens and the pasture and plow-

Land laws of Tiberius Gracchus.

land of It′aly was in the hands of a few proprietors. Rome was mistress of the world, while the great mass of her citizens lived in misery. The conquered territories in It′aly, an immense domain, instead of being sold for the common good or allotted to needy citizens at a low rate of rental or purchase, was allowed to fall into the hands of a few patrician families who paid nothing for its use. The relief lay in the redivision of the soil among the people. That was the principle of the legislation of Licin′ius. This is the Sempro′nian law of Grac′chus : That all public lands privately occupied should revert to the State; that a commission of three men should determine all questions of dispute concerning proprietorship and should allow each occupier to retain from 500 to 1,000 *ju′gera* (300 to 600 acres), and should distribute the rest of the recovered public domain among the citizens and the Ital′ian allies, awarding homestead farms of eighteen acres each to worthy applicants.

Such was Grac′chus's great proposal to the Assembly of the Centuries. It was wise and just, but the way to its enactment was very hard, and its enforcement was harder still. The Senate, packed with landed nobles, refused to entertain the proposition, and secured the aid of a tribune, Mar′cus Octa′vius, to annul the acts of the bold reformer. The latter destroyed the power of the former's veto by persuading the people to depose Octa′vius from the tribunate. Such a thing had never been done before, but the people obeyed their young champion and set aside the creature of the landlords. The Sempro′nian law was passed, and its author, with his father-in-law, Clau′dius, and his brother, Cä′ius Grac′chus, were named as commissioners to enforce it. They encountered violent opposition from the landholders, and Tibe′rius, whose year of office was expiring, feared the consequences in case he should lose the protection of his

Opposition of Senate.

official title. He seems to have been led astray by the dangers of his position, and to have made high bids for popularity and re-election. The king of Per'gamon, in A'sia, had lately bequeathed his kingdom to Rome. The senators, as usual, meant to administer the estate to their own advantage, but Grac'chus asked the populace to vote the bequest for stocking the farms of the new proprietors. Then he asked their votes for a second term of office. The partisans of the Senate postponed the election and raised the cry that Grac'chus aspired to be king. The consul refused to suppress him, and a band of young Ro'man lords rushed from the Senate-house, struck down the tribune with their bludgeons, and killed three hundred of his followers (133 B. C.). Here was the muttered thunder of an approaching storm. Tibĕ'rius Grac'chus fell the first martyr to the contest of the classes. His cousin, Scip'io Æmiliā'nus, followed him a few years later (129 B. C.), and his brother, Cā'ius, ended a good fight in the same tragic fashion in the year 121 B. C.

Death of Tiberius Gracchus. 133 B. C.

The vacancy in the land commission was filled and the work of allotment went on for several years as Tibĕ'rius had planned. The measure certainly afforded relief; but in 129 B. C. a dispute with the Lat'in proprietors, on the ground of infringement of title, brought the work to a close. In that year Scip'io Æmiliā'nus, the hero of the destruction of Car'thage, was assassinated. He was the leader of the senatorial party and a wise and prudent statesman. Who murdered him was never discovered, but his opposition to the Grac'chan reforms had been bitter, and it is credibly asserted that he was removed for a political purpose.

Reforms blocked.

The Senate tried to stop the progress of reform by dispersing the reformers. The energetic pair, Cā'ius Grac'chus and Ful'vius Flac'cus, were sent out of the country, the former as

quæstor in Sardin'ia, the latter as proconsul in that part of
Gaul which is now southeastern France. The
work of subjugation which Flac'cus began was
carried out a few years later, and the Span'ish
possessions were connected with Cisal'pine Gaul by a new
Ro'man province, Gal'lia Narbonen'sis, founded in 120 B. C.

<small>Tactics of Senate.</small>

In 123 B. C. Ca'ius Grac'chus left his province to take up his
brother's work at Rome. He was a man of far greater genius
than the martyred Tibē'rius, and his reforms
looked beyond the relief of the poorer citizens to a
genuine revision and reform of the political condition of the city. He was elected tribune of the
people for 123 B. C., and re-elected for the succeeding year.
The legislation of this brief period is a monument to his
tremendous energy, resembling Cæ'sar's. Grac'chus, like his
brother, went to the people for his authority, and disregarded
the Senate until he should accumulate sufficient power to
break down the opposition of that dignified body. He first
won the friendship of the city rabble by a law providing that
grain should be furnished to them by the State at a nominal
price. This politic but radically unsound enactment allured
thousands of indigent citizens to Rome, eager for bread and
ready to support the leader who provided it without toil.
Having cemented his popularity with the masses by these
largesses of grain, by reasserting the Sempro'nian land-law
which was no longer enforced, and by founding colonies in
It'aly and abroad, the reformer attacked the aristocracy.
First he divided it, separating the landholding senators from
the capitalist knights (*eq'uites*) by granting certain valuable
privileges to the latter. Thus to the knights was given the
collection of the revenues of A'sia and the jury duties and
consequent fees at Rome. The gain of the equestrian order
was the Senate's loss; and the lawmaking power which the

<small>Proposals of Caius Grac-
chus. 123 B. C.</small>

Comitia of the Centuries was now exercising at the beck and nod of the tribune threatened that the Senate would be left behind in the development of the new constitution, as the Comitia of the Curies had been stranded long since and as the English House of Lords has been robbed of its power by the rise of the Commons.

But Grac′chus overestimated his hold upon the populace. The Senate was aroused to fight for its very existence, and the tribune's proposal to extend full Ro′man citizenship to the Lat′ins, with other liberties to the Ital′ians, repelled the Ro′mans themselves, more jealous than ever of their misused rights. The Senate put up a tribune, M. Liv′ius Dru′sus, who promised the populace more favors than Grac′chus had offered, and the fickle citizens cast off their old love for the new. In the elections for 121 B. C. the once popular tribune was defeated. The Senate declared him a public enemy, and the consul took arms against him. His friends rallied to his defense on the Av′entine Hill, but the authorities broke down their barricades. Cā′ius, with a single slave, succeeded in crossing the Ti′ber, and in a grove on its farther shore their pursuers found the dead bodies of both. With the death of the Grac′chi ended a sincere effort for reform. The Senate saved itself at the expense of the lives of two genuine patriots and much bloodshed. How well it deserved to live and govern was shown by the events of the next twenty years.

Defeat and death of Caius Gracchus. 121 B. C.

The war with Jugur′tha (111–105 B. C.) is an index of the sad condition into which the Ro′man government had sunk. The following is its disgraceful history:

By the terms of the second settlement with Car′thage, Rome assigned the rich Af′rican kingdom of Numid′ia to Massinis′sa, her ally in the second Pu′nic war. His son, dying, left the kingdom in common to his own two sons and his nephew, Jugur′tha, a brilliant young noble who had served in the Ro′man army at Numan′tia, and knew the frail stuff which composed the nobility of the city that ruled the world. Confident of his ability to shield himself, Jugur′tha killed one of his royal cousins and laid siege to the other, who straightway appealed to Rome for the protection which the Senate owed. A senatorial commission came to investigate, took Jugur′tha's bribes, and, to obey their orders, gently urged him to spare his cousin. The disrespectful monarch heard their speeches, sacked the town, and slew Rome's royal ward with cruel tortures. More than that, he slew Ro′man citizens, and the tribune Mem′mius, in the citizen assembly of Rome, called the Senate to account for its scandalous perfidy. The Senate declared war and sent a consular army to Af′rica, but the generous Jugur′tha sent the commanding consul home a millionaire without a battle. Again Mem′mius, the honest tribune, denounced the taker of bribes, and the sluggish Senate summoned the king to Rome for trial. But no one condemned. The unpurchasable Mem′mius alone accused. The other tribunes slunk away with heavy purses. Jugur′tha was so confident of safety that he dared to let loose his assassins upon a rival Af′rican prince then resident at Rome. This heinous murder was too much. The Senate granted the popular demand for war, and the king returned to Af′rica pronouncing his famous judgment upon Rome: "O venal city; thou, too, shalt perish when a purchaser shall appear!"

Jugurthine war. 111-105 B. C.

Bribery at Rome.

The second invasion of Af′rica failed as miserably as the first. Jugur′tha routed the consular army, and sent it under the yoke of three spears (*sub ju′gum*), which was the acme of disgrace. The consul made a craven peace which the powers at Rome would not ratify. Metel'lus, the able but aged senator, who commanded the next expedition, had two men in his army of whom the world was to hear much—they were Ca'ius Ma'rius and Lu'cius Cornelius Sul'la. The latter was a young and hitherto reckless patrician of no reputation. The former was forty-eight years old and a plebeian. Ma'rius was born on his father's little farm at Arpi'num, in 157 B. C. Some have called him a day laborer's son. Outdoor work hardened his constitution to bear the strains to which his later life subjected it. He joined the army, and served at Numan'tia with credit though without distinction. The popular party in the city made him tribune and afterwards prætor. His faithfulness and his genuine interest in his soldiers and exertions in their behalf gained some recognition for him among military men, and doubtless led Metel'lus to select him as his second in command.

<small>Caius Marius.</small>

For two years the Ro'mans accomplished little, and Ma'rius accordingly conceived the idea of applying for the consulship and the chief command. Metel'lus scouted the possibility of his election, and advised him not to humiliate himself by going to Rome as a candidate. Ma'rius not only went, but won, *no'vus ho'mo* as he was. As consul (107 B. C.) he displaced Metel'lus, reorganized the army, enlisted soldiers from the city rabble, and drilled them into perfection of discipline. These legions followed their horny-handed general now as they had not followed the exquisite senatorial chiefs. The really weak Jugur'tha was easily crushed the moment a man of honesty and energy opposed him. The ability of Sul'la as quæstor under Ma'rius hastened the close of the war (105 B. C.). Jugur'tha was taken and brought to Rome, where he died in prison.

<small>Marius and Sulla in Africa.</small>

The military significance of the Jugur'thine war was

nothing, and the whole affair might be dismissed with a
line of comment were it not for the exhibition
Significance of Jugurthine war. which it furnishes of the utter weakness of the Ro′man Commonwealth. The wretched business of the earlier campaigns showed that the highest offices in the State were filled with bribe-takers. The successful candidacy of Ma′rius showed that a popular general might ride to the highest place on the suffrage of the people. Two new characters, Ma′rius and Sul′la, have been introduced, and the praise which Sul′la has won from the Ro′man aristocracy for his part in Jugur′tha's capture has soured the temper of the jealous and vindictive democratic consul.

During the Af′rican campaigns the Ro′man armies in Eu′rope were marching from one disaster to another under
the direction of incompetent leaders. Rome had
Rome threatened by Germans. 113-100 B. C. no civilized enemy on the continent, but her soldiers found more than their match in the half barbarous Ger′man, or Teuton′ic, tribes which were in turbulent commotion north and east of the Alps, and from time to time sent hostile hordes over the mountain barrier into the tempting plains of It′aly. In 113 B. C. the Cim′bri defeated a consular army on the northeastern frontier, but turned aside to Gaul (modern France) without pursuing their advantage. In 109 B. C. and 107 B. C. the Ro′man commanders in Gaul met the Cim′bri and were repeatedly defeated. In 105 B. C. these same barbarians destroyed two Ro′man armies on the lower Rhone.

The citizens were panic-stricken. Their armies seemed useless, their generals incapable of victory. The
Marius defeats the Germans. 102-100 B. C. Jugur′thine war had just closed and the populace assigned the command against the Cim′bri to their hero, Cā′ius Ma′rius. A sudden change in the movements of the barbarians granted an interval for

preparation. In defiance of law and custom Ma′rius was made consul five times in succession (104–100 B. C.). He made a few marked changes in military organization and tactics, inspired his men with a share of his own confidence, led them into Transal′pine Gaul, and there, in 102 B. C., routed the Teu′tones in the renowned slaughter of A′quæ Sex′tiæ. The Cim′bri had meanwhile swept around the Alps and entered the valley of the Po, chasing before them the army of Cat′ulus, the patrician consul. Ma′rius met them at Vercel′læ, broke their formation of battle, and, aided by Cat′ulus, inflicted such a blow upon them that they abandoned forever their schemes of Ital′ian conquest.

The populace now had nothing too good for Ma′rius. Their hero had become their idol. He was "the third Rom′ulus,"
"the second Camil′lus." His very boorishness of manner, which disgusted the aristocrats, commended him to the democracy as an "old-fashioned Ro′man." He had another element of strength—the veteran army. The military reforms had altered the character of this force. It was no longer a national guard of militiamen, called from shop and plow for a season and returning to their work at the close of the campaign. The wide extent of the realm and the attitude of the frontier tribes compelled the State to support a standing army of regular soldiers—men whose only business was war. The victories of Ma′rius bound these hardened regulars very closely to his fortunes. Henceforth the leader of an army was a political factor.

The popular hero.

But Ma′rius, the soldier, was no statesman. He was too honest to engage with all his heart in the wilder schemes of Glau′cia and Saturni′nus, the leaders of the populace with whom he formed his first political partnership. These three men obtained the high offices for the year 100 B. C., and the tribune Saturni′nus re-

Fresh democratic reforms.

vived the laws of Grac'chus. New colonies were to be formed, and the public lands were to be assigned to the Ma'rian soldiers and the Ital'ian allies. The promise of rations at nominal rates secured the favor of the mob of city voters.

The demagogues had overreached themselves. The turbulence of their followers frightened the capitalists of the equestrian order, whom the Grac'chan tax-and-jury-laws had attached to the popular party, and even Ma'rius wavered in their support. Saturni'nus and Glau'cia grasped at illegal power, and the Senate commanded Ma'rius, as consul, to protect the State. He obeyed, and marched against his own political friends. A bloody battle was fought in the forum, December 10, 100 B. C.; the senatorial party, led by the ex-chief of the people, triumphed, and the two popular leaders, together with many of their followers, were put to death without a trial. Ma'rius was checked in his political career. The ungrateful Senate had no further use for him, and the people hooted him in the streets. He left the city at the expiration of his sixth consulship, hating both citizens and aristocrats, but cherishing the dark prophecy that he should once more rule at Rome. "Seven times consul," an old witch had said of him.

Marius suppresses the popular outbreak. 100 B. C.

Mar'cus Liv'ius Dru'sus, "the Grac'chus of the aristocracy," made a noble effort to cure the evils which preyed upon the State. He was a true aristocrat, and had the support of the most enlightened men of his order, but they were in a minority. His laws aimed to strengthen the Senate, to relieve the poorer citizens and the Ital'ian allies. He proposed to transfer the lucrative jury-privilege from the knights to the senators, but to enroll three hundred new senators from the equestrian order. To placate the people he would extend the distribu-

Drusus attempts reform.

tions of grain, offer homesteads to the idle citizens, and finally raise the Ital'ians to political equality with the Ro'mans. But the jealous citizens charged Dru'sus with high treason. The dregs of the populace and the dregs of the Senate turned against him. An assassin struck him down (91 B. C.) and the Senate canceled his legislation.

Discontent with the failure of their hopes of liberty, based on the laws of Dru'sus, led the Ital'ians to revolt. The Social war (war with the allies or *so'cii*) began in Picē'-

Social war. 90-88 B. C. num, in 90 B. C. The whole peninsula rose against Rome. Corfin'ium, under the new name Ital'ica, was made the capital of a rebel Ital'ian State. But the bonds between the allies were loose and their organization poor. Rome pulled her forces together for the struggle. By the Va'rian law the partisans of Dru'sus were expelled from the Senate. A large army was raised, and both Ma'rius and Sul'la offered their services to the war department. Sul'la was appointed to the leadership of the southern army and Ma'rius was assigned to the central division. To break up the confederacy the Julian law (90 B. C.) offered Ro'man citizenship to the Ital'ians not yet in revolt, and the Plau'tio-Papir'ian law, a few months later, granted the same concession to all Ital'ians who should apply for it within sixty days. By such seductions and by superior discipline the dangerous insurrection was crushed (88 B. C.); but it left

New perils. a harvest of bitter fruits for the city. The Senate had lost its ablest men by the Va'rian law; the Ital'ians were dissatisfied with the restrictions which were fixed upon their newly acquired citizenship; Ma'rius, the democratic general, and Sul'la, the aristocratic commander, were rivals and enemies. At the same time the Senate declared war against Mithrida'tes, king of Pon'tus, who was plundering and murdering Ro'man citizens in A'sia

Mi′nor. Sul′la, with the army of the south, was ordered to A′sia to conduct operations against him.

To settle some of the harassing problems the tribune Pub′lius Sulpi′cius devised several laws. The Senate was to be rehabilitated by the expulsion of its bankrupt members and the restoration of the Va′rian exiles. The Ital′ian citizens were to have full political rights in the city. The Senate, led by Sul′la, opposed the Sulpi′cian reforms. Ma′rius allied himself with the tribune, who persuaded the populace to transfer the conduct of the Mithrida′tic war from the champion of the Senate to the old time friend of the people, the aged conqueror of Jugur′tha and the Cim′bri. Sul′la, at Brundis′ium, appealed to his soldiers to protect the constitution; they clamored to be led against Rome. Ma′rius and Sulpi′cius could not collect a sufficient army to hold the city, and for the first time Rome was taken by Ro′mans (88 B. C.). The offensive tribune was put to death but Ma′rius was reserved for fresh vicissitudes, escaping from one place of refuge to another until his opportunity should reappear. Sul′la forcibly quelled the democratic opposition, greatly increased the authority of the Senate, and after a few months in the city hurried to A′sia Mi′nor to prosecute the war.

<small>Sulla takes Rome. 88 B. C.</small>

Ever since the subjection of Antī′ochus the Great (189 B. C.) A′sia Mi′nor had been in a disturbed condition. Half a dozen discordant kingdoms, more or less under Ro′man influence, preyed upon each other. The remoteness of Rome itself and the corruptibility of the commissions of senators which were sent out to protect her interests gradually brought Rome into contempt abroad. Mithridā′tes, king of Pon′tus, despised her authority as heartily as did Jugur′tha of Af′rica. This Mithridā′tes was a remarkable man, of unusual stature, of surpassing bodily

<small>Mithridates.</small>

accomplishments, and of a tremendous mental and physical energy. The hard struggle which he gave the Ro′mans led them to believe the current stories of his almost superhuman strength. They did not doubt that he had so inured himself to poisons that he was safe from the usual terrors which haunted Eastern sultans and was hardly able to take his own life.

Mithridā′tes extended the boundaries of his ancestral kingdom, Pon′tus, on the Eux′ine or Black Sea, until they included the eastern and northern shores of that water. Having gathered wealth and power by these annexations he began a course of similar encroachments on the west upon territories in which Rome had an interest. Sul′la, then governor of Cilic′ia, forced the king to respect the decrees of the Senate (92 B. C.). During the Social war in It′aly Mithridā′tes repeated his aggressions so insultingly that war—

First Mithridatic war. 89-81 B. C.

the first Mithrida′tic war—was declared by Rome (89 B. C.). But the city had scarcely troops enough to man her armies in It′aly; her allies were in revolt, and for a year the Pon′tic king met no real opposition. He overran the adjoining kingdoms and the Ro′man province of A′sia, proclaiming himself to Greeks and Asiat′ics as a liberator. All the Ital′ians in the province—numbering at least 80,000—were murdered, without distinction, at his cruel command in a single day. Only a few small districts in A′sia remained faithful to Rome, and without waiting to reduce them the conquering army crossed the Ægē′an to liberate Greece. The poor Greek cities, constitutionally unable to stand alone, had already suffered "liberation" at the mercy of Mac′edon and Rome; but they were ready for more, and Ath′ens led the welcome to the invader.

We have now reached the point where Sul′la, having

composed the affairs of the city and propped the Senate on its doubtful seat, took the field against Mithridā′tes. With 30,000 men he crossed to Greece (87 B. C.) and drove the invaders out of Ath′ens and the Piræ′us. An overwhelming army under Archelā′us opposed him at Chæroneʼa in Bœō′tia, but was beaten in an action in which the aristocratic commander exhibited brilliant military genius.

Sulla in Greece. 87 B. C.

Meanwhile there had been a democratic overturn at Rome, and the popular party had voted to depose Sul′la, and sent Flac′cus, one of its own men, to take his place. But it had become one thing to vote the deposition of a successful commander and quite another thing to compel him to give over his army. Sul′la gave no heed to the mandate of the comitia. He had no dealings with Flac′cus, and continued his campaign against Mithridā′tes, proposing to finish with the business in hand and then to settle in person with the unruly democrats at Rome. Flac′cus left Greece and crossed over to A′sia with the democratic army. Sul′la inflicted a second defeat on the Asiat′ics at Orchōm′enus in 85 B. C. and then led his devoted troops into A′sia by the land route. The civil war at Rome deluded Mithridā′tes into the belief that he could purchase peace with one party by offering his aid to crush the other. But Sul′la was a hard man to hoodwink. He guarded his own interests well, but he did not neglect his duty. Mithridā′tes signed a treaty with him in 84 B. C. whereby the king agreed to give up all his conquests and prisoners, to dismiss most of his army and navy, and to pay the expenses of the war. The revolted province of A′sia was mulcted of a heavy fine ($24,000,000), and the few faithful towns were richly rewarded. The army of Flac′cus now mutinied and joined the Sul′lan victors. The conqueror

Democratic revolution at Rome.

Sulla prosecutes the war.

had finished the business in hand and now turned his hard face toward Rome.

There was need of him in It′aly. He had left an aristocrat, Octā′vius, and a democrat, L. Corne′lius Cĭn′na, in the consulate at Rome. The latter was a firebrand. No sooner was Sul′la safely in Greece and his back turned than Cĭn′na provoked a civil war (87 B. C.) by attempting to restore the lately canceled Sulpi′cian laws and to recall the popular leaders whom Sul′la had banished. The senatorial party broke up the comitia by violence and killed many of the multitude. For the safety of the State the Senate outlawed the democratic consul, but Cĭn′na lingered in It′aly and all the malcontents gathered about him.

Cinna.

Return of Marius. Ma′rius, bowed with years, but still awaiting his promised seventh consulship, hastened from his Af′rican retreat. The many outlaws of the Sul′lan revolution and the dissatisfied Ital′ians helped to swell the democratic army. The rapid growth of the insurgent force created a panic at Rome. It was difficult for the Senate to raise troops and impossible to select a fit commander. Cĭn′na cut off the sources of the grain supply and laid siege to the city. A pestilence within the walls helped his cause. Cā′ius Ma′rius, and Quin′tus Sertō′rius supplied the military genius which Cĭn′na lacked. Their presence foreshadowed the result of a siege, and men from the garrison nightly deserted to the Ma′rian camp. Without awaiting an attack the Senate surrendered, trusting Cĭn′na's promises of mercy (87 B. C.). Ma′rius had promised nothing, and his will was stronger than Cĭn′na's. He had been cast out by the city which once had hailed him as its savior. The aristocrats had used him as their tool and thrown him aside in contempt. Their dragoons had hunted him out of It′aly and harried his rest even in foreign lands. He was now seventy years old, ignorant as ever, still narrow in mind and changed only in the deepened intensity of his hate. At his command the soldiers disregarded the pledge of Cin′na and slaughtered indiscriminately all the senatorial adherents who could be found. The list of more than 1,000 dead includes some famous names, but no noble name could slake the thirsty vengeance of the maddened Ma′rius. The prophecy which had nourished his hopes during his later years was now fulfilled—by his own order—and on the 1st of January, 86 B. C., he entered on his seventh consulship. One of his first acts was to give office to his nephew, Julius Cæ′sar, then an elegant and intellectual youth of sixteen years. Two weeks later the old man died in a raging delirium, furnishing in life and death an awful exhibition of the intensity of uncontrolled passions.

Marian slaughter of optimates.

Death of Marius. 86 B. C.

The democratic leaders triumphed in the blood of the aristocracy; but there was a specter left to haunt their dreams for the next four years. Sul′la, the greatest of the senators, was in Greece fighting for his country at the head of 30,000 devoted men. Flac′cus, the successor of Ma′rius, was sent to relieve him of his army and the conduct of the Mithrida′tic war (86 B. C.). How he fared in Greece and A′sia we have already seen. Sul′la went on with his campaigns as if his commission from the Senate had not been revoked. He was now legally an outlaw; but an outlaw at the head of a conquering army was a dangerous man to deal with, and his army was being recruited constantly by the arrival of members of the senatorial party who no longer dared to remain at the capital. Still he was absent and fighting. There were the perils of war, of camp, and pestilence to take him off; perhaps he would never return. So, it may be, Cin′na reasoned for a time. It may be that he hugged the delusion the more closely as it showed

Tyranny of Cinna.

signs of vanishing quite. Year after year he made himself consul and ruled Rome as if there were to be no day of reckoning. His power was practically absolute. He was what no one dared whisper that he was—a Ro'man king. The weakened Senate and the fawning rabble passed his laws. All Ital'ians south of the Po were accepted as genuine citizens of Rome, and the city mob drew its daily dole of grain from the government stores.

In 84 B. C. the outlaw Sul'la wrote to the Senate. He had fulfilled his mission in A'sia. Mithridā'tes had acknowledged Ro'man supremacy and made amends for his misdemeanors. Sul'la was now about to return, and he announced his intention of coming at the head of his army to restore the constitution as he had settled it in 88 B. C. At the unwelcome news Cin'na started to meet him with an army, but his soldiers mutinied and slew him (84 B. C.). The leadership fell to Car'bo, the younger Ma'rius, and Serto'rius. Norba'nus and Lu'cius Scip'io were consuls for 83 B. C., the year in which Sul'la landed at Brundis'ium with forty thousand men. Many senators came to his camp; one young knight, Cnē'ius Pompē'ius (Pom'pey), led three legions of volunteers from Picē'num and presented them to the delighted commander, who hailed him "Imperator." Sul'la's aim was to gain possession of the capital and reestablish the rule of the aristocratic Senate. He could not hope to reverse all the legislation of the democracy without estranging the allies, and he accordingly guaranteed to the Ital'ians the fullest citizenship. The army of one consul he defeated, and that of the other deserted in a body to his camp (83 B. C.). The next year the armies of the government were more ably led, and the Sam'nites, always the hardiest of the allies, joined in the opposition to Sul'la. But his general-

Return of Sulla. 83 B. C.

Pompey joins Sulla.

ship was unequaled among his opponents. His blows were sudden and heavy. With the odds against him he triumphed signally. The final battle was fought at the gates of Rome, in November, 82 B. C. Young Ma′rius commanded his slaves to kill him; Sertō′rius escaped to Spain. For the third time the Ro′mans had taken Rome.

Sulla recaptures Rome. 82 B. C.

Sul′la's former capture of the city had been comparatively bloodless. But Ma′rius and Cĭn′na had reddened the forum with the blood of aristocrats, and now Sul′la's acts eclipsed even the Ma′rian massacres in horror. He was not a man to be swept by passion, like the other revolutionists; revenge was not his inspiration, neither did he covet absolute power. Himself an aristocrat of the aristocrats, he believed that his order was the only one capable of governing the State. Of the despised common people he feared nothing if left to themselves. It was when led by the deserting optimates—the Grac′chi, and Cĭn′nas, and the like—that they were dangerous. He would, therefore, exterminate the chiefs of the moderate party, the agitators of the dull-souled masses. This was the policy of the "Sul′lan proscriptions." Lists were drawn up of all the prominent men throughout It′aly who had sided with Cĭn′na, sentences of exile or death were pronounced against the proscribed, and their property fell to the State and the informer. Nearly five thousand names of "evil-minded" citizens were so blacklisted, and most of them suffered the execution of the sentence. Their lands were distributed among the soldiers of Sul′la's army and their slaves were made free citizens.

Proscriptions of Sulla.

The victor did not care for personal power; all his measures were bent on giving the Senate monopolistic control of the State. He doubled the number of its members, gave them the jury-powers which the knights had lately possessed, and abolished the power of the

The Sullan constitution.

censors to expel senators. The tribunes were disqualified from holding any higher office, and in general the popular assemblies were deprived of authority. They could not even meet, except at the call of the Senate, and the Senate's sanction was indispensable to the validity of every law. With their political rights the populace also lost the free-grain grants which Grac'chus had inaugurated.

Sul'la held the position of dictator for two years—a genuine king in power—and then, as soon as his " Cornē'lian reforms " were established, withdrew to private life. He died, in 78 B. C., in the full tide of his prosperity and in the enjoyment of the pleasures and successes for which he gave himself the title of Fē'lix, "the Fortunate." His death left the Senate in control of the State, but, unfortunately, without self-control. Burdened with the responsibility of absolute power it staggered along to its destruction without guide or leader.

Death of Sulla. 78 B. C.

The task of preserving the Sul'lan constitution was difficult in itself—quite enough to occupy the attention of the Senate ; but the problem was complicated by revolts abroad and insurrections at home.

At Sul'la's death the consul, Mar'cus Lep'idus, a member of the popular party, made an effort to overthrow the recent reforms. But the other consul, Căt'ulus, backed by the Senate, the survivors of Sul'la's army, and the troops of Pompē'ius, crushed this movement (78-77 B. C.). The soldiers of Lep'idus who escaped made their way to Spain, where the democratic cause had found a stout champion in the person of Sertō'rius, a fugitive officer from Cĭn'na's army.

Rising of Lepidus. 78-77 B. C.

Sertō'rius, when exiled from It'aly, founded an independent kingdom among the Lusita'nian mountains in Spain, and for eight years (80-72 B. C.) successfully resisted the senatorial armies, led by such men as Metel′lus and Pompē′ius. A jealous officer murdered him (72 B. C.), and was himself defeated and put to death by Pom′pey.

While the latter general, who was the best soldier of the Senate after Sul′la's death, was engaged in Spain a dangerous outbreak occurred in It′aly. At Cap′ua was a school where athletic slaves were trained for the sword-fights which were a popular feature of the public games at Rome.

Spartacus and the Servile war. 73-71 B. C. One of these gladiators, Spar′tacus, a Thrā′cian, inspired his fellows, mostly his countrymen and Gaul′ish prisoners of war, to kill their guards and escape. Their plan succeeded, and the liberated bandits infested the sleeping crater of Vesū′vius and terrorized the neighboring hamlets and farms. Other gladiators followed their bold example. Slaves crowded to them from the neighboring barracks. Spar′tacus defeated the troops which Rome sent against him, and soon felt strong enough to fight his way out of It′aly toward home. But his subordinates were unruly, and the temptation of rich spoils kept them in the peninsula, which they ravaged, like Han′nibal, unchastised for two whole years (73–72 B. C.). In 71 B. C. the prætor, Mar′cus Cras′sus, scattered the slave army, and with the assistance of Pom′pey, just returned from Spain, put an end to this disgraceful Servile war. A pack of half-armed slaves (*scr′vi*) had roamed through It′aly for three years. Surely the reformed Senate was no more capable than in the days of Jugur′tha!

Pompē′ius and Cras′sus received the consulship as a reward for ridding the State of Sertō′rius and Spar′tacus. They sig-

Pompey and Crassus consuls. 70 B.C. nalized their year of office (70 B. C.) by forming an alliance with the popular party to cut away several of the newly set props of the Senate. The tribunes were reinstated in their old privileges; the jury duties were divided between the senators and knights, and the power of removing senators for cause was restored to the censors. Thus the chief clauses in the Sul′lan constitution were canceled by two men who had fought in his army, but who now took sides with the common people. The grain largesses had already been restored, so that the city rabble peaceably regained nearly all that it had lost in the aristocratic revolution of Sul′la.

It was the absence of strong government in It′aly which allowed the Servile war to grow to dangerous proportions, and it was the same weakness abroad which allowed the pirate power to flourish in the Mediterra′nean and Mithridā′tes to recommence his aggressions upon the provinces and allied kingdoms of Rome in A′sia Mi′nor.

A period of weakness.

The second Mithrida′tic war (83-81 B. C.) made no change in the terms of peace as Sul′la had arranged them in 84 B. C.; but in 74 B. C. a third contest opened between the Senate and the ambitious king. Tigrā′nes, the son-in-law of Mithridā′tes, was now King of Arme′nia and the most powerful ruler in Western A′sia. He refused his aid to Mithridā′tes, but Sertō′rius, in Spain, and the pirates who swarmed in all the eastern seas lent valuable assistance. Lu′cius Lucul′lus led the Ro′man army in eight campaigns (74-67 B. C.). He fought on sea and land, captured numerous fleets, and destroyed powerful armaments. In 73 B. C. Mithridā′tes fled to the court of Tigra′nes, whither Lucul′lus followed him. The veterans won the famous battle of Tigranocēr′ta, 69 B. C., and then crossed the Euphrā′tes in pursuit of the kings. Here the army mutinied and clamored to be led home (68 B. C.). The people at Rome had authorized the discharge of the veterans, and there was no alternative for Lucul′lus but to abandon his advantage and

Second Mithridatic war. 83-81 B. C. Third. 74-63 B. C.

Lucullus in the East. 73-66 B. C.

leave the two kings unconquered. In 66 B. C. Pom'pey superseded him in the command.

While Lucul'lus had been performing wonders among the deserts and mountains of A'sia another set of generals had been marring their fortunes in the war with the pirates. These buccaneers had organized governments, with fortified harbors and strong castles, and no part of the Mediterra'nean was free from their depredations. Their fleets levied contributions from isolated towns, seized the Ro'man grain and treasure-ships, captured travelers and held them for ransom. In Crete and Cili'cia their strongholds were especially numerous. In 78 B. C. their audacity aroused the wrath of the Ro'man Senate, and throughout the next ten years expeditions were sent against the pirates. Cili'cia was wrested from them in 75 B. C. and Crete in 68 B. C. Although two of their nesting places were broken up the foul brood was not destroyed. There was need of a more comprehensive plan and more energetic action. In 67 B. C. the Gabin'ian law clothed Pom'pey with unlimited power over the waters of the Mediterra'nean and its coasts for fifty miles inland. Whatever he wanted of money, ships, or men, he had full warrant to take, and he was allowed three years for preparation and execution. It was a decree of the people, not a law of the Senate, which conferred this unprecedented royal authority. Pom'pey acted rapidly, and within three months swept the pirate power from the seas.

The pirates.

Pompey conquers the pirates. 67 B. C.

On the strength of this brilliant exploit the tribune Manil'ius proposed Pom'pey as the man to take up the war against Mithridā'tes, which had languished since Lucul'lus was recalled. The "Manil'ian law" was passed, and Pom'pey thus added the full command of A'sia to his proconsular power over the

Pompey conquers the East. 66-63 B. C.

seas and coasts. He was already on the ground, and received from the reluctant Lucul'lus the travel-worn legions. In 65 and 64 B. C. he drove Mithridā'tes from Pon'tus and conquered Tigra'nes. The new Ro'man possessions were assigned to vassal kings. Mithridā'tes' spirit broke at last, and he killed himself (63 B. C.). Pom'pey took Jeru'salem and set up Ro'man authority there (63 B. C.), and lingered in the East several years longer before returning to Rome for his triumph (61 B. C.).

While Pom'pey, the favorite general of the Senate and the leading Ro'man, remained in the East, the city itself

Plots at Rome. was the scene of a deep-laid and well-nigh successful conspiracy to overthrow the government. By some unexplained circumstance the plot to make Cras'sus dictator, with Ju'lius Cæ'sar his lieutenant, for the year 65 B. C., failed. In 64 B. C. a new conspiracy was hatched. This time such great men as Cras'sus and Cæ'sar kept aloof from the plotting or at least acknowledged no connection with it. The leadership was left to an entirely different set of men. Foremost among them was Lu'cius Ser'gius Catili'na (Cat'iline), a patrician and a senator

Catiline's conspiracy. whose ability was as marked as his profligacy. Cat'iline was well qualified for his dangerous work. He had the boldness and the wickedness of a hardened criminal and was so deeply in debt that only robbery could extricate him. His followers were a motley set. "Outcasts from honor, fugitives from debt, gamblers, and ruffians," said Ci'cero. These men had no higher aim than plunder, but many believed that behind this anarchistic screen the real leaders of the democracy, even Cæ'sar himself, were concealed. Cat'iline had the audacity to stand for the consulship for the year 63 B. C., but he was rejected, and a new man (*no'vus ho'mo*) gained the coveted office. This man was the Ro'man Demos'thenes, Mar'cus Tul'lius Ci'cero.

Ci'cero had come to the city in his youth from his country home at Arpi'num, the birthplace also of Ca'ius Ma'rius.

Marcus Tullius Cicero.

Weak of body, but strong of mind, his ambition kept him out of the usual military paths to honor and office and directed him to the arduous way to the Senate-house which led through the forum and the law-courts. Ci'cero was neither rich nor favored by influential friends, but his intellect and his brilliant oratory conquered the difficulties of public life. Keeping generally on the side of the Senate in the strife of parties, Ci'cero made his way through the various grades of office until, in this conspiracy-year, 63 B. C., he was consul. The senatorial party were inclined to sneer at this countryman of no ancestry who had pushed his way among them, and the sensitive and conceited orator suffered intensely from their coldness toward him.

In 63 B. C. Cat'iline's plans were matured. He would stand for the consulship, kill his competitors, summon the non-

Cicero frustrates the plot. 63 B. C.

descript army which he had collected in Etru'ria under his friend Man'lius, and give over the city to fire and plunder. By the agency of a woman the consul Ci'cero discovered the plot, and on November 8, B. C. 63, laid his information before the Senate. Cat'iline, the impersonation of audacity, sat in his place among the senators and listened to Ci'cero's famous harangue beginning: "How long, O Cat'iline, wilt thou abuse our patience?" The arch-conspirator fled from the city, leaving trusted agents to kill Ci'cero, fire the city, and open the gates to him as he should return with Man'lius' army. These agents bargained for an alliance with the envoys of the Allöb'roges, a Celt'ic tribe. But Ci'cero's men captured the envoys as they were leaving Rome and found upon them treasonable letters to the Celt'ic chiefs. The conspirators in the city were also arrested. The papers were opened and read in the Senate. There was no longer any doubt of their guilt. The question arose as to what should be done with the conspirators. Ci'cero refused to decide, and laid the matter before the Senate. Some favored death, others imprisonment. Capital punishment was unusual at Rome, and could not legally be inflicted except after trial by due form of law and by the sanction of the citizens.

<small>Illegal execution of the conspirators.</small>

But the danger was pressing; Cat'iline was marching on the city; the whole State seemed to be undermined and ready to explode. Cæ'sar voted no, but Ca'to—the younger of that name—turned the tide. He denounced the milder senators as partners in the crime. There was a hurried change of votes, and the Senate decreed the immediate execution of the prisoners. They were strangled in prison a few hours later. Ci'cero flattered himself that his consulship had saved the State. Ca'to hailed him *pa'ter pa'triæ*, "father of his country," and he retired from his year of office steeped in glory, as his letters still extant amply testify. The wretched army of Cat'iline and Man'lius—"and such an army!"—was defeated at Pisto'ria (62 B. C.) and the renowned Catilina'rian conspiracy was thus brought to an end. Its leader fell on the field.

It is reserved for another chapter to relate how a stronger brain and steadier hand than Catiline's, planned and accomplished the overthrow of the commonwealth.

ANALYSIS OF CHAPTER V.

I. *The Beginnings of Party Strife*, 100-108:
   Preliminary, 100.
   The new aristocracy, 101.
   The new parties, 102, 103:
      The aristocrats (Optimates), 102.
      The democrats (Populares), 102.
      The equestrian order (Equites), 103.

The Gracchan Popular Reforms, 103-108:
    The Gracchi, 103.
    The Tribunate, 104.
    The Sempronian law, 105.
    Death of Tiberius Gracchus, 106.
    Proposals of Caius Gracchus, 107.
    His defeat and death, 108.

II. *The Army in Politics*, 108-117:
    The war with Jugurtha, 108-110.
    Marius and Sulla in Africa, 110.
    Marius saves Italy from the Germans, 111, 112.
    Rising of Saturninus and Glaucia, 113.
    The attempted reforms of Drusus, 113.
    The Social war, 114.
    Sulla captures Rome, 115.
    First Mithridatic war, 115-117.

III. *The Popular Revolution*, 118-120:
    Cinna and Marius at Rome, 118.
    Slaughter of aristocrats, 119.
    Sulla defies the government, 119.
    Tyranny of Cinna, 119, 120.

IV. *The Aristocratic Revolution*, 120-128:
    Return of Sulla, 120, 121.
    Proscriptions of Sulla, 121.
    Democratic risings,—Sertorius, Lepidus, 122.
    Spartacus and the Servile war, 123.
    Pompey and Crassus consuls, 123.
    Second and Third Mithridatic wars, 124.
    Lucullus and Pompey conquer the East, 124, 125.
    Plots against the aristocracy, 126-128:
        The first plot, 126.
        Catiline's conspiracy, 126-128:
            Marcus Tullius Cicero, 127.
            The plot frustrated, 127.
            The conspirators executed, 128.

REVIEW EXERCISE.

Third Period. The Roman Republic. Part III. (a) *133-63 B. C.*

1. Describe the "new aristocracy."
2. What change came over the Comitia Centuriata?
3. How was the party of the optimates made up?

4. Describe the composition of the populares.
5. What was the political position of the knights?
6. Who were the Gracchi?
7. How had the tribunate been altered?
8. What was the Sempronian law?
9. What was the fate of Tiberius Gracchus?
10. What reforms did Caius Gracchus attempt?
11. How did Caius Gracchus lose his popularity?
12. What did the Jugurthine war discover?
13. What was the origin and early history of Marius?
14. What great service did Marius perform for Rome?
15. How did Marius lose the popular favor?
16. What reforms did Drusus attempt?
17. Give an account of the Social war.
18. What was the first capture of Rome by the Romans?
19. What induced the first Mithridatic war?
20. Describe Sulla's operations against Mithridates.
21. Describe the triumph of Marius and Cinna.
22. With what purpose did Sulla return to Italy?
23. What young knight joined Sulla?
24. What were the features of the Sullan reforms?
25. What armed opposition confronted the aristocratic government?
26. Who was Spartacus?
27. What distinguishes the consulship of Pompey and Crassus?
28. Describe the campaigns of Lucullus.
29. By whom were the pirates put down?
30. What was the "Manilian law"?
31. What was the Catilinarian conspiracy?
32. Describe the early career of Cicero.
33. What irregularity marked Cicero's treatment of the conspirators?

CHAPTER VI.

SECOND PERIOD (*Continued*).

THE ROMAN REPUBLIC.

Part III. (*Continued*). (*63–31 B. C.*).

FROM THE CONSPIRACY OF CATILINE TO THE END OF THE REPUBLIC.

THREE figures—members of the First Triumvirate—the wealthy Cras'sus, the fortunate Pom'pey, and the masterful Cæ'sar, loom above the turmoil of the last years of the republic.

Mar'cus Licin'ius Cras'sus was the type of the Ro'man knight. His family was good, though not of patrician blood, and his ability was mainly in the line of money-getting.

Crassus.

The vast extent of Ro'man possessions afforded a wide field for a man of such conspicuous business talent as Cras'sus possessed. He was the Roths'child of his time; a banker with nations for his clients, a contractor upon public works—in short, a bold and successful manipulator of capital. He had some military talent, and had put down the Servile insurrection. He had much political ambition, and had been consul with Pom'pey in 70 B. C. The consuls of that year had signalized their term by an alliance with the popular party to modify the aristocratic legislation of Sul'la. In this way Cras'sus had lost caste with the Senate, without being fully adopted as a leader of the democracy.

Cnē′ius Pom′pey was also of the knights. His family were outside the sacred pale of the aristocracy, and his father had been thought lukewarm in his support of the Senate and yet had incurred Cin′na's high displeasure. Pom′pey was born in 106 B. C., and was reared as a soldier. We saw him, a handsome youth of twenty-three (83 B. C.), raising recruits for Sul′la, and so gaining the dictator's approbation. That leader sent him to quench the democratic fires in the Sicil′ian and Af′rican provinces (80 B. C.), and on his return allowed him, young as he was, the honors of a formal triumph, and the title of Mag′nus— "the Great." As the general of the Senate Pom′pey ended the Serto′rian war in Spain, and was in at the death with Cras′sus when the gladiators of Spar′tacus were captured. With Cras′sus, too, as consul (70 B. C.) he had helped the knights and democrats to strip the Senate of its privileges. He gained rich rewards from the people by the Gabin′ian and Manil′ian laws (67, 66 B. C.), which intrusted the entire military strength of the realm to him for three years. He cleared the sea of pirates and A′sia of enemies. Lucul′lus had raided the East; Pom′pey conquered it. An inscription in Rome declared that "Pom′pey, the people's general, had in three years taken 1,500 cities and reduced to submission 12,000,000 human beings." All parties were afraid of him, and had he combined his soldierly qualities with statesmanship he might have mastered the government as another ambitious general did twenty years afterwards. But Pom′pey had lived too long in camps. He had little facility in dealing with the populace or the politicians, and he had no oratory with which to sway the Senate. He thought the grateful nation should grant him all his requests out of thankfulness for his victories, and he sulked at home when his demands were denied. He was "out" with the Senate, which feared him, and no longer "in" with the democracy, which had found in Cæ'sar a most sagacious leader.

Ca'ius Ju'lius Cæ'sar, the head of the popular party, was born in Rome, July 12, 102 B. C. (otherwise stated 100 B. C.),

Cæsar. of excellent patrician family. The Ju'lian *gens* had numbered many consuls and prætors in its list of honors, but this baby boy was destined to eclipse them all. Cæ'sar's aunt, Ju'lia, married Ma'rius, the rough democratic soldier, and just before he died the "seven times consul" honored his nephew by appointing him a *fla'men dia'lis*, a high-salaried officer under the State religious establishment. Young Cæ'sar married the daughter of the consul Cin'na, and showed his mettle by defying Sul'la's command to divorce her at a time when Pom'pey meekly yielded to a similar mandate. He was outlawed, and his estate confiscated, but he escaped death in the proscription, though it is reported that in granting his pardon in response to the petition of powerful friends the dictator said, "In this young Cæ'sar there is many a Ma'rius." After Sul'la's death he served as quæstor in Spain (67 B. C.), and later sank his fortune under a load of debt by the magnificence of his administration as ædile at Rome (65 B. C.). In 63 B. C. the people elected him *pon'tifex max'imus*, supreme head of the State religion, in spite of the fiercest senatorial opposition.

Cæ'sar was the only great man in Rome. Pom'pey and Cras'sus, at the head of their legions or their loans, were

Cæsar's plan. rendered prominent by circumstances; but Cæ'sar alone saw exactly the weakness of the State and a way to set it right. He formed a purpose and arranged his plans for its execution. His purpose was to put an end to the murderous strife of parties by crushing both in his own mailed hand. But, as yet, the hand held no weapon of offense. To carry out his plan an army, stronger than Pompey's, more loyal to himself than to the State, was a necessity. To secure such a command for himself Cæ′sar joined the First Trium′virate (60 B. C.).

Rome had become accustomed to civil strife, and the return of Pom′pey from the East was awaited with alarm. But the conqueror came back as a private citizen, merely asking the Senate to ratify his acts in A′sia, to reward his soldiers, and grant him the honor of a triumph. The demands were not excessive, but the Senate, fearful of raising any man too high, denied them. The politic Cæ′sar, who had lately returned from Spain much improved in fortune, showed himself a friend to the slighted general, married his relative Pompe′ia for a third wife, and interested both Pom′pey and Cras′sus in an arrangement for the benefit of all three. By this private bargain—the First Trium′virate—the three magnates divided the offices among themselves. Cæ′sar's share was one year of consulship (59 B. C.) to be followed by five years as governor (proconsul) of Gaul. This was his opportunity to pay his debts and train an army. Pom′pey was to have what the Senate had refused him—a triumph, the ratification of his Asiat′ic policy, and farms for his soldiers. Cras′sus took nothing, but secured certain privileges for his order, the knights. In his consulship Cæ′sar fulfilled his promises to Pom′pey, the Senate, led by Mar′cus Por′cius Ca′to, an old-fashioned aristocrat, vainly opposing. Disregarding the obstructionist measures of the senators, he pursued his own course, in co-operation with the assembly enacting a series of wise and permanent laws. In 58 B. C. he went to his province, which included Gaul on both sides of the Alps (France, Switzerland, Lombardy, and the Rhine Provinces of Germany). Pom′pey remained in It′aly to watch over the distribution of lands among his disbanded

The First Triumvirate. 60 B. C.

veterans. To cripple the Senate, the democracy, led by Pub′lius Clo′dius, sent Ca′to to the East on a public mission, and banished Ci′cero from It′aly for killing the Catilina′rian conspirators without trial.

The details of Cæ′sar's Gal′lic wars are not to be followed here; it is enough to say that in eight years he subdued to the Ro′man authority those Celt′ic tribes living in the countries now known as France, Bel′gium, and the Neth′erlands, crossed the Rhine and chastised the Ger′mans, crossed the Channel and commenced the conquest of Brit′ain. His campaigns left Gaul thoroughly pacified and partially Ro′manized; the Lat′in language took hold of its people, and it rapidly assumed an important place in the Ro′man State. In this warfare Cæ′sar developed the rarest military traits. He was prompt, energetic, and brave, fertile in resource, and careful of his men. He bound the army to him by kindness, by liberality, and by complete mastery of his profession as a soldier.

Cæsar in Gaul. 58–50 B. C.

While Cæ′sar the politician was in Gaul, making a new reputation for Cæ′sar the general, Pom′pey was doing police duty at Rome—watching the parties and endeavoring to shape a course between the factions. Clo′dius, the disreputable demagogue, was outbidden by the demagogue Mi′lo, who persuaded the populace to recall Ci′cero. Ca′to's term expired, and he, too, came back to Rome (57 B. C.). The consequently increased prestige of the Senate led the triumvirs Pom′pey and Cras′sus to meet Cæ′sar at Luc′ca in his province, 56 B. C., to arrange a new program. Cæ′sar stipulated for the extension of his term for another five years. At its close he was to be elected consul for 48 B. C., and was to be excused from the legal requirement of coming to Rome as a candidate. Pom′pey and Cras′sus were to be consuls (55 B. C.), followed by five years of proconsular

The meeting at Lucca. 56 B. C.

government, the former in Spain, the latter in Syr'ia. The terms of the bargain were partially carried out. Cæ'sar went on with his conquests; Cras'sus went to Syr'ia, where he was killed, after the Par'thians had defeated him in the great battle of Car'rhæ. Pom'pey sent lieutenants to manage his Spanish province, but himself lingered menacingly at Rome. It began to appear that his services might be indispensable to the Senate in case of a breach between Cæ'sar and the aristocrats.

The death of Cras'sus destroyed the Trium'virate. The death of Cæ'sar's daughter, Pom'pey's wife, dissolved the family tie that joined the two leaders. The aristocrats feared Cæ'sar's return more than the greatness of Pom'pey. The disorders in the city seemed to warrant the Senate in proclaiming martial law. Pom'pey was ordered to enforce the measure; he accepted the commission, thus becoming the open defender of the aristocracy and the foe of Cæ'sar's friends, the democrats.

End of Triumvirate.

The breach between Cæ'sar and the Senate was openly made and widened rapidly. Cæ'sar was safe while in Gaul at the head of an army; but under the laws he could not return to the city without resigning his command. The special law which made him proconsul for five years had declared that he might be a candidate for the consulship for 48 B. C. without complying with the usual formality of presenting himself in person to the city electors. The Senate insisted that this law was invalid, and that Cæ'sar must resign if he sought office before his term of command in Gaul expired. In the excited state of the city at that time he would certainly have been imprisoned upon his return, even had he escaped assassination.

Breach with the Senate.

Throughout the years 51 and 50 B. C. Cæ'sar and the Senate fought a battle of diplomacy on this point. Cæ'sar was absent, to be sure, but he had become wealthy in Gaul and could buy the support of consuls and tribunes as he needed it. His creature, the tribune Cu′rio, accepted the Senate's bill deposing Cæ′sar, but demanded that Pom′pey should lay down his power and betake himself to his Span′ish province at the same time. Pom′pey refused. The struggle, which was nominally between the Senate and Cæ′sar, became actually a duel for the supremacy which must end in the monarchy either of Cæ′sar or Pom′pey. The latter assumed command of the army in It′aly in December, 50 B. C., at the request of the consuls-elect. On January 1, 49 B. C., a final letter from Cæ′sar was read in the Senate. While maintaining the justice of his position, he offered to give up the greater part of his provinces and all but one of his legions if he might stand for the consulship in his absence. But the Senate, which had pinned its faith upon the generalship of Pom′pey, declared Cæ′sar a traitor if he should not immediately resign all his command. Cu′rio and An′tony hastened to him at Raven′na with the news. It was expected. The Senate had declared war, and there was no time to lose. "The die is cast," said Cæ′sar, as he led his devoted army southward across the little river Ru′bicon which divided his own Gaul′ish province from his native It′aly.

Cæsar crosses the Rubicon. 49 B. C.

In the Civil war there is nothing more remarkable than the consummate military genius exhibited by Cæ′sar. Pom′pey the Great, the conqueror of the East, was a soldier of more than ordinary talents. But his reputation had outstripped his merits. The fame of his early achievements under Sul′la, his share in the Serto′rian and Ser′vile wars, his suppression of piracy, and final victory over Mithridā′tes and the East, constituted an unbroken series of successes whose marked contrast with the sorry failures

Pompey and Cæsar.

of most senatorial generals, made him seem to the aristocracy—and, doubtless, to himself—invincible. Cæ'sar, on the contrary, had left Rome eight years before with no military record. He was now a conqueror, but surely, reasoned the nobles, it was not so hard for a Ro'man to subdue the half-civilized Gauls and Ger'mans. It would be a different matter to make head against Cnē'ius Pompe'ius Mag'nus! So they thronged to the headquarters of the Pompe'ian army in Campa'nia confident of victory, and eager for the battle which should put an end to Cæ'sar's presumption. But Pom'pey was too cautious to oppose Cæ'sar's practiced legions with a small or an undisciplined army. While he awaited recruits at Cap'ua Cæ'sar was in vigorous action. His veterans were hurried into It'aly, the young men of Cisal'pine Gaul, to whom he had promised Ro'man citizenship overtook him on the march and poured into his camps. He waited for nothing, but hastened down the eastern side of the peninsula, sending Mar'cus Anto'nius (Cleopa'tra's Mark An'tony) over the Ap'ennines with a detachment to take the road to Rome. Pom'pey lingered at Cap'ua and did nothing. He expected the Ital'ians to enlist under him, but there was scarcely an Ital'ian town on Cæ'sar's route that did not welcome the democratic leader. Not only the Ital'ian citizens, but the Ro'man garrisons in their citadels hailed the conqueror of Gaul as a friend. The patrician, Domi'tius Ahenobar'bus, occupied a mountain fortress and attempted to block the path of invasion. His troops mutinied and gave him up to Cæ'sar, who pardoned him and his companions. Pom'pey waited for recruits no longer. In April, 49 B. C., he crossed the Adriat'ic from Brundi'sium to the Illyr'ian coast of Macedo'nia with his army and a baggage-laden throng of senators and aristocrats, abandoning It'aly with-

Mark Antony.

Pompey quits Italy. April, 49 B.C.

out a battle. Thenceforth It'aly was Cæ'sar's, but the empire was yet to be won. The Pompe'ians held Spain and Af'rica in the West and the entire Ro'man dominion in the East. Macedo'nia was a convenient recruiting-ground, and from his station there Pom'pey could gather strength until fit occasion offered to recross the narrow seas and give battle to the usurper.

Cæ'sar did not follow; he had no fleet, and he was confident that Pom'pey would not soon feel strong enough to attempt the reconquest of It'aly. Rome was without defenders and Cæ'sar entered the city unopposed.

Cæsar at Rome.

If the aristocrats had feared the treatment which the massacres of Ma'rius and Sul'la gave them reason to expect they were pleasantly disappointed. Life and private property were spared. The remnant of the Senate declined to grant Cæ'sar's request for the consulship, and he accordingly assumed the responsibility of government. With the authority of the popular assembly he drew money from the public treasury and hastened to Spain to crush the Pompe'ian party there. Before the end of the year he completed the work and returned to Rome. The people named him dictator, but he resigned this office and was chosen consul for 48 B. C., the office which had been promised him at the meeting of the triumvirs at Luc'ca in 56 B. C., and from which the aristocrats had endeavored to exclude him. A majority of the Senate was now abroad with Pom'pey, holding sessions in the camp and going through the motions of government.

Dictator.

Cæ'sar stayed but eleven days in Rome, and then hastened to Brundi'sium, to forestall, if possible, Pom'pey's return. The latter had collected a great army of Ro'mans and allies, and a numerous co-operating navy. By his own good fortune, or by the stupidity of the commander of

Dyrrachium.

the senatorial fleet, Cæ'sar with half his force crossed the sea unopposed. The other half, under Mark An'tony, was cooped up at Brundi'sium. The Pompe'ian army was encamped at Dyrrä'chium. Cæ'sar had landed south of that point. An'tony ran the blockade and landed further north. The two armies united before Pom'pey was aware of their temporary isolation. But he broke through their lines and marched into Thes'saly in the spring of 48 B. C.

Pharsalus. Aug., 48 B. C. This slight success convinced his party that the next battle would be Cæ'sar's ruin. The next battle was fought at Pharsä'lus, August 9, 48 B. C. The Pompe'ians were utterly routed. Thousands were killed, and twenty-four thousand surrendered to Cæ'sar and his twenty-two thousand. Pom'pey fled to the seashore and took ship. On landing in E'gypt he was murdered by order of the king of the country. His lieutenants dispersed throughout the provinces, fearful of Cæ'sar's vengeance.

It was the conqueror's purpose not to build until he had laid sure foundations. The Ro'mans heaped their honors upon him—the consulship for five years, the tribunate *Cæsar in the East.* for life, the dictatorship for one year; but he did not return to the city while enemies remained in the provinces. E'gypt was his first destination. Here the rise of the Alexan'drines and the Ro'man garrison placed him in extreme peril, from which he was saved by courage and promptitude. With timely re-enforcements he defeated the Egyp'tian army. The beautiful Cleopä'tra was established as queen, and then "that dull cold-blooded Cæ'sar" hurried off to A'sia Mi'nor. Pharna'ces, the son of Mithridä'tes, had extended his dominions, thinking to go unnoticed and unpunished in the tumult of the Civil war; the proconsul had opposed him in vain. Leaving Alexan'dria, Cæ'sar hurried through Syr'ia and A'sia Mi'nor to Pon'tus, demanded the submission of Pharna′ces, and compelled it after a five days' campaign. "*Ve′ni, vi′di, vi′ci*," "I came, I saw, I conquered," is the famous form in which he announced his victory.

The East and most of the West were now at Cæ′sar's feet. His mastery of the Ro′man world was assured, although the two sons of Pom′pey, with Ca′to and other irreconcilables, hopelessly defied him in Af′rica and elsewhere. Ci′cero had cut a poor figure in the affairs of the past two years. By nature and training a conservative, he had clung to the senatorial party, though he did not abandon It′aly with its leaders. After the death of Pom′pey he accepted Cæ′sar's government as an established fact, and was thereupon read out of the senatorial party. Still he took no earnest part in public affairs, and was regarded as a political trimmer whose course was determined by his personal safety rather than by principle. The men who had the most to fear from Cæ′sar—Labiĕ′nus, who had been his lieutenant in Gaul, Sex′tus and the young Cnæ′ius Pom′pey, Afra′nius, and Petre′ius—and such fanatical adherents of the lost republican cause as Ca′to, collected a formidable army at U′tica, near the ruins of Car′thage, in Af′rica. On his return from the East by way of It′aly, Cæ′sar had to face a new peril. His successes thus far had been won by the fidelity of the legions which he had trained in the Gal′lic wars. They had sympathized with his cause and had shared his campaigns. They now demanded rewards and release from service. The Tenth Legion, which had borne the brunt of the hardest service in Gaul, broke into open mutiny and appealed to Cæ′sar to redress their wrongs. He satisfied them, and by a wonderful display of coolness and tact won them back to renewed devotion. Losing little time at Rome, Cæ′sar crossed to Af′rica (47 B. C.) and routed the

Cæsar in the West.

republican army on the field of Thap′sus. His soldiers, wearied with chasing rebellion around the Mediterra′nean, granted no mercy; 50,000 men were killed; Ca′to, "the last of the Ro′mans," died a republican, falling on his own sword rather than accept pardon from Cæ′sar. Labiē′nus and the sons of Pom′pey rallied a new army in Spain, but Cæ′sar, who had already neglected It′aly too long, returned to Rome (46 B. C.). There he celebrated four magnificent triumphs—for Gaul, E′gypt, Pon′tus, and Af′rica—and delighted the populace with splendid shows and games.

The republic survived in form alone. Cæ′sar was really king or emperor of Rome. The Senate—what was left of it after the Civil war—and the public assemblies existed only to give formal assent to his decrees.

<small>Settling the State.</small>

He wore the purple robe of royalty, but the old prejudice against kings denied him the title and crown. Yet he was made dictator for ten years, and then became censor and high priest for life. Uniting these offices in himself he set about his reforms. These measures were not intended to revive the old constitution. In the struggles of the hundred years' war the Grac′chi had tried to save the State by magnifying the power of the popular assemblies, and Sul′la had strengthened the Senate with the same end in view. Cæ′sar allowed both Senate and assemblies to exist, but deprived them of real power. All responsible authority centered in himself as monarch of the Ro′man Empire. Candidates for public office, like the laws, must have his approval. In the army, the legislature, and the Church, he was supreme. The ancient republican forms, Senate, comitia, consuls, prætors, and tribunes, remained, but their life was extinguished. From the chief executive power in the State the Senate was degraded to the place of an advisatory council. Its membership was raised to nine hundred, the new men Cæ′sar's nominees, and its aristocratic exclusiveness was invaded by the admission of prominent men not only from the Ital′ian cities but from Gaul and Spain. Besides these foreigners even some of the liberated slaves were admitted to seats in this old chamber of the nobles. The Cisal′pine Gauls were confirmed in the rights of citizenship which Cæ′sar had promised them. The great body of Ro′man law was reduced to systematic form and published to guide the decisions of the law courts. Even the calendar was reached in this comprehensive scheme of reform, and the Ju′lian solar year of three hundred and sixty-five days and six hours computed by Egyp′tian astronomers, superseded the inexact Ro′man year of twelve lunar months, by which time had hitherto been computed.

<small>Cæsarian reforms.</small>

In the midst of these plans of reorganization Cæ′sar was called to Spain by the defeat of his lieutenants. He took with him Octavia′nus Cæ′sar, his grandnephew and adopted heir. The Pompe′ians offered battle on the plain of Mun′da, near the modern Cor′dova, March 17, 45 B. C. They knew the temper of Cæ′sar's soldiers and understood that defeat meant death. The two armies were of nearly equal strength, and both were ably led. There was no skirmishing, no exhibition of tactics; the men fought fiercely at close range with sword and spear, their leaders in the thickest of the fight. Cæ′sar's desperate efforts and his personal bravery won the victory. Thirty thousand Pompe′ians, including many of rank, fell, but Sex′tus Pom′pey escaped to the mountains. Mun′da was Ju′lius Cæ′sar's last battle; after restoring his authority in Spain he returned to Rome.

<small>Cæsar in Spain.</small>

<small>Munda. 45 B. C.</small>

Measures for the consolidation and defense of the empire occupied the great mind of the man. The provinces had hitherto suffered from the loose government of the Senate; Cæ′sar made the financial officers of the provinces responsible to himself. Criminals had escaped through the right of appeal to an easily influenced populace; Cæ′sar abolished the right of appeal except to himself as supreme judge. Short terms of office and frequent changes had diminished the authority of the magistrates, and enhanced the power of the perpetual Senate; Cæ′sar held office for life and gained the power to name his successor. Other generals had made conquests and organized provinces without regard to the interests of the empire; Cæ′sar endeavored to form a "scientific" and easily defended frontier. The Rhine, the Alps, the Dan′ube, the Cau′casus, the Euphra′tes, were the natural boundaries of the empire, and he recognized the folly of gaining a precarious foothold beyond them. At one important point the frontier of Rome was still weak, and the dignity of the Ro′man arms was not respected. It was on the borders of Syr′ia, where the Par′thians had defeated Cras′sus, the triumvir (53 B. C.). Cæ′sar planned to avenge that insult, and made preparations for a Par′thian campaign. A republican conspiracy prevented their completion.

An imperial policy.

Cæ′sar had pardoned his enemies, but they had not forgiven him. The aristocrats who had escaped alive from the Civil war were not proscribed. On the contrary, the dictator treated them with kindness and forbearance, gave them honors, seats in the Senate, and provincial governorships. But his effort to attach them to his person was a failure. The remnant of the ancient aristocracy, whose incapacity to govern had brought on the evils that Cæ′sarism was trying to correct, still plotted in secret for the old constitution. Ci′cero was, in heart, at least, with this republican faction, though his voice was on the side

Republican plots.

of Cæ'sar. The leading conspirators—nearly all senators of high birth—were M. Ju'nius Bru'tus, Cas'sius, Dĕc'imus Bru'tus, Trebo'nius, Cim'ber, and Dolabel'la. Marcus Ju'nius Bru'tus deserves especial mention. He was the nephew and son-in-law of Ca'to, the sturdy patriot who had killed himself at U'tica rather than survive the republic. Bru'tus shared his uncle's devotion to the republican form of government; he was honest, and held a high place in the esteem of Cæ'sar and of the Senate. But the conspirators persuaded him that Rome was suffering from another tyranny like that of the Tar'quins, and that, as in the ancient days, a Bru'tus must bring back liberty. It was easy to work upon his sentimental and superstitious temperament, and he was soon won over, notwithstanding the tokens of Cæ'sar's confidence which he had received.

M. J. Brutus.

The trappings of the dictatorship aroused the Ro'man prejudice against kings. Cæ'sar's purple robe and golden chair, his concentrated power, and his selection of his own successor, were sufficient evidence of the regal nature of his position; still he put away the offered crown. As the Ides of March (March 15, 44 B. C.) drew near preparations for his assassination were perfected. Sixty senators were implicated in the plot, and rumors of their purpose were rife in the city. Cæ'sar was warned, but took no precautions and provided no bodyguard. As he entered the meeting-place of the Senate on the morning of the fatal 15th the " liberators " crowded upon him and attacked him with their daggers. Pierced with twenty-three wounds he fell and died at the foot of a statue of Pom'pey. Bru'tus, the fanatic, dipped his blade in Cæ'sar's streaming blood and brandished it in the face of Ci'cero, crying, " Liberty is restored!"

Assassination of Cæsar. Mar. 15, 44 B. C.

But liberty was not restored, as the " liberators " themselves learned. Mark An′tony was consul and an executor of Cæ′sar's will. He made alliance with Lep′idus, Cæ′sar's lieutenant, who was at the gates with an army. Veterans of the Gal′lic wars, who cared more for their former leader's memory than they did for the republic which he had overthrown, were in the city awaiting the lands which had been promised them. An′tony, Lep′idus, and the army had not figured in the conspirators' calculations, and their sudden appearance altered the footing. Instead of treating Cæ′sar as a traitor the liberators humored the temper of soldiery and populace by granting his body honorable sepulture. The remains were placed in the forum, and there Mark An′tony addressed the people. He read the dead man's will, which bequeathed money to every citizen and his gardens to all. Gaining their favor thus, he played upon their feelings, showed them that it was as their champion that Cæ′sar had risen and triumphed, and as their friend that the aristocrats had struck him down. He inspired them with frenzied devotion to Cæ′sar and fierce hatred of the conspirators. In solemn enthusiasm they built a funeral pyre in the forum, and there burned the body of their dead hero.

Failure of the revolution.

Antony to the people.

The conspirators, alarmed by the popular horror at their deed, dispersed in haste. To several of them provinces had been assigned by Cæ′sar. Mar′cus Bru′tus was to govern Macedo′nia, and Dec′imus Bru′tus was to have Cisal′pine Gaul. An′tony had fully determined to succeed to Cæ′sar's power, and had no mind to allow these two neighboring and wealthy provinces to remain in the hands of the leading conspirators. He accordingly persuaded the people that the late dictator had changed his intention regarding the appointments. Mar′cus and Dec′imus Bru′tus were, therefore, assigned by popular de-

Antony attacks the conspirators.

eree to other offices, and the government of both Macedo′nia and Cisal′pine Gaul was given to An′tony himself. But the governors had already reached their provinces and must be expelled. Dec′imus Bru′tus, in northern It′aly, was the first to be attacked. While An′tony was in the field against him the young Octavia′nus returned to Rome from Greece, accompanied by his friend, Agrip′pa.

The adopted son and heir of Cæ′sar was in his nineteenth year when the news of his uncle's death and his own preference in the will aroused his ambition. He Cæsar
Octavianus. hastened to It′aly, taking the adoptive name Ca′ius Ju′lius Cæ′sar Octavia′nus. With the adroitness of an older hand he ingratiated himself with Ci′cero and the Senate, posing as the friend of the republic and the foe of An′tony. Cæ′sar's old soldiers hailed with pleasure the handsome youth whom they had seen in Cæ′sar's company. His personality had elements of strength, and the Senate was in sore need of a champion. Ci′cero's keenness had penetrated the purposes of An′tony, against whose ambition the orator was now thundering his "Philip′pics." By his marvelous eloquence he aroused the Senate to action. The boy Octavia′nus received a prætorship and a military command, and was sent northward with the two consuls of 43 B. C. to crush An′tony, who was declared an outlaw.

Both consuls perished in the war, and the heir of Cæ′sar was thus left at the head of an army. The Senate had intended to throw him over as soon as he had The Second
Triumvirate.
43 B. C. served its purpose, and now refused him the consulship which he demanded. He, too, crossed the Ru′bicon and, contrary to the Senate's express command, entered the city and compelled the assembly to elect him consul. This chief magistrate, barely twenty-one, secured a decree of outlawry upon Cæ′sar's assassins and then returned to the North. Lep′idus, Cæ′sar's former "master of the horse," and An′tony, joined their forces and routed Dec′imus Bru′tus. Octavia′nus threw over the Senate's cause as readily as the Senate would have abandoned him for its own advantage. With his uncle's friends, An′tony and Lep′idus, he formed the Second Trium′virate (43 B. C.) "for establishing the republic." For the present there was to be no division of power among the three generals. They were to have equal consular authority for five years, and their acts were to be beyond the jurisdiction of Senate or assembly. The "republic" which they established was really the Cæsa′rian government, with a tripartite dictatorship. Such a government was destined to last only until dissensions should reduce the triune dictatorship to a monarchy.

In It′aly the triumvirs had equal authority; Spain and the West were assigned to Lep′idus, An′tony took Gaul, on both sides of the Alps; Af′rica, Sic′ily, and Sardin′ia fell to Octavia′nus. The East was prudently reserved for later division, as it was already in the hands of the conspirators. Bru′tus was in Macedo′nia, assembling the troops which Cas′sius and others had collected in A′sia. This republican army was formidable in numbers and composition, and really threatened the discomfiture of the triumvirs. Before assuming charge of their provinces the latter resolved to attack Bru′tus. Previous to leaving It′aly, however, they secured a formal vote of the people legalizing their actions, and then in cold blood set about the proscription of their private and political enemies. The lists of the proscribed included hundreds of honorable citizens who were the victims of personal spite or of the informer's greed. The patriotic Ci′cero, the matchless orator whose vanity and political indecision do not alter his claim to the second place in the Ro′man honor

The division of the world.

Death of Cicero. 43 B. C.

roll, was murdered to gratify the hate of An'tony (Dec. 7, 43 B. C.).

The republican army numbered 100,000 men, gathered from all the Ro'man East. Extortion and plunder supplied the funds for its support. In 42 B. C. An'tony and Octavia'nus passed over to Epi'rus with a force of equal if not greater strength. The heirs of Cæ'sar and his murderers met at Philippi, in Thrace, afterwards famous as the home of the first Christian church in Europe. Two battles were fought here in November, 42 B. C. On the first day Cas'sius was defeated by An'tony and killed himself in despair, ignorant that the division of Octavia'nus had meanwhile been driven back by Bru'tus. The death of Cas'sius deprived the republican army of its real leader. Bru'tus was a philosopher, but no ruler of men, and his soldiers broke loose from all restraint. Twenty days after the first battle a second was fought. The result was doubtful, till Bru'tus, despairing of success and deserted by his legions, took his own life. The triumvirs triumphed, and the last struggle for the old republic was at an end.

Battle of Philippi. 42 B. C.

Lep'idus, rich and indolent, had been neglected in the late campaign, and was slighted in the redistribution of the provinces, receiving only "Af'rica,"—that is, the Ro'man province of that name. Already the theoretical equality of the triumvirs was disturbed, and the two naturally stronger men were asserting their authority. From Philip'pi An'tony marched through A'sia, reclaiming the East. In Syr'ia he met the far-famed "Serpent of the Nile," Cleopä'tra, the woman whose beauty had captivated Ju'lius Cæ'sar and won for her the throne of E'gypt. The rough triumvir was an easy conquest. He accompanied her to Alexan'dria, her capital, and lived there with her in

Decay of the Triumvirate.

Antony and Cleopatra.

the most shameless and extravagant debauchery. His wife, Ful'via, and his brother, Lu'cius Anto'nius, were in It'aly, and stirred up a civil war in the hope of summoning him to Rome. They thwarted the efforts of Octavia'nus to regulate affairs at home and to reward his soldiers by grants of land and the foundation of new colonies. In conjunction with Lep'idus he took up arms against the Anto'nians and captured their stronghold, Peru'sia (41 B. C.). These disorders recalled the pleasure-loving An'tony to his senses. He hurried to It'aly with an army, and there came to an understanding with his colleagues. Lep'idus was content to retain the administration of his single province, while Octavia'nus took the West, with It'aly, and An'tony the East, with Cleopā'tra. The marriage of An'tony and Octa'via, young Cae'sar's sister, sealed the bond of reunion.

This partition of the Ro'man lands did not convey the sovereignty of the sea. Sex'tus, that indomitable son of Pom'pey the Great who had escaped death at Pharsā'lus, Thap'sus, and Mun'da, had gathered a fleet and placed himself at the head of the Mediterra'nean pirates. He did not care to renew the battle for the republic, but he had his father's death to avenge and his family fortune to recover. Rome's food supply came from Sic'ily, A'sia, and Af'rica by sea, and the ships of Sex'tus, by the capture of the grain-fleet, held the city in constant peril of famine. To buy him off, the triumvirs, in 39 B. C., signed the treaty of Mise'num, in which they agreed to restore his father's confiscated millions and allow him full control of Sic'ily, Sardin'ia, and a large part of Greece. But Sex'tus offended Octavia'nus by seizing an Ital'ian coast town, and the triumvirs soon reopened the war. In 37 B. C. the Sex'tian fleet was soundly beaten and its buccaneering admiral deprived of power.

Sextus Pompey.

Lep′idus asked that Sic′ily be now added to his department; but the western ruler, jealous of his territory, not only refused this favor, but took Af′rica for himself, thus thrusting Lep′idus out of the Triumvirate (36 B. C.). In 38 B. C. the three ruling men had extended their term of office for a second five years, and Octavia′nus and An′tony had thus three unexpended years of power. The former adopted the policy of Cæ′sar and undertook campaigns against the Illyr′ians, who intervened between the Ro′man province and the River Dan′ube, the natural boundary of conquest in that direction. In his military and naval operations the triumvir, still under thirty, had the advice of Mar′cus Vipsa′nius Agrip′pa, and in all business of civil government that renowned knight and patron of poets, Cil′nius Mæce′nas, was his trusted counselor. In the East An′tony held royal court at Alexan′dria in the luxurious splendor of an oriental monarch. The Egypt′ian, Cleopā′tra, was favored, and Octa′via, his proud Ro′man wife, was put aside. His expedition against the Par′thians, 36 B. C., was an utter failure; but a later raid into Arme′nia yielded the honor of a triumph which, to the disgust of the Ro′mans, was celebrated in Alexan′dria instead of at Rome. This report fed the current suspicion in It′aly that Cleopā′tra had persuaded An′tony to discrown the queen city of the world and remove the capital of the Ro′man realm to Alexan′dria. An′tony's treatment of Octa′via widened the breach between the triumvirs.

Lepidus expelled from the Triumvirate. 36 B. C.

Rivalry of Antony and Octavianus.

In 32 B. C. the smoldering rivalry of East and West flamed into war. An′tony and Cleopā′tra collected an enormous armament for the invasion of It′aly. Four Asiat′ic kings contributed to the army, and the ships of many nations composed the fleet. The delay consequent upon the assemblage, transportation, and

War of East and West. 32-31 B. C.

sustenance of such a force enabled Octavia′nus and his lieutenants to summon the utmost of his comparatively meager resources. The East was populous, wealthy, and full of ships and seamen. The West was inferior in all these particulars, but immeasurably superior in the personality of its present leader. An′tony was broken by dissipation, infatuated with a reckless woman, and could not command the confidence of his motley array. Octavia′nus Cæ′sar had the advantage of a great name, of ten years' honest and capable administration, of a united and devoted following, and of Agrip′pa's constant counsel and encouragement.

The two armies confronted each other for a time in Greece. Desertions from An′tony's army alarmed him. On the 2d of September, 31 B. C., the two fleets engaged in battle at Ac′tium in the western waters of Greece. After the first encounter Cleopā′tra turned her vessel's prow toward E′gypt. An′tony saw the movement, joined her on board, and the craven pair deserted the seafight, which became a scene of rout and destruction. Octavia′nus was completely victorious, thanks to good fortune and the skill of Agrip′pa. The Anto′nian army surrendered as soon as the fate of the fleet was known.

Battle of Actium. Sept., 31 B. C.

The next year (30 B. C.) the victor invaded E′gypt. An′tony's resistance was but half-hearted, and his troops refused to fight. Even Cleopā′tra, foreseeing his ruin, and bent on making good terms with the new master, turned from the lover whom she had dragged to ruin. When her servants falsely told him of her death, Mark An′tony, the friend of Cæ′sar and the ruler of the East, destroyed his miserable life. Alexan′dria surrendered to Octavia′nus, but the conqueror did not bend the knee to the city's queen. She had hoped to lead captivity captive as she had done before; but the new Cæ′sar was

Octavianus in Egypt. 30 B. C.

forewarned of her wiles. He spared her life to grace his triumph at Rome, but she escaped that humiliation. In some unknown way, perhaps by the sting of an asp, as the old stories have it, her spirit followed the ruined An'tony out of the world in which it had so delighted.

Death of Antony and Cleopatra.

The deposition of Lep'idus and the death of An'tony reduced the triumvirate to its lowest terms. The power which this governing board of three had usurped in the confusion after Cæ'sar's death was now concentrated in the single survivor, Octavia'nus.

Octavianus, master of Roman world.

Ju'lius Cæ'sar had forever answered in the negative the question whether the republic could longer exist. The hundred years of civil war from Grac'chus to Cæ'sar had proved the incapacity of the Senate as a governing body, and the reformers, the Grac'chi, Dru'sus, Sul'la, had successively failed to create a competent and stable government out of either of the elements at hand, the aristocracy or the democracy. A king was inevitable, and years of proscription and civil murders taught the Ro'mans the folly of resistance. What the republic could do it had already done.

So long as its citizen-body and its aristocratic Senate were simple, sober, frugal, and patriotic, its power extended. The citizen armies of Rome conquered It'aly, Car'thage, the western and the eastern world, and made the Mediterra'nean Sea a vast Ro'man lake. But wealth and power brought to the aristocrats decay of morals, greed of power and gain. The slave system destroyed free labor and exterminated the middle class of citizens. With a corrupt nobility and a beggared populace the State lost its balance. The provinces were misgoverned and robbed; successful generals seized the civil power. At last a general and a statesman crushed the whole frail fabric of the republic

Why the republic failed.

and made himself monarch of the Ro′man world. He fell a victim to the sentimental attachment which a few still cherished for the old Commonwealth, but the republic never got upon its feet again; after a dozen years of divided sovereignty the Cæsa′rian power was reunited in the person of Cæ′sar Octavia′nus, the nephew of Ju′lius, and the very person whom the great founder of the empire had chosen to succeed him. Thus the worn-out republic expired, and a greater monarchy took its place, a little less than five centuries after the last Tar′quin king was banished by the first Bru′tus and the patrician revolution.

When the first monarchy closed, Rome was supreme among the Lat′ins, the farmers who tilled the soil of La′tium; the new monarchy found Rome the capital of the world.

ANALYSIS OF CHAPTER VI.

I. *The First Triumvirate*, 131-136:
    Three eminent Romans, 131-133:
        Crassus, 131.
        Pompey, 132.
        Cæsar, 133.
    The Triumvirate organized, 134.
    Cæsar's wars in Gaul, 135.
    The meeting of the triumvirs at Lucca, 135.
    Death of Crassus dissolves Triumvirate, 136.

II. *The Struggle of Cæsar with the Senate*, 136-140:
    Cæsar's right of candidacy disputed, 136.
    The Senate's mandate, 137.
    Cæsar invades Italy, 137.
    Pompey evacuates Italy, 138.
    Cæsar at Rome, 139.
    Defeat of Pompey at Pharsalus, 140.

III. *The Reign of Julius Cæsar*, 140-147:
    Cæsar conquers the East, 140.
    Defeat of republicans at Thapsus, 141, 142.
    Settling the affairs of state, 142.

The Spanish campaign, Munda, 143.
The imperial policy, 143, 144.
The plot and assassination, 144, 145.
Failure of the revolution, 146.
Antony aims at Cæsar's place, 147.
Advent of Octavianus, 147.

IV. *The Second Triumvirate*, 147-154:
The Second Triumvirate organized, 147.
The partition of the world, 148.
The republicans defeated at Philippi, 149.
Antony and Cleopatra, 149.
War with Sextus Pompey, 150.
Lepidus expelled from the Triumvirate, 151.
Rivalry of Antony and Octavianus, 151.
Battle of Actium, 152.
Octavianus in Egypt, 152.
Octavianus sole master of the Roman world, 153.

REVIEW EXERCISE.

Second Period. The Roman Republic. Part III. (b.) 63-31 B. C.

1. What three men formed the First Triumvirate?
2. Describe briefly the career of Crassus.
3. What were the elements of Pompey's strength and weakness?
4. Narrate the events of Cæsar's early life.
5. For what did Cæsar require an army?
6. What did the First Triumvirate accomplish?
7. Give a brief account of Cæsar's work in Gaul?
8. What was determined in the meeting at Lucca in 56 B. C.?
9. What brought the First Triumvirate to an end?
10. Upon what constitutional point did Cæsar and the Senate disagree?
11. What did Cæsar signify by "crossing the Rubicon"?
12. Why did Pompey evacuate Italy?
13. What civil honors did Cæsar receive at Rome?
14. Where and when was Cæsar's decisive victory won?
15. What events gave rise to Cæsar's saying, "*Veni, vidi, vici?*"
16. Describe the events leading up to the battle of Thapsus.
17. What was Cæsar's position at the close of the wars?
18. What was Cæsar's attitude toward the old republican institutions?
19. What lasting reforms did Cæsar introduce?

20. What was Cæsar's last great victory?
21. What was Cæsar's foreign policy?
22. Who were the leaders of the republican conspiracy?
23. Describe the circumstances of Cæsar's assassination.
24. Describe the movements of Antony immediately after Cæsar's death.
25. What view did Cicero take of Antony's activity?
26. What was Octavianus' first public commission?
27. Who were the members of the Second Triumvirate?
28. How did the triumvirs divide the Roman world?
29. In what battle did the triumvirs conquer the republicans?
30. What famous woman captivated Antony?
31. Give an account of the war with Sextus Pompey.
32. What change took place in the Triumvirate in 36 B. C.?
33. What fostered the rivalry between Antony and Octavianus?
34. Describe the battle of Actium.
35. Describe Octavianus' operations in Egypt.
36. What course of events brought Octavianus to the supremacy of Rome?

CHAPTER VII.

THIRD PERIOD.

THE ROMAN EMPIRE FROM AUGUSTUS TO CONSTANTINE.
(354 YEARS.) 31 B. C.—323 A. D.

THE defeat of An'tony at Ac'tium (31 B. C.) established Octavia'nus, the crafty nephew and adopted son of the great Ju'lius, in the sole mastery of the many lands which the Ro'man republic had conquered. After years of foreign warfare and intestine strife the civilized world—that part at least of Eu'rope, A'sia, and Af'rica, which bordered the Mediterra'nean—was at peace. At Rome the double doors of the old temple of Ja'nus which always were flung wide in war time, were closed for the third time in their history—once in the reign of the half forgotten King Nu'ma, and again after the second war with Car'thage. Having crushed all opposition in the East, Octavia'nus returned to Rome to celebrate the triumph which he had earned and to organize a system of government for the vast realm of which he was the undisputed lord.

<small>Peace. The triumph of Octavianus.</small>

In this arduous labor he was aided by those tried counselors, Agrip'pa and Mæce'nas, to whose ability and foresight quite as much as to his own combination of subtlety and force he owed his eminence, and he was admonished by the example of his uncle, who, confronted with the same task had called down his own destruction by too bold assumption of royal prerogatives

<small>The sources of his success.</small>

and symbols. The nephew was no genius, yet he succeeded where his great kinsman failed. The very fact that there had already been a Cæ'sar perhaps abated something from the common dread of an absolute ruler. Moreover, during the protracted civil wars a generation had grown to manhood which had no personal experience of the better days of the republic, and which acquiesced in the new *régime* with its assurances of peace and prosperity rather than hazard life and property in fresh struggles for the re-establishment of the doubtful blessings of the Commonwealth. The new despotism disguised its more obnoxious forms in the familiar robes of the republic and the time-honored institutions faded by scarcely noticeable gradations into the new empire.

Octavia'nus kept aloof from the title and trappings of a king. "Impera'tor" was a name long since applied to military officers of superior rank. Ju'lius Cæ'sar had assumed it as commander-in-chief of the army; it was inherited by his nephew and it is this word which, softened to "emperor," is so familiar to our ears. Impera'tor Cæ'sar also united in his own person the honors and functions of the ancient constitutional offices. He not only commanded the army, but as consul he could convene the Senate; as prince (*prin'ceps sena'tus*) he was its leader; as censor he could enroll or expel members of that body; as tribune he was the especial magistrate of the commons, and possessed the veto power; and as pon'tifex max'imus he was the supreme earthly director of the great ritual machinery of the State religion. A new title was needed to comprehend this manifold authority and it was found in 27 B. C. when the Senate decreed to Octavia'nus the surname of Augus'tus ("consecrated by the Au'gurs"), a title which may be roughly compared to our form of address "his majesty." This name was borne with

Augustus. First emperor. 31 B.C.-14 A. D.

A new title.

equal right by his successors, but to Octavia'nus, its first owner, it seems to belong in an especial sense and it is his most familiar appellation. Sexti'lis, the sixth month in the Ro'man calendar, was henceforth (from 8 B. C.) called Augus'tus (August) in his honor, as Quinti'lis, the fifth, had been named Ju'lius (July) for his noble kinsman.

All power, military, legislative, judicial, executive, was concentrated in the hands of Augus'tus, but the outward forms of the old constitution still stood in empty but delusive array. The assemblies (Comi'tia Centuria'ta and Tribu'ta) continued to sit and vote. Officers of the old titles but with impoverished authority, consuls, prætors, quæstors, and ædiles were still elected, though it was noticed that the emperor's nominees were never rejected. The Senate was treated with much consideration and its opinion was frequently consulted, but at best it could do nothing against the man who had the legions at his beck and call.

Republican survivals.

It had been a fruitful source of Ro'man ills that the Senate of the republican era had applied no satisfactory system to the government of the provinces which had been carved out of the conquered kingdoms. To hold a nation down by military power while a prætor or proconsul plundered its treasury had been the too common policy and practice. The senatorial governors had robbed and harried their poor subjects and plunged their territories into abject misery.

Senatorial government of the provinces.

The accession of Augus'tus brought a sweet relief. In 27 B. C. he assorted the provinces into two classes. Ten,* distinguished for their quiet and order, were to be administered

---

*The ten senatorial provinces were Africa, A'sia, Acha'ia, Illyr'ia, or Dalma'tia, Macedo'nia, Sic'ily, Crete with Cyre'ne, Bithyn'ia, Sardin'ia, and South Spain.

by the Senate's governors as before, except that a financial agent of the emperor attended to the collection of such taxes as belonged to the crown. The remaining provinces, being those of more recent conquest or more exposed situation, were called imperial* and were directly subject to the emperor, who governed them through deputies ("legates," "procurators," or "prefects") of his own appointment. The governors and deputies received fixed salaries, the collection of the taxes was systematized, and shorn of its more oppressive features, and it was made easy for the provincial to appeal to the ear of the emperor himself. As the empire became more firmly established the provincials were encouraged to aspire to the full rights and privileges of Ro'man citizenship to which the Lat'ins, Ital'ians, and Cisal'pine Gauls had been successively admitted. Under the process of Romanization, which went silently on, it was not many years before the contented and happy population of the Mediterra'nean world forgot their struggles against the conquering Ro'mans and learned to look upon themselves as fellow-countrymen of the great Ital'ians and partakers in the glories of the empire. Gauls, Span'iards, Greeks, Asiat'ics, Af'ricans, and Egyp'tians, were proud of the name of Rome, acquired her language, obeyed her laws, imitated her architecture. Numbers of provincials settled in the eternal city, which now began to take on character as the mother city (metro-polis) of the world.

Averse to luxury himself, and living on a scale of democratic simplicity, Augus'tus had far-reaching plans for his capital. Rome was to be adorned in a manner worthy of her exalted station. The buildings of the old town were low and shabby, the streets narrow

---

* In 27 B. C. the twelve imperial provinces were: North Spain, Lusita'nia, the four Gauls, Upper and Lower Ger'many, Syr'ia, Cili'cia, Cy'prus, and E'gypt.

and steep, the public squares untidy, and the temples and public buildings generally far below the splendor of such subject towns as Ath'ens, An'tioch, and Alexan'dria. The revenues which should have been expended for the public good had been wasted in the long term of civil war. The return of peace and settled order brought the emperor both the opportunity and the means to beautify the city. By his order hundreds of buildings were razed, more ample squares were laid out, fine residences erected, temples renovated and the walls strengthened. Ro'man architecture, which had borrowed the arch from its Etrus'can inventors and combined it with the columns and gables of the Greek style, rose to its best estate in this reign. The new Cæ'sar completed the extensive buildings projected by his uncle and added many of his own. Wealthy citizens imitated his example. Agrip'pa, always foremost in executing the emperor's designs, built the Pan'theon ("the all-holy place") in 27 B. C., the best extant example of the Ro'man builder's art. His, too, were the *ther'mae*, the first of the splendid public baths in which the Ro'mans of the empire took such high delight.

The benefits of a strong government went further yet. A police force preserved order throughout the city. The magnificent roads which radiated from Rome through the peninsula were extended throughout the empire, and a governmental postal system facilitated rapid communication with distant provinces. An age of material prosperity was dawning which went on unchecked even amid the wild caprices of the succeeding emperors. Peace and order loosed the fetters of commercial enterprise. Freedom of trade throughout the Mediterra'nean basin laid the foundation of such unexampled prosperity as the warring kingdoms of the world had never known before.

The city of Rome had no natural means of support for its swarming citizens. It was neither a great commercial market like Lon'don nor a manufacturing center like Par'is; indeed the prevalence of slavery had cast dishonor upon manual labor and left the mass of citizens poor indeed but too proud to labor. The republic early undertook to control the price of bread in the interest of its hungry voters, and successive bids for popularity on the part of ambitious politicians, reduced this price until in 58 B. C. any Ro'man householder might have his grain for the asking. In 46 B. C. 320,000 were not too proud to ask and there were sullen murmurs when Augus'tus cut down the number of recipients to 200,000 and fixed it there.

Doles of food.

In allusion to his extensive municipal improvements it is often said of Augus'tus that "he found Rome built of brick and left it built of marble," but his reign has left us something more enduring than the choicest product of the Pa'rian quarries; for these years mark the "golden age" or "Augustan age" of literature. Until the closing century of the republic the Ro'mans had cared little for the arts of literary expression either in prose or poetry. In the last gasps of the Commonwealth Cæ'sar, Ci'cero, and Sal'lust stand forth as masters of Lat'in prose. Under the protection and sometimes by the subsidy of the knight Mæce'nas, the emperor's confidential counselor, now sprang up a whole chorus of poets: Ver'gil (70–19 B. C.), whose "Æne'id" glorified the reigning dynasty; Hor'ace (65–8 B. C.) the master of graceful song; the elegiac poets, Tibul'lus (54–19 B. C.), Proper'tius (49–15 B. C.), and Ov'id (45 B. C.–17 A. D.); and the justly celebrated prose historian Liv'y (59 B. C.–17 A. D.).

"The Augustan Age of Letters."

The wars of Augus'tus were waged chiefly with the border tribes and kingdoms remote from the capital. Scarcely an in-

THE ROMAN EMPIRE—AUGUSTUS TO CONSTANTINE. 163

surrection within the broad limits of the empire ruffled the peace or shook the allegiance of a province. By steady advances the imperial generals carried the sway of the Cæ'sar to the shores of the Dan'ube (29-15 B. C.), the last free Span'ish mountaineers were subdued (27-19 B. C.), and the fierce Par'thians, who had overwhelmed with barbarism the rich lands of Western A'sia once subject to Cy'rus, Xer'xes, and Alexan'der, though they had not yet paid for their insult to the Ro'man eagles at Car'rhæ (53 B. C.), sued for peace and sent back with honor the trophies of that dolorous day. Gaul, the field of Ju'lius Cæ'sar's conquests, was in process of rapid and thorough Romanization from the Pyr'enees to the Rhine. But the free Ger'mans who cultivated the fields and roamed the forests beyond that river remained a constant menace to the peace of the empire in the West. On the Rhen'ish frontier accordingly the Ro'man armies were concentrated. Here the antiquary still may trace the moats and ramparts of the camps of the Ro'man legions, which were real fortresses in strength and permanence. Frequent raids were made across the stream, not so much to conquer Ger'many as to strike dread of Rome into the Ger'man breast and so preserve the peace of Gaul. Thither the princes, Dru'sus and Tibe'rius, sons of Liv'ia Augus'ta, whom the emperor had taken to wife, were sent to win their spurs. There Dru'sus met his death, but the brother, whose name is famous in Ro'man history, achieved distinction in those wars and even helped to extend the Ro'man power on the farther shore of the Rhine and in Panno'nia (Hun'gary).

The wars of Augustus.

In these border wars, some of them fierce and bloody, the legions were led by the imperial generals, for Augus'tus usually remained at Rome. He was never a military genius and as he grew older he had little love for a soldier's life. His active career had begun

The gloomy close of the reign.

at a very early period in his life and the enormous responsibilities of the government now weighed heavily upon his somewhat enfeebled physical frame. His last years were clouded with trouble. The fortune which smiled upon his public acts had no favors for his family. The emperor had no son of his body to succeed him. Of the two Ne′ros, his stepsons by Liv′ia, Dru′sus the favorite was dead. His daughter and granddaughter disgraced the Ju′lian name by their flaunting vices and were justly banished. His grandsons, Ca′ius and Lu′cius Cæ′sar, died in early manhood, leaving him only an idiot heir. It was whispered at Rome that the empress was not guiltless of these untimely deaths and was showing a more than motherly solicitude for the future of her own surviving son Tibe′rius, who lived, now a prince at Rome, now a general on the Ger′man frontier, now a gentleman at Rhōdes, growing old in exasperating uncertainty whether he or another should succeed Augus′tus. An awful disaster to the Ro′man army deepened the gloom which was settling down over the emperor's mind. In the year 9 A. D. at a time when tribes east of the Rhine seemed to be yielding to the blandishments of Ro′man commerce, an army of three legions commanded by Quintil′ius Va′rus was lured by deep-laid strategy into the heart of Ger′many and massacred almost to a man by a national uprising of the Ger′mans under their chief, Armin′ius, who, under the name of Her′mann, has become a hero of his race. The news of this slaughter in the Teutobur′ger Forest sent a shudder through the capital. Again, as in the times of Bren′nus, of Han′nibal, of the Cim′bri and Teu′tones, an awful peril seemed to impend. Though past his seventieth year, weak in body and disturbed in mind, the emperor prepared to avenge the loss and avert a fresh attack. Thoughts of the catastrophe haunted him awake and asleep

The slaughter at Teutoburg. 9 A. D.

and he was heard to cry out, "Va'rus, Va'rus, give me back my legions!" Death soon relieved him. He met his end like a Ro'man, at No'la, near Na'ples, in his seventy-sixth year, having held the reins of power steadily and alone for nearly forty-five years (31 B. C.-14 A. D.).

By his very name "Augus'tus" Octavia'nus was set apart from and above ordinary mortals. The decay of the ancient re-

The deification of the emperor.

ligions of Rome and Greece had left men's minds in an expectant attitude toward supernatural things. Some looked for a return of the "Satur'-nian times," a mythical golden age of the remote past; the Jews looked for their Messi'ah. In the eastern provinces first, and later in the West, there sprang up a veneration of the emperor scarcely comprehensible to modern monotheists. Ju'lius Cæ'sar, imperator, had claimed some of the honors of a god and after his death the triumvirs had formally awarded him the name and honors of deity (*Di'vus Ju'lius*). In like manner when Octavia'nus died the Senate publicly proclaimed his divinity (*Di'vus Augus'tus*) and established a new college of priests (*Augustā'les*) to superintend his worship. Later emperors found this practice advantageous to the dignity of their office and it became the custom on the death of each emperor for his successor to propose and for the Senate to pass a resolution placing him among the deified rulers. Upon the walls of one of these imperial temples at Ancy'ra (Angō'ra), a town of the Gala'tians, tablets have been discovered bearing in Greek and Lat'in the first emperor's own story of his life, copied and fixed there by the priests. Plainly and proudly as befitted a Ro'man, he sets down the "list of deeds done by himself." But of

Birth of Jesus. 4 B. C.

the single event which the world now esteems the greatest, he himself knew nothing. For in Beth'-lehem of Jude'a, an obscure village of his dominions, in the

166   ROME AND THE MAKING OF MODERN EUROPE.

twenty-seventh year of his reign, the Savior of the world was born.

Augus'tus had established his throne so quietly that the Ro'mans still spoke of the republic as if it yet existed. The hereditary principle was by no means admitted and there was no law to regulate the succession.

<small>The question of the succession.</small>

By right of adoption, however, his stepson, Tibe'rius Ne'ro, was the heir of the emperor's property. The troops on the Ger'man frontier urged their general, Cæ'sar German'icus, Dru'sus Ne'ro's son, to assert his claim, to which they pledged their support. But the popular soldier declined in favor of Tibe'rius who was at Rome and whose interests were jealously watched by his widowed mother.

The Senate renewed for Tibe'rius the honors of his stepfather. He took the name of Cæ'sar, was entitled Augus'tus, imperator, tribune, censor, pon'tifex max'imus, and the rest, and acquired without bloodshed or intrigue the absolute authority. Parts of the threadbare apparel of the republic were now cast off. The rights and powers of the citizen assemblies were still further depleted, the Senate being apparently the gainer, though few dared gainsay the emperor by rejecting his laws or his nominees for office.

<small>Tiberius. Second emperor. 14-37 A. D.</small>

The ruler's authority was made more complete by the laws against treason and by the development of the so-called "prætorian guard." The laws were calculated to protect the emperor in person, property, and dignity, and the slightest word that could be offensively construed made its owner liable to crushing penalties. Informers (*delato'res*) were paid to ferret out and accuse such political offenders and the most trivial utterance reflecting upon the ruler or his government was punished with exile and confiscation. The prætorian guard was the

<small>Laws against treason. *Delatores*.</small>

necessary accompaniment of despotism. The republic had been overthrown by force and the emperor must have a visible force at hand to uphold his decrees.

The prætorian guard.

Accordingly Augus'tus had reserved a body of troops for special duty in the city and in It'aly, and now a permanent camp was fortified just outside the city and garrisoned with 10,000 picked men, mainly veterans. The commanders of these prætorians were in a position to be most useful or most dangerous to the emperor and were selected with the greatest care.

Until her death (29 A. D.) the empress-mother, Liv'ia Augus'ta, exercised the chief power jointly with her son, and she seems to have been the stronger character and the abler mind of the two. Before her death the knightly German'icus had defeated Armin'ius, the Ger'man hero, thereby gaining such favor with populace and soldiers that the jealous government thought best to send him to Syr'ia on a dangerous mission from which he never returned.

Livia Augusta.

Cæsar Germanicus.

Tibe'rius was already past middle life when his stepfather died, and age came rapidly upon him. By degrees he let himself be ruled by one Seja'nus, the commander of the prætorians and the man by whose advice the city battalions had been concentrated in a single camp. In 27 A. D. the emperor retired from the cares of state to the island of Ca'pri, near Na'ples, where he threw away the remnant of his life in sickening vice and frightful cruelty. Meanwhile the favorite Seja'nus remained at Rome, the actual ruler of the empire, securing the imperial sanction for his most lawless acts of tyranny. Tibe'rius never entered his capital again, but news came to him at Ca'pri that Seja'nus was plotting to usurp his place. Then the old Ro'man spirit took fire.

The favorite, Sejanus.

Tiberius at Capri.

The favorite was seized without warning and hurried to death (31 A. D.). The emperor's horrid existence, growing more foul and cruel year by year, lasted until death took him in 37 **A. D.** The groveling Senate did not begrudge divine honors to this human monster. In his later years under Pon'-tius Pi'late, one of his governors in Jude'a, Je'sus of Naz'areth was crucified (30 A. D.) at Jeru'salem upon an accusation of treason—having, as the false witnesses swore, proclaimed himself "King of the Jews," who had no king but this Tibe'rius Cæ'sar.

<small>Crucifixion of Jesus, 30 A. D.</small>

Ca'ius Cæ'sar, son of German'icus and Agrippi'na, had perhaps been designated by the dying ruler as his heir or joint-heir. Thanks to the fair fame of his noble father he was high in the good graces of people and prætorians at Rome and easily slipped into the vacant place and the Senate could but ratify what the troops and populace approved. This third emperor, Ca'ius Cæ'sar German'icus, is known to history as Calig'ula ("Boots"), the nickname which his father's soldiers had given him when, as the baby of the legion, he toddled about the camps in his soldier-suit. He was a willful and weak-minded tyrant, vexing the empire with extravagant and insane undertakings and encouraging by his own gross immoralities the vices which were already too common in high life at Rome. Claiming to be a god, he required his subjects to worship him, and horrified the Jews by requiring them to erect his statue in their sacred places. The old books are full of stories of this silly tyrant who could command the world to execute his crack-brained projects. He built a bridge of boats across a bay "that he might tread on water"; he led an army to "the conquest of the ocean," halting them on the shore to gather seashells as trophies of their victory. After bearing with his whims for four years

<small>"Caligula." (Caius Cæsar.) Third emperor, 37-41 A. D.</small>

<small>His feebleness and folly.</small>

(37–41 A. D.) two of his officers stabbed him to death in the theater.

The young Calig′ula left no heir, and the Senate sprang to its opportunity, reasserting its ancient claims and proposing to rule unhampered by a Cæ′sar. But the prætorians demanded an emperor and ranging through the palace they found Clau′dius Ne′ro, a "poor relation" of the imperial family, dragged him to camp and hailed him as the sovereign of Rome. The Senate yielded with such grace as it could muster and Clau′dius was duly clothed with authority. During the lifetime of his nephew Calig′ula, this man, who was deformed and of unbalanced mind, was the butt of the court. As emperor he cared little for the business of government, leaving such matters to the fawning freedmen and loose women who formed his household. The day of great officials—secretaries, chamberlains, and seneschals—had not yet come and the civil service of the empire was in the hands of slaves and freedmen. By ministering to his pleasures the latter gained entire control of Clau′dius. Two men especially—Pal′las, his steward, and Narcis′sus, his secretary—conducted his affairs and enriched themselves by the shameless sale of offices and privileges. Fe′lix, whose conscience may well have been stung by Paul's reasoning of "judgment to come," was another of these wretched parasites. The influence of the worst of women came in to deepen the palace intrigues. The name of Messali′na, the empress, has been for eighteen centuries synonymous with insatiate and reckless lust. As cruel as she was licentious, the accusations of Narcis′sus at last moved the emperor to consent to her execution.

Agrippi′na, the younger, Calig′ula's sister and the emperor's niece, was chosen to console the dotard. Her first husband, one Ahenobar'bus, was a man of notorious temper and her own qualities were not of the most womanly. Her absorbing care was to make the fortune of her boy Domi'tius, who exemplified the evil traits of his parents. She managed to have Clau'dius adopt him although he already had two children by Messali'na. Of these the boy was thrust aside and the girl Octa'via was married to Agrippi'na's son, whom we shall know henceforth by his adoptive name of "Ne'ro." When her plans were ripe a pinch of poison gave Clau'dius his quietus and her son the scepter of the world (54 A. D.). The reign had yielded few events of public record. The Ro'mans had resumed with vigor the conquest of Britain, which had been left nearly to itself since the days of Ju'lius Cæ'sar. Within its borders the empire was quiet and prosperous. "The empire is peace" became a proverb and it is probably true that the personal foulness, cruelty, and weakness of the later Ju'lian emperors did not affect materially the condition of commerce and society outside of Rome and It'aly. But the deeds of Agrippi'na's son were to horrify the civilized world.

"The empire is peace."

The efforts of his mother had given Ne'ro the empire (54 A. D.). Bur'rhus, the prætorian general, was on her side and the Senate made a virtue of necessity and awarded to him the customary honors. For several years his true character was disguised. Agrippi'na attended to the government and left him to his tutors and to the music and drama which were his chief delight. His guardians, the honest Bur'rhus and the philosopher Sen'eca, whose name tradition links in friendship with St. Paul's, labored faithfully to fit him for his responsibilities. But the young man preferred the stage to the state. He even acted in the public theaters and forced high-

Nero. Fifth emperor. 54-68 A. D.

Burrhus and Seneca.

born senators to equal degradation. With all his fondness for art he showed the brutality of a fierce-tempered tyrant to whom absolute power brought no sense of the necessity of self-restraint. He was ungrateful to his faithful teachers and even had the pious Sen'eca put to death. To divorce Octa'via, and poison her brother Britan'nicus, and to kill his second wife, Poppæ'a by a kick, these were bad enough, but the heartless murder of his gray-haired mother, who would have died for her incorrigible son, passed the bounds of Ro'man cruelty, and insured him an immortality of infamy.

In 64 A. D. a great fire swept for six days through the most densely built sections of Rome. Men said—though, it seems, with little of truth—that the flames had been spread by the emperor's orders, and that he viewed the scene from a palace roof " fiddling while Rome burned," and comparing the sight with Homer's story of the fall of Troy. Such rumors were distasteful to the court and the generally misunderstood and distrusted disciples at Rome of that Jew whom Pi'late had crucified in Judea a generation before were made the scapegoats to bear the emperor's guilt. Thus arose the first imperial persecution of the Chris'tians, and Ne'ro lavished his artistic sense in devising strange and horrible modes of torturing the innocent sufferers. The burnt district was seized as public property and laid out upon a splendid scale with parks, gardens, and magnificent edifices. Upon the construction of his own palace, the "Golden House," were expended the revenues of a kingdom. Such extravagance and such cruelty were unheard of. Augus'tus had been called penurious ; Tibe'rius at his worst had been less cruel and bloody ; Calig'ula and Clau'dius could scarcely be held responsible for their wild caprices. But now the provinces felt the drain of taxation to supply the emperor's purse

Great fire at Rome. 64 A. D.

First persecution of the Christians.

The "Golden House."

and the greatest men of the realm were slaughtered to satisfy his anger or suspicion. Bur'rhus and Sen'eca, the guardians of his youth, the poet Lu'can, whose genius rebuked the emperor's attempts at poetry, the senator Pæ'tus, who adorned his stoic philosophy by the manner of his taking off, and Cor'bulo, the best soldier of his day, had fallen victim to his displeasure. There were mutterings of conspiracy at Rome against the monster. In Ro'man Gaul, the chieftain Vin'dex, roused his countrymen to throw off a yoke so disgraceful. At the same time Sulpi'cius Gal'ba, commander of the troops in Spain, was hailed as "imperator" by his soldiers and set out for Rome at their head to wrest the purple from the Cæ'sar. Deserted by all around him, Ne'ro fled to the house of one of his former slaves and there finding escape impossible put an end to his miserable existence (68 A. D.). He was the last of the so-called "Ju'lian emperors," connected by blood or adoption with the line of Ju'lius Cæ'sar. Thenceforth the names Cæ'sar and Augus'tus are borne by all the emperors merely as titles of honor, for the family which had made the names glorious was extinguished. Even after the empire had vanished the potency of the surname of Ju'lius lived on and to this day lives as the Ger'man "Kai'ser" in the West and the Slav "Czar" in the East.

Nero's cruelty.

Risings in the provinces. Vindex.

Galba invades Italy.

Death of Nero. Last of the Julian line. 68 A. D.

Having passed out of the Ju'lian line the sovereignty of Rome became for a time a prize to be scrambled for by the strongest and for the first time in a hundred years It'aly suffered the horrors of a civil war.

Galba. Sixth emperor. 68–69 A. D.

Gal'ba reigned but for a few months (68–69 A. D.). He had come at the head of an army and the Senate had conferred upon him the customary honors; but he was an old man and turned out to be a puppet

THE ROMAN EMPIRE—AUGUSTUS TO CONSTANTINE.

in the hands of unprincipled courtiers. O'tho, a senator, and a former comrade of Ne'ro in his revels, conspired against him and secured the good will of the prætorians. Too late the aged ruler tried to save himself by associating Pi'so, a young noble, with him in the government, but the guards proclaimed O'tho emperor and killed both Gal'ba and his colleague (69 A. D.).

Otho. Seventh emperor. 69 A. D.

The disorder spread apace. If the Span'ish legions could confer the scepter, why not the Ger'man or the Syr'ian? So reasoned soldiers and ambitious commanders. The legions on the Rhine set out for It'aly to put their candidate, the drunken glutton Vitel'lius, in Cæ'sar's seat. O'tho's military ability was limited but the prætorians stood by him; and the troops in Illyr'ia and the East were loyal. If the latter could arrive in time he might be saved. But the Vitel'lians were the first to pass the Alps. The wretched force of prætorians, marines, and gladiators, which O'tho had assembled near Cremo'na was routed and the emperor of a few months killed himself.

Disorder in the army.

Plunder and outrage marked the southward march of Vitel'lius. The servile Ro'man Senate honored this purple-faced reveler with the title of Augus'tus, and for his brief day of power he ate and drank in the palace of the Cæ'sars. But his lease of power was brief. From Illyr'ia and Syr'ia came the belated succors which O'tho had summoned. Anto'nius with the vanguard defeated the Vitel'lians near the scene of O'tho's disaster. Rome again changed hands and the abject emperor was dragged from his hiding place in a kennel and killed like a dog (69 A. D.). The combined reigns of these three so-called "legionary" emperors, Gal'ba, O'tho, and Vitel'lius, aggregate little more than a year.

Vitellius. Eighth emperor. 69 A. D.

The "legionary" emperors.

The first century of the empire seemed to have brought the throne to the verge of its fall, when the strong hands of the Fla′vian rulers grasped it and set it firm again. The first of them, Vespa′sian,—or, if writ large, Ti′tus Fla′vius Vespasia′nus—had no clearer title than his three immediate predecessors. There was no Ju′lian blood in his veins. Indeed, men said that his great-grandfather was a farm laborer. His father certainly was a tax-gatherer or something of that despised sort. In Ne′ro's reign, Vespa′sian had served with credit in the army and as a capable provincial governor, but he lacked the graces of a courtier, even falling asleep in the theater while the actor-emperor was on the boards, and so forfeiting the monarch's esteem. The mad uprising of the Jews in Pal′estine (66 A. D.) called for Rome's best military talent and the command fell to Vespa′sian. He took with him his son Ti′tus, leaving behind at Rome his brother Sabi′nus and his younger boy Domi′tian. The war was prolonged by the stubborn resistance of Jeru′salem and the news of the fall of the last of the house of Ju′lius and the usurpations of Gal′ba, O′tho, and Vitel′lius found Vespa′sian still in the East. His son and his soldiers urged him to claim the empire for himself by the right of the strongest army. He yielded, with a show of reluctance, and went to Rome, already in the hands of Anto′nius.

"The Flavian family." Vespasian, Titus, Domitian.

Vespasian. Ninth emperor. 69–79 A. D.

The Gauls and Ger′mans, sensitive to the signs of Ro′man discord, rose in rebellion under Civi′lis, but the generals of Vespa′sian quelled the rising before it had gone far (71 A. D.). Ti′tus, who had been left before the walls of Jeru′salem, reduced the city after its memorable three years' siege (70 A. D.). The Ro′mans were exasperated by the obstinacy of the defense and the Jews resisted even after the walls were carried. The city was given

Titus takes Jerusalem. 70 A. D.

over to pillage, burning, and slaughter, blood ran in the streets, the stately temple of Jeho'vah was flung down so that not one stone was left upon another. In his splendid triumph at Rome the victor displayed his trophies, and upon the Arch of Titus may still be seen the sculptured figures of the seven-branched candlestick and the sacred furniture of the Jew'ish sanctuary which commemorate the fall of Jerusalem.

Vespa'sian is reckoned one of the "good emperors." In contrast to Tibe'rius and his successors his tastes were simple, his temper mild. By careful economies and shrewd management he refilled the empty treasury of the State. Men who had reveled with Ne'ro said that this commoner was a miser; but his money was honestly gained and wisely expended for the improvement of the city. His death in the tenth year of his reign (79 A. D.) closed a well-spent life.

Character of Vespasian.

Ti'tus, the second Fla'vian, succeeded his father. Indeed during Vespa'sian's lifetime this energetic son had been admitted to a large share in the direction of affairs. To his liberal policy we owe many of the chief monuments of the empire. The Arch of Ti'tus stands almost uninjured by the eighteen centuries which have passed over it. His Fla'vian amphitheater, where gladiatorial combats were fought to please the populace, is the most stupendous ruin of the Ro'man world. The massive strength of this building inspired the lines:

Titus, Tenth emperor. 79–81 A. D.

> "While stands the Colosse'um Rome shall stand;
> When falls the Colosse'um Rome shall fall;
> And when Rome falls—the World!"

Ti'tus outlived his father by but two years (79–81 A. D.) but his subjects admired and loved him and sincerely mourned his death.

The reign of Ti'tus is marked by a succession of awful

calamities : a conflagration at Rome, a plague in It'aly, earthquake shocks in Campa'nia, followed by the most memorable disaster in history, the eruption of Vesu'vius. For centuries this volcano had slumbered. The cities of Pompe'ii and Hercula'neum at its foot were favorite places of resort for the wealthy. Suddenly the pent-up forces were let loose. The crater vomited ashes and stone upon all the country around. The townspeople fled whither they could. Many were struck down by flying coals, suffocated by the noxious gases, or entombed in the cellars and temples in which they had sought refuge. The younger Plin'y has preserved a graphic description of the scene as he saw it from the bay. His uncle and namesake, the distinguished naturalist, went ashore to study the phenomenon, but was stifled to death by the gases. The exhumation of these cities in recent times has been our chief instructor in the domestic life of the Ro'mans of the first century.

Eruption of Vesuvius. Pompeii buried. 79 A. D.

The first two rulers of the Fla'vian family were of ripe age when they came to power and the elevation did not make their hard heads dizzy. But Domi'tian was only a lad when the good fortune of his father Vespa'sian made him an emperor's son. During the lifetime of Ti'tus the wild young prince was kept in curb ; indeed to conceal his real character it is said that he assumed the cloak of foolishness and filled the mouths of gossips with stories of his fly-killing exploits. He came to the throne in 81 A. D. and gave early promise of a mild and equable reign. But the wars which he undertook against the half barbarous tribes along the Dan'ube river brought disaster to the Ro'man arms and disgrace to the cowardly sovereign. To protect himself against conspiracy and to replenish his war-drained treasury he made tremendous use of his despotic power. The worst of his predecessors was scarcely his equal

Domitian. Eleventh emperor. 81-96 A. D.

in murders and confiscations. He trusted no one, and those stoic philosophers and Chris′tians whose theory of life raised them above the fear of death, were objects of his especial suspicion and dread. His own wickedness and cowardice made him fear the virtuous and brave. Agric′ola, a noble Ro′man worthy of the best days of the republic, fell a victim to his distrust. Even his own empress discovered that he had determined to kill her. But she forestalled his purpose and had him murdered in the palace. Agric′ola's successful campaigns in Brit′ain (78-84 A. D.) are the sole glory of this reign. Elsewhere the eagles were defeated, and to crown the ignominy, the Da′cians, who dwelt along the lower Dan′ube, compelled Rome to purchase their peace by annual presents—little less than tribute.

Incredible cruelties.

Agricola in Britain. 78-84 A. D.

The prætorians asserted themselves upon the death of Domi′tian and compelled the Senate to award the purple to one Mar′cus Cocce′ius Ner′va, a senator of high character. He signalized his brief term (96-98 A. D.) by his ardent endeavors to undo the wicked acts of the previous administration. He annulled the laws concerning treason, which had been so abused that no wealthy citizen had been safe from the greed or malice of the informers; the political outlaws of the Fla′vian days were recalled and the burdensome taxes for wars and public works were reduced. He moreover forestalled the interference of the soldiers at his death by selecting his own successor during his lifetime.

Nerva, Twelfth emperor. 96-98 A. D.

Mar′cus Ul′pius Traja′nus—to give at length the name of Tra′jan—was a native of Spain, the first Cæ′sar born beyond the Alps. Ner′va did wisely in designating this man for the throne. He was of good Ro′man lineage, though of provincial birth; a soldier

Trajan. Thirteenth emperor. 98-117 A. D.

of proved abilities, he was fitted to preserve internal peace, to guard the border, and even to extend the imperial boundaries; while as a statesman he was liberal and prudent, not only adding greatly to the splendor of his capital, but exercising a vigilant and helpful care in the remotest provinces. Tra′jan was with his army corps in Ger′many when his young kinsman Ha′drian brought him the news of Ner′va's high favor. For a year he made no haste to return to the city, although he accepted the imperial dignity. He came at last as a citizen-emperor, entering Rome unostentatiously with his good wife Ploti′na, with whom he lived in all frugality and simplicity, expending his surplus income for the good of his people. The revenues of the empire were laid out in works of public benefit. The capital was furnished with an increased supply of pure water brought from the distant hills upon lofty aqueducts of stone, several of which remain in use unto this day. The theater was enlarged and remodeled with an eye to the comfort of the populace. Artificial harbors were constructed near the mouth of the Ti′ber and at Anco′na on the Adriat′ic coast. Provision was made in Ploti′na's name for the support of orphaned children and other purposes which indicate the ruler's enlightened policy and his real interest in the welfare of his people.

His excellent rule.

Ner′va, Tra′jan, and Ha′drian, who followed, are sometimes called the three "statesmen" emperors; the name is well applied, but it should not disguise the tremendous energy and military genius of Tra′jan. The Ro′man arms had little to boast of since the days of Ju′lius Cæ′sar. A century of almost incessant campaigning had scarcely made an impression beyond the Rhine and the North Brit′ons were still free. The Da′cians had humiliated Domi′tian and even exacted tribute-money.

Trajan as general.

Tra′jan discontinued these payments and war was declared. Da′cia, under its king Deceb′alus, lay north of the Dan′ube in a mountainous country now comprised in Rouma′nia and portions of Hun′gary. In 101 A. D. the Ro′mans, led by the emperor himself, crossed the Dan′ube by a bridge of boats, penetrated the mountains (the Transylva′nian Alps), and exacted terms of peace. Three years later the war was renewed. This time the Ro′mans flung a massive bridge of stone across the broad blue river near the point where it breaks through the mountains (the Iron Gate). This time the subjection was complete. Deceb′alus killed himself in the moment of defeat (107 A. D.) and his kingdom became a Ro′man province (Da′cia). The stately Ro′man roads traversed its plains and climbed its mountains; Ro′man colonies were planted on eligible sites; and the customs, the language, the very name of Rome were impressed upon the conquered nation. To this day the people of Da′cia call themselves "Roma′nians," and their speech is clearly akin to the Romance tongues of It′aly, France, and Spain.

<small>Conquest of Dacia.</small>

Tra′jan celebrated his triumph with the most elaborate gladiatorial shows that the spectacle-loving populace had ever seen. As a monument of victory he laid out a public square, the "Forum of Tra′jan," entered through a massive arch and inclosed by a colonnade of marble. Within rose the magnificent "Column of Tra′jan," a hollow shaft of marble 124 feet high and 10 feet in diameter, around whose exterior surface in a spiral band 200 feet long winds a sculptured panorama of the Da′cian war. The column still stands where the emperor placed it, but his gilded effigy on its summit gave place three hundred years ago (1587 A. D.) to the bronze figure of St. Peter.

<small>Trajan's Forum and Column.</small>

The imperial soldier found his chief pleasure in the field.

In 113 A. D. he went to Syr'ia to take command in a fresh war with Par'thia, the hereditary enemy of Rome. But the Par'thian spirit had lost its ancient fierceness and made but feeble resistance. Tra'jan's conquests in A'sia carried him farther eastward than any Roman general had yet penetrated. He saw the ruins of Nin'eveh, the old, old cities of Bab'ylon and Su'sa, and reached the waters of the Per'sian Gulf. On his return his body yielded to the stress of long and arduous labors and at Seli'nus in Cili'cia he breathed his last (117 A. D.), naming as his successor in almost his latest breath, that Ha'drian who, twenty years before, had hurried to his camp in the northwest with tidings of the honor which Ner'va had bestowed on him.

Trajan in the East.

The emperor Ha'drian—Pub'lius Æ'lius Hadria'nus—was a worthy follower of the aggressive Tra'jan. His predecessor had brought the empire to its widest extent; Ha'drian's ambition was to guard and maintain it. He recognized, however, that the defense of far-away Asiat'ic possessions, lying outside the circle of the Mediterra'nean countries would be a killing burden for the Ro'man arms, already taxed by the frequent assaults of the uncivilized races of Central Eu'rope, who looked with greedy eyes upon the rich provinces along the border. For the good of the empire he abandoned Tra'jan's conquests beyond the Euphra'tes and made that stream the eastern boundary of the empire.

Hadrian. Fourteenth emperor. 117-138 A. D.

Trajan's conquests abandoned.

Although no lover of war, Ha'drian was too busy with the multifarious duties of his government to spend much time at Rome. He journeyed throughout his vast dominions, directing the construction of public works, superintending the defenses, and stimulating the arts and sciences, of which he was an eager and accomplished student. From Gaul, now almost as Ro'man as

Hadrian's activity.

It′aly itself, he crossed to Brit′ain, where only one emperor, the crazy Clau′dius, had preceded him. Here he pursued his policy of defense by building the triple rampart known as "Ha′drian's Wall," across the island to shield the Romanized Brit′ons of the province from the forays of the Picts and Scots of the Caledo′nian highlands.

Coins and inscriptions still dug up in the most diverse parts of the empire declare the emperor's widespread activity. Like Alexan′der, he visited the ruins of ancient Troy; the name of his empress is scratched upon the "singing statue" of Mem′non in E′gypt; an engraved tablet found in an Alge′rian camp shows his presence in Africa. In Greece the humane emperor lingered with especial delight. His love for her arts kindled a love for Ath′ens which Rome, his birthplace and capital, could not inspire. He loved to adorn the old Greek city with new buildings, and under his patronage a new quarter, "the City of Ha′drian," was added to the historic town. Curiosity led him to pry into all religious and philosophic systems which he found in his journeyings and he was generally tolerant. But it is worthy of remark that he allowed divine honors to be paid to the memory of Antin′öus, a beautiful shepherd lad who loved him and who died in his service.

<small>Antinöus canonized.</small>

Other emperors had filled Rome with palaces; Ha′drian left his tomb as his monument in the city—the massive tower on the Vat′ican now known as the papal fortress of St. An′gelo—and built his palace in the country, at Tiv′oli, where, in the grounds about his famous villa, were represented the most famous scenes recorded in the literature of Greece and Rome.

<small>Hadrian's tomb and villa.</small>

Two events of Ha′drian's reign must be noticed even in this summary: the codification of Ro′man law and the dispersion of the Jews. Hitherto the Ro′man prætors, acting as judges in the courts, had established certain principles of law, which were now reduced to a system by the jurist Sal'vius Julia'nus and by the emperor's command now received the force of law. This "perpetual edict" of Ha'drian served as a guide for law-officers in all parts of the realm and was the basis of the still more important code of Justin'ian, the *Cor'pus Ju'ris Civi'lis*, compiled in the sixth century.

"The perpetual edict."

After the devastating Jude'an wars of Ti'tus the Jews still looked for a Messi'ah. Many false prophets appeared, raised the national standard, and perished under the Ro'man sword. In 132 A. D. a new prophet, Bar-Coch'ba, called upon his countrymen for a fresh struggle. The case was hopeless, but so desperate were the rebels that the best generals of the empire were baffled for three years, and half a million He'brews fell. The poor remnant was widely dispersed over the face of the earth.

The revolt of the Jews.

In his last years Ha'drian lost his frankness and became suspicious of those around him, and cruel in many of his acts. Yet he blessed the world in the choice of his heir, Ti'tus Aure'lius Antoni'nus. He died in 138 A. D. and his ashes were laid in the great mausoleum which he had raised with so much pride on the banks of the Ti'ber.

Hadrian's end and his successor.

Antoni'nus remained by Ha'drian's bedside to soothe the last hours of his delirium, and then, returning to Rome, accepted the Senate's proffer of imperial honors. For the late monarch, the cruelty of whose closing months had almost obliterated the record of many years of moderation, the new emperor secured the decree of deification which might have been withheld. For himself, though seeking nothing, he received much. "Augus'tus" he was already by custom and "Cæ'sar" he was by the

Antoninus Pius. Fifteenth emperor. 138–161 A. D.

established usage of the sovereigns since the extinction of the Ju'lian line; but he must have treasured most the name of "Pi'us," which signified in brief "the kind, the gentle, the devoted." History, fond of wars, finds little to record in the long reign of Antoni'nus Pi'us (138-161 A. D.). Peace reigned to the farthest corners of the realm; the Da'cians turned at times against their conquerors, and the Jews, wherever they could gather force, struck a blow for their despised race, but the general peace was undisturbed. The emperor dwelt at Rome in unaffected simplicity, doing his duty by his household as by his dominions. The Senate was treated with respect, the legions were well cared for and loyal, the prætorians lay quietly in their camp beyond the gates. The unfinished public works of Ha'drian were completed. In Gaul, the family home of Antoni'nus, great buildings were erected at his charge. The state prospered, and foreign kings and their envoys flocked to Rome to lay their disputes before a judge so wise, so just, as the first of the An'tonines. In Rome or in his country seat in Etru'ria, the ruler divided his time between the public interests and the education of the boys, Mar'cus Aure'lius and Lu'cius Ve'rus, whom Ha'drian had commended to his care. The former lad grew to a manhood after the adoptive father's own heart, and when the old man died (161 A. D.) he ascended the throne as Mar'cus Aure'lius Antoni'nus.

"Pius."

Peace and prosperity.

When but a child the manners of Mar'cus Aure'lius had caught the notice of the watchful Ha'drian. Æ'lius Ve'rus, the emperor's colleague, had adopted him and later the pious Antoni'nus had selected him as his successor. Thus from a child the sun of the monarch's favor beat upon the boy. Yet his tastes were scholarly, and his character sweet and pure. His teachers—

Marcus Aurelius, Sixteenth emperor. 161-180 A. D.

the rhetorician Fron'to, and the philosopher Rus'ticus—were worthy of their apt pupil, and strongly influenced his career. In early manhood he became a convert to the stoic philosophy—the noblest creed of human invention—and made its self-denying precepts the guide of his life. He was a tender and affectionate father, a wise and liberal ruler, sagacious in statecraft, and formidable in war. In Mar'cus Aure'lius the philosopher, monarchy vindicated itself, for the one man who was raised up to give the law to his fellow-men was the ablest man of his generation, Carlyle's "kenning" or "knowing" man, the genuine king.

"The philosopher."

For eight years his adoptive brother, Lu'cius Ve'rus, shared the throne with the philosopher, but the incapacity of the former prince has hurried him out of history even as his dissipations hurried him out of the world.

Verus, Joint-sovereign.

The conduct of a defensive war against the Par'thians (162-165 A. D.) fell to Ve'rus and his abler subordinates. The latter won the victories for which the pleasure-loving prince claimed credit, though he had dawdled at An'tioch while his generals were breasting the foes of Rome. In the absence of his colleague Mar'cus Aure'lius conducted the government with distinguished talent. To the Senate, which some of his predecessors had quite excluded from the government, he restored many of its republican privileges. He preferred to guide rather than dictate its legislation.

But there was little peace for the peace-loving emperor. The prosperous empire was begirt by enemies like a treasure-house beset by robbers. Within its boundaries it had assembled all the civilized nations of earth and had even taught civilization to the Span'iards, Gauls, and Brit'ons. Within these limits dwelt many races—perhaps 120,000,000 souls—peaceful and happy, trading freely in all the Mediterra'nean ports, secure

Rome and the barbarian world.

in the enjoyment of their religion, familiar with the Lat'in tongue, obedient to the code of Ro'man law; beyond the natural and man-made barriers of the realm in North Brit'ain, in the forest-clad Ger'man plains, among the Aus'trian mountains, on the treeless steppes of Rus'sia, were other inchoate nations as tough of thew and as stout of heart as any Ro'man. They had reached varying degrees of culture, from savagery to civilization, but to the haughty Ro'mans all were barbarians. The sight of the wealth of the Ro'man provinces was ever tempting these tribes across the boundaries in quest of plunder or of permanent abodes. By garrisoned fortresses, by unbridged rivers, by long lines of ramparts (as Ha'drian's across Brit'ain and the "Ro'man limit" connecting the upper courses of Rhine and Dan'ube) Rome strove to shield her riches, but her thirty legions could not hold a thousand miles of frontier against an ever-present and multifarious foe. In the reign of Mar'cus Aure'lius frequent incursions from the North awoke her to a new sense of her peril. From 166 to 180 A. D.

Continual border wars. the emperor was almost continually at the front, beating against the surges of the tide of Ger'man invasion that threatened It'aly. The hungry plague which the army of the East brought home from Syr'ia carried off his colleague, the slothful Ve'rus, and left Mar'cus Aure'lius alone on the throne. Of his many wars on the Dan'ube little need be said. The chastisement of one fierce tribe seemed in no wise to terrify its neighbors, and the north-land swarmed with restless nations eager to take the places of the fallen. Some submitted, others were lured off by bribes, but such arrangements could but be temporary; the final reckoning between Rome and the barbarians was merely postponed, but that day was surely coming. Before his warfare was accomplished a fever, caused by long exposure to the perils of campaigning, took the gentle pagan out of the world. He is supposed to have died near the place which we call Vien′na, in the year 180 A. D.

Among the noblest passages in heathen literature are those of the "Meditations," in which the philosopher-emperor records his thoughts upon the problems of life. Yet great and good as was his rule, and faithful to the right as it was given him to see the right, this same Mar′cus Aure′lius authorized a bitter persecution of the Chris′tians. This "Jew′ish sect" as it was commonly and ignorantly called, gained the hatred of the generally tolerant Ro′mans, because it was hopelessly out of joint with the heathen world; its members could not with a clear conscience mingle with their neighbors in many of the commonest observances of life with which the worship of idols was interwoven; from nuptial and general rites, from the customary sacrifices in temple and law court, from the worship of the deified emperors, the follower of Je′sus turned in undisguised condemnation. To the pagans this aversion from the vice and idolatry that was in the world seemed like a hatred of mankind which in some of its forms was treasonable. Ne′ro had struck at the Chris′tians as soon as the gospel began to root in Rome. The second persecution helped to gratify Domi′tian's cruel whim. Tra′jan, Ha′drian, and the An′tonines in their zeal for good government and for the upholding of the old forms of constitution and religion harried thousands of innocent Chris′tians to death. Even under the philosopher-emperor died Pol′ycarp of Smyr′na, the friend and companion of " the disciple whom Jesus loved."

Meditations of M. Aure′lius.

Persecution of Christians.

The moral descent from Vespa′sian to Domi′tian was not so startling as that from Mar′cus Aure′lius to the level of his son and heir Commo′dus. This degenerate scion abandoned the defense of the frontier to his officers and even purchased such peace as he

Commodus. Seventeenth emperor. 180-192 A. D.

could, for he preferred the luxury of the seraglio to the hardships of tent and saddle. This "last of the An'tonines" as we may call him—though several later emperors assumed the name to borrow of its luster—was a bloodthirsty and lustful despot. Jealous of the influence of the Senate he again let loose the informers to prey upon its leaders. During his reign the Chris'tians went unscathed, perhaps because the laws everywhere were slackly enforced, or it may be accounted for by the influence attained by Chris'tians in the very palace of the Cæ'sars. Commo'dus outbid even Ne'ro in his disgraceful public exhibitions of himself. That imperial amateur had sought distinction in the gentle arts of Greece; Commo'dus courted honor in the bloody sports of Rome. He won seven hundred and fifty sword-fights, say the annals—no great marvel, for what poor gladiator would venture to flesh his sword upon the master of the world? Lions, tigers, and elephants were brought to Rome that he might "hunt" them in the amphitheater and he boasted that he had slain one hundred lions with one hundred arrows. His shocking vices befoul the pages of Ro'man history. Like Domi'tian he was slain (192 A. D.) by the men and women of his own demoralized household who slew him to escape his fury.

An imperial gladiator.

Up to the death of Commo'dus the Ro'man realm, though hard beset without and honeycombed within, remained intact. The barbarian nations had been beaten or bought off, and, although their incessant assaults had been a grievous burden, no Ro'man territory had yet been yielded to them. It is noticeable, moreover, that the legions on the frontier—now largely recruited from the barbarian races—although they had more than once asserted and established the right of their favorite commanders to the purple, had not ventured to disintegrate the empire by

Growth of military influence.

splitting off fragments and erecting them into independent states. In the era which opens with the last decade of the second century the military power is supreme in the state. Again and again the legions select the emperor and civil discords like those at the death of Ne′ro waste the resources of the State.

The conspirators who had removed Commo′dus were prompt to fill his place. Their choice fell upon Per′tinax, a prominent senator, and a man of sterling qualities not at all to the taste of the lawless prætorians, who murdered him in the third month of his reign. Then, most shameful to relate, the greedy guards offered the imperial honor for sale to the highest bidder. Did′ius Julia′nus, an aged senator, a glutton, and a millionaire, was the purchaser, his bid being something more than one thousand dollars (6,250 drachmæ). But the prætorians, though they might overawe sovereign, Senate, and capital, could not deliver the goods which they had sold. The frontier armies everywhere cried out against the indecent action of the Ro′man garrison and the powerful army in Illyr′ia nominated as emperor one of its own officers, Septim′ius Seve′rus. From the West and from the East came similar tidings of rebellion. But the Illyr′ian proved himself the master. First flinging himself upon It′aly, Seve′rus brushed the stupid Julia′nus from the throne, and for precaution banished the old guard from the peninsula and replaced it by a garrison of 50,000 choice troops to defend himself and Rome. Then turning on his rivals with a force and precision that recalled the great Cæ′sar, he crushed the eastern rebels in A′sia and those of the West in Gaul. Having secured his own seat to himself and his sons he resumed the defense of the imperiled frontier. In Par′thia at one end

Pertinax, emperor.

The empire sold to Didius Julianus.

Septimius Severus. 193-211 A. D.

of the line and in Brit′ain at the other his army were successful. In the midst of his arduous labors at Ebor′acum (York) in the latter island, his life and long reign ended, 211 A. D.

His two miserable sons, Bassia′nus and Ge′ta, succeeded the impetuous Septim′ius Seve′rus. The elder was nicknamed "Caracal′la" from the hooded greatcoat which the Gauls called by that name and for which he set the fashion among the Ro′man dandies. He soon slew his brother and became sole Cæ′sar. He ranks with the worst of the emperors in personal character and in governing ability, yet his reign is one of the most memorable. The public baths which he erected are among the most imposing relics of Ro′man architecture. The money needed to build this elaborate and beautiful structure, to retain the favor of the garrison, and to support the inglorious military expeditions, was exacted from the provinces by gross injustice. It was, indeed, for the purpose of extending the range of his tax-levies that the emperor issued his famous order—"the edict of Caracal′la"—opening the privileges of Ro′man citizenship to all free men within. Thus the last civil barrier between the mother city and her children was removed and the sense of national unity was intensified.

Caracalla. 211-217 A. D.

The Empire.

Caracal′la fell (217 A. D.) by the dagger of a disappointed office-seeker. For two generations after him affairs drifted from bad to worse. A score of emperors attained the throne within that period, commonly winning and for the moment defending their authority by force alone. Among them were few over whose names we need linger. For some history has a contemptuous silence; others have mounted by their misdeeds to horrid eminence; a few deserved the purple. Elagab′alus (218-222 A. D.), the twenty-second Cæ′sar, was the worst. He was the high priest of the Syr′ian sun worship whom the army of the East

Elagabalus. 218-222 A.D.

foisted upon the Ro′man people. After four years of lavish and abominable vice this effeminate young man was murdered.

Alexander Severus. 222-235 A.D.
His cousin and successor, Alexan′der (222-235 A. D.), who took the name Seve′rus, was, on the contrary, a man of well-furnished mind and temperate life, who restored to the empire something of the order and mild government which it had known in its prime. The distinguished lawyer Ul′pian continued the work which his forerunner, Papin′ian, had begun in the reign of the earlier Seve′rus, namely, the systematic arrangement of the multifarious body of Ro′man law. Under Alexan′der the empire was ably defended; wars were waged against the Per′sians who had now replaced the Par′thians as the disturbers of the eastern provinces, and against the ever-changing Ger′man hordes which menaced the Rhine provinces and defeated all endeavors to Romanize their own fatherland.

After Alexan′der the sovereigns grow less conspicuous. We speak of the insignificant Phil′ip (emperor 244-249 A. D.) *Philip. 244-249 A.D.* merely because in his reign fell the millennial of the founding of the city by Rom′ulus, an anniversary which was celebrated with extravagant splendor (April, 248 A. D.). Under his successor, De′cius, *Decius. Persecutions.* was inaugurated a general persecution of the long-suffering Chris′tian church, before whose conquering progress among the common people heathenism was already trembling. Most of the emperors in these dreary years either fell in battle with the barbarians or were murdered by their own soldiers, incited by some ambitious general. Vale′rian (253-260 A. D.) *Valerian. 253-260 A.D.* was taken by the Per′sians, whose king used his living body for a horse-block and after death had his skin stuffed in the likeness of life. The legions in the several sections of the empire set up as many as nineteen claimants to Vale′rian's throne, and these years of division are well called the "age of the Thirty Tyrants."

"Thirty Tyrants." Such anarchy was the opportunity of the northern barbarians. The Goths launched their light barks on the Black Sea and swooped down upon its rich old trading cities and darted through the Bos′phorus to prey upon the crowded harbors of A′sia Mi′nor. They might have made booty of Rome itself had not Clau′dius

Claudius II. 268-270 A.D. II. (268-270 A. D.) aided by a destroying pestilence dispersed their invading host. The brave emperor himself proved to be a shining mark for this same fatal plague, but his worthy successor, the soldier

Aurelian. 270-275 A.D. Aure′lian (270-275 A. D.), continued his work. He rallied all his resources in a strenuous effort to save It′aly from the Ger′man Alleman′ni, who had passed the Alps and were already ravaging the valley of the Po. The marauders were annihilated but Rome had received an unmistakable warning. It boded ill for the imperial city that her armies could no longer hold the barbarians in check. Yet the melancholy confession was clearly made when Aure′lian undertook the construction of massive walls of defense around the city, which had not been threatened by foreign foe since Ma′rius crushed the Cim′bri nearly four centuries previous. Another admission of weakness was the abandonment of Da′cia—Tra′jan's conquest—whose position beyond the Dan′ube exposed it to the perpetual incursions of the Goths. Yet Aure′lian brought some semblance of order into the confusion of the empire, overturned the independent thrones which had been set up in the border

Palmyra overthrown. Zenobia. lands in the times of the tyrants, and so gained the title "restorer of the realm" (*restitu′tor or′bis*). Not the least of his brilliant achievements was the overthrow of the kingdom of Palmy′ra, whose high-spirited queen, Zeno′bia, was brought to Rome in golden fetters to grace his gorgeous triumph.

Five emperors in rapid succession came to the throne within the decade after Aure′lian's assassination. Tacitus (275 A. D.), of the family of the historian, the Illyr′ian soldier Pro′bus (275-282 A. D.), who repulsed fresh sallies of the barbarians, strengthened the two hundred miles of stone wall which joined the upper waters of the Rhine and Dan′ube, and who introduced the plan of enlisting barbarians for service in the legions; Ca′rus (282-283 A. D.), another energetic soldier, took his place, to be superseded after a few months by his two sons, Nume′rian and Cari′nus. Again the empire, vexed within and without, disorganized in civil affairs and defended by ill-disciplined troops, seemed hastening to its ruin. But the times produced in Diocle′tian, the forty-second emperor, a man who re-established the government upon a basis which, as further developed by Constantine, prolonged its life for two centuries.

The Illyrian emperors.

The parents of Diocle′tian (284-305 A. D.) had been slaves, and the freedman's son had gained a responsible military command and the good will of his men by genuine ability. His soldiers raised him to the purple and fortune removed his rivals. With a statesman's mind he saw that the defense of an empire so vast and so surrounded by active enemies could no longer be conducted by a single ruler. Accordingly he raised to the rank of Augus′tus the peasant-born Maxim′ian, a general of approved valor and prudence. Diocle′tian undertook the defense of the East, holding his court at Nicome′dia in Bithyn′ia, which soon became a populous city; Maxim′ian's headquarters were in the West, commonly at Mediola′num (Mil′an) in It′aly, which took on the magnificence of a capital. There was one empire, but two har-

Diocletian. 284-305 A.D.

Two Augusti.

monious Augusti of equal authority. The success of this device led to an extension of the reform. The two Augus'ti took to themselves colleagues with the rank of "Cæ'sar." Diocle'tian intrusted a share of the East, together with the Danu'bian frontier to Gale'rius, while Constan'tius relieved the second Augus'tus of the government of Brit'ain, Gaul, and Spain and guarded the Rhine provinces. Marriage ties cemented this imperial partnership. The effects of the change were immediately evident in the increased vigor of military and civil administration. They were noticeable too in the growth of imperial prestige. The emperors, no longer resident at Rome, discarded the remnants of republican forms, left the Senate to languish in impotence, and surrounded themselves, especially in the East, with the trappings of royalty. To contribute to the uniformity of the realm Diocle'tian inaugurated the last general persecution of the Chris'tians (303 A. D.). There was no escape from the law's strong arm. The number of victims mounted into the hundreds of thousands. The believers were outlawed, deprived of their goods and lands, and every means was taken to extirpate the obnoxious sect. Indeed, the government believed its efforts to be successful, and coins of the period have been found which commemorate the "annihilation of the Christians." In 305 A. D. Diocle'tian and Maxim'ian withdrew from active life and the board of emperors was remodeled. New Cæ'sars were appointed, but the self-seeking of individual members plunged the State into confusion. Con'stantine, son of Constan'tius, assumed the title of Augus'tus, and the army of the West pronounced for him. Other claimants sprang up until six generals at once were clamoring for the imperial title. But none could cope with Con'stantine. By force and craft he plotted and fought his way to

Two Cæsars added.

Constantine's triumph. 323 A. D.

power. Progress was gradual, but one competitor after another was beaten down and the year 323 A. D. saw the scepter of the united empire firmly settled in the hand of Con′stantine, whom history calls "the Great."

Thus we have followed the history of the Ro′man Empire for three centuries and a half. But the forces which have been gathered for its destruction have long been at work and we must now turn to a consideration of the barbarian flood which ingulfed the empire in the fourth and fifth centuries, and out of which emerged by slow degrees the partly Ro′man, partly Ger′man nations of Modern Eu′rope.

ANALYSIS OF CHAPTER VII.

I. *The Julian Emperors,* 157–172:
    Octavianus Augustus, 157–165:
        Sources of his success, 157.
        The title of "Augustus," 158.
        Republican survivals, 159.
        Government of provinces, 159, 160.
        Public buildings, 160, 161.
        Doles of food, 162.
        "Augustan Age of Letters," 162.
        Wars of Augustus, 163, 164.
        Death and deification, 165.
        Birth of Jesus, 165.
    Tiberius, 166–168:
        The succession, 166.
        Laws against treason, 166.
        The prætorian guard, 167.
        Sejanus, the favorite, 167.
        Crucifixion of Jesus, 168.
    Caligula, 168.
    Claudius, 169:
        His favorites, 169.
        His wives, 169.
    Nero, 170–172:
        His youth, 170.

His cruelty, 171.
Fire at Rome, 171.
Persecution of Christians, 171.
Death, 172.

II. *The Legionary Emperors*, 172-173:
Galba, 172, 173.
Otho, 173.
Vitellius, 173.

III. *The Flavian Emperors*, 174-177:
Vespasian, 174, 175:
Capture of Jerusalem, 174.
Titus, 175, 176:
The Colosseum, 175.
The eruption of Vesuvius, 176.
Domitian, 176, 177:
Incredible cruelties, 177.
Agricola conquers Britain, 177.

IV. *The Good Emperors*, 177-186:
Nerva, 177.
Trajan, 177-180:
His excellent rule, 178.
His Dacian conquest, 179.
His forum, 179.
His eastern wars, 180.
Hadrian, 180-182:
Abandons Trajan's conquests, 180.
His activity, 181.
His buildings, 181.
"The perpetual edict," 182.
The Jewish revolt, 182.
Antoninus Pius, 182-183.
Marcus Aurelius, 183-186:
Verus, joint sovereign, 184.
Rome and the barbarians, 184, 185.
Border wars, 185.
Meditations of the philosopher-emperor, 186.
Persecution of the Christians, 186.

V. *The Third Century of the Empire*, 186-192:
Commodus, the imperial gladiator, 186, 187.
Emperors created by soldiers, 187-192:
Growth of militarism, 187.
Pertinax, 188.
The empire at auction, 188.

Septimius Severus, 188.
Caracalla, 189:
    Edict of citizenship, 189.
Elagabalus, 189.
Alexander Severus, 190.
Philip, 190:
    Millennial celebration at Rome, 190.
Decius, 190:
    General persecution, 190.
Valerian, 190.
"Thirty Tyrants," 191.
Aurelian, 191:
    Palmyra and Zenobia, 191.
The Illyrian emperors, 192.

VI. *Reorganization of the Empire by Diocletian*, 192-194:
Diocletian, forty-second emperor, 192, 193:
    The partnership plan, 193.
Triumph of Constantine, 193, 194.

REVIEW EXERCISE.

Third Period. The Roman Empire. (a) *31 B. C.-323 A. D.*

1. Why did Octavianus succeed where Julius failed?
2. Who were the two best counselors of Augustus?
3. What offices did Augustus absorb?
4. What was the policy of Augustus toward republican institutions?
5. How was the provincial administration improved?
6. What is said of the buildings of Augustus?
7. To what extent were the public doles of food carried?
8. What famous writers adorn the reign of Augustus?
9. Describe the military operations of Augustus.
10. What cast a gloom over the closing years of Augustus?
11. What remarkable honor was paid to the emperors?
12. What was the greatest event of Augustus' reign?
13. What were the laws of Tiberius against treason?
14. What gave the prætorian guard its power?
15. Describe the career of Sejanus.
16. What was the character of Caligula's reign?
17. Who controlled the fourth emperor?
18. Who were Messalina and Agrippina?
19. What philosopher was among Nero's guardians?

20. Narrate the chief features of Nero's reign.
21. Name the five Julian emperors.
22. What modern titles perpetuate the name of "Cæsar"?
23. Who were the three "legionary emperors"?
24. Under what emperor was Jerusalem destroyed?
25. Describe the catastrophe which marks the reign of Titus?
26. Who was the most noted victim of Domitian's cruelty?
27. How did Nerva forestall the interference of the soldiers in selecting his successor?
28. Describe the character and conquests of Trajan.
29. What and where is "Trajan's column"?
30. What is memorable in Hadrian's reign?
31. What was the character of Antoninus Pius?
32. What emperor is called "the philosopher"?
33. What peril menaced the northern frontier?
34. Why were the Christians persecuted?
35. What power did the legions exercise in the third century?
36. What soldierly emperor died in Britain?
37. What was the cause of the famous edict of Caracalla?
38. When was the millennial of Rome's foundation celebrated?
39. What was the "age of the Thirty Tyrants"?
40. What emperor humbled Palmyra?
41. What was Diocletian's measure of reform?
42. What was Diocletian's attitude toward the Christians?
43. Who reunited the empire after the death of Diocletian?

CHAPTER VIII.

FOURTH PERIOD.

FALL OF THE EMPIRE IN THE WEST.

FROM CONSTANTINE TO THE FIRST CARLOVINGIAN KING OF THE FRANKS. (429 YEARS.) 323—752 A. D.

Apparent permanence of the empire. — For three and a half centuries the Ro'man Empire maintained unbroken sway over Southern Eu'rope, Northern Af'rica, and Western A'sia. Internal peace, a common language, and a universal law prevailed throughout this vast assemblage of once independent states. Many generations of men were born and died under its beneficent rule, until the world grew into the belief that the empire was to be perpetual. However harassed on its borders by barbarians, however vexed within by rival claimants for the great prize of its sovereignty, no thought of its possible overthrow had entered the mind of man. In the present chapter we are to consider briefly the causes which led to its decay and note the stages on its road to ruin.

In the latter days of the third century, Diocle'tian, who had risen to the purple from the humblest origin, had devised a new system for the defense and government of the empire. For one capital he had substituted four; for one ruler he had established a partnership of four—two Augus'ti and two Cæ'sars, each administer-

Diocletian's reforms.

FALL OF THE EMPIRE IN THE WEST.

ing his own prefecture for the common good. But under his successors this orderly arrangement soon degenerated into a scramble for power by a half dozen ambitious generals.

Out of the confusion into which the wreck of the partnership system plunged the empire, emerged the one strong arm and brain which was to restore order and peace. The new founder of the empire was Con'stantine, to whom history has awarded the name of "Great." This man, the son of Constan'tius, one of Diocle'tian's partners, and Hel'ena, was hailed as emperor by the Brit'ish legions upon the death of his father at York in 306 A. D. A seasoned soldier and a politician of rare sagacity, he accepted the trust. After six years of successful combat with the Franks, who had crossed the lower Rhine into Gaul, and with rival emperors, he forced his way into It'aly and made himself sole master of the West (312 A. D.). Ambitious and untiring, he encroached upon the eastern prefectures until Licin'ius, the eastern Augus'tus, was crowded into two wars for their defense, the first of which cost him three precious provinces, the second (323 A. D.) his throne and his life.

Career of Constantine.

Once more the Ro'man world obeyed a single ruler, and Con'stantine devoted his matured faculties to the problem of so reorganizing the empire that the evils of loose administration and disunion, so prevalent in the last century, might not again recur. His revolutionary plans included (1) radical changes in the administrative system, (2) the removal of the seat of government from the West to the East, and (3) the formal recognition of a new religion.

Union of empire under Constantine.

Con'stantine disbanded the prætorian guard which had made and unmade so many emperors. He parted the realm among four prefectures: the East, Illyr'icum, It'aly, and Gaul, which were subdivided into thirteen dioceses and these into one hundred and sixteen provinces. Both the military and the civil authority centered in the person of the emperor, but he now deprived his generals of their civil power, which he confided to a swarm of officials covering the whole empire and responsible to himself alone. His court was organized upon the oriental system, with numerous chamberlains and gorgeous ceremonials. The simplicity of manners, with which the Ju′lian emperors had humored the partisans of the republic and which had been many times revived by the rough generals who had cut their way to the throne, was now finally cast aside and the imperial court began to accumulate the paraphernalia of monarchy,—robes and diadems, scepters and jeweled sandals, and high-sounding titles of honor.

Pomp of the new monarchy.

We have said that Rome had unified the civilized world, yet it must be remembered that the empire which she had brought under one scepter was composed of two distinct elements, the Greek and the Ro′man. East of the Adriat′ic were the populous and wealthy provinces upon which the language, thought, and arts of Greece had made a lasting impression at a time when Rome was scarcely known outside of It′aly. The Ro′man conquest of the East extended Ro′man law and order in these countries and gave a certain official establishment to the Lat′in language, but in other respects the East remained Greek. The West, on the contrary, had been barbarian until the Ro′man conquest brought civilization. The rude tribes of Gaul and Spain and Brit′ain, the men of the Rhine and the Dan′ube, owed to the Ital′ian city all that they had of progress. In language and law, in customs of life and thought, they were disciples of Rome, rather than of Greece. Thus the united empire was really Græ′co-Ro′man. The East

Two elements in the empire.

The Greek East.

The Roman West.

FALL OF THE EMPIRE IN THE WEST. 201

was Greek, the West, Ro′man, and the subject Greeks but thinly disguised their contempt for the culture of their conquerors. This line of separation was brought out more clearly than ever when Con′stantine removed the capital of the reconstituted empire from the West to the East. He abandoned the old Rome on the Ti′ber and founded a New Rome (*No′va Ro′ma*), on the Bos′phorus.

The site of the New Rome, soon called the "City of Con′stantine," or Constantino′ple, was chosen with eminent wisdom. On the shore of Eu′rope, with A′sia in full view, possessed of a noble harbor, the "Golden Horn," the natural market of the nations about the Black Sea and the Eastern Mediterra′nean, its commercial ascendency was assured. Easily defensible by sea at the straits of the Bos′phorus and Dardanelles′, it was fenced off from northern invasion by a mighty river and by range on range of mountains. For a thousand years the Greek colony of Byzan′tium had reaped the advantages of this location when the reforming monarch fixed upon it for his capital. The work on palaces, residences, and walls was now pushed with characteristic energy. It is said that forty thousand Goths were employed upon these buildings. In May, 330 A. D., the New Rome was formally dedicated—not in the name of Lat′in Ju′piter or Greek Apol′lo, but to the Jew′ish Ma′ry, the virgin mother of that Je′sus whom the procurator of the second Cae′sar had crucified between two thieves.

<small>New Rome ("Constantinople"). Founded 328-330 A. D.</small>

The religion of Je′sus Christ was zealously preached throughout the empire within a generation after the Sa′vior's ascension, and it took firm and speedy root, not only among the common people, who had gladly heard its first proclamation, but with some of the imperial household and with not a few Ro′mans

<small>Progress of Christianity.</small>

of high rank. With increased numbers came bitter persecution for the rising Church, which was thought to threaten not only the old religions, but the very existence of the State. Thousands of martyrs had perished for their faith when, in the first years of the third century, Diocle′tian believed that he had at last crushed out the new "superstition" which had emptied the heathen temples of worshipers. Twenty years later Christian′ity was the official religion of the empire.

Con′stantine had shown friendliness to the Chris′tians from the first days of his power, but his so-called "conversion" seems to date from about the year 312 A. D., during his campaign for supremacy in the West. As he afterwards told the tale, he was standing at noonday at his tent door when he saw in the heavens a flaming cross inscribed, "By this conquer," or, in the common Lat′in version, *In hoc sig′no vin′ces.* A dream enforced the meaning of the vision and afterwards, by his order, the eagles of the legions gave place to the *lab′arum*, a standard bearing the initials of the Greek word for Christ. By the "Edict of Mil′an," in 313 A. D., Con′stantine and his colleague gave the Chris′tians full equality with other religionists throughout the empire, and not a heathen temple was allowed within the walls of the new capital.

Conversion of Constantine.

"In hoc signo vinces."

It is of small consequence to us whether Con′stantine's conversion was sincere, but it is of the greatest interest and importance to know that he saw in the Chris′tian Church a valuable ally in his work of re-establishing the empire. The Chris′tian churches as they had multiplied had been forced to devise some plan of organization and supervision for themselves, and they had naturally adopted the imperial system which lay ready to their hands. Accordingly each province had its bishop, and from

Organization of Christian Church.

a very early time the bishops of the apostolic churches and especially the bishop of Rome, the successor of Pe′ter, exercised superior authority. Con′stantine placed himself at the head of this imperial Chris′tian system. Under his auspices the first general council of the chief authorities of Chris′tendom was held at Nicæ′a ("Council of Nice"), in 325 A. D., which assembly condemned the A′rian heresy (that Christ was God-like and not very God), and formulated a statement of belief, the Ni′cene Creed. Yet with all his favors for Christian′ity, the emperor seems to have grasped its truths but feebly. He was tolerant of paganism, and more than once honored Apol′lo, the sun god. He still consulted the soothsaying haruspices in times of perplexity, and he postponed his own baptism until near death's door.

<small>Council of Nice, 325 A. D.</small>

Con′stantine died in 337 A. D. He had settled the government on new principles which endured for a thousand years in the city in which he planted them. His name survives in that of his splendid capital, and his act in allying Christian′ity with the secular powers of the empire had consequences of which we of to-day have not seen the end.

The sons and nephews, to whom Con′stantine bequeathed his power, showed no ability to carry out their great kinsman's designs. After years of contention the empire was reunited under Constan′tius, the second son, and in 361 A. D., he, too, died while engaged in a civil war with his cousin Ju′lian, who as his lieutenant had rescued Gaul from a devastating incursion of Franks and Aleman′ni, and made too great a name for himself in the West.

<small>The sons of Constantine.</small>

Ju′lian, the only survivor of the family of Con′stantine, reigned only two years (361–363 A. D.). He was a soldier, like

Tra'jan, and a philosopher, like Mar'cus Aure'lius. History calls him "the Apos'tate," because, though tutored by a bishop, he endeavored to retrace the step which his uncle had taken and to re-establish the old religion, reformed in accordance with Chris'tian ethics. The attempt, though prosecuted with craft and zeal by a monarch whose own life was a model of virtue, ended in failure. For the faith in the living Jeho'vah was surely conquering its way, and after the Apos'tate had fallen in battle with the Per'sians, his successor Jo'vian (363, 364 A. D.), restored the Church to its full privileges. Soon we find the old conditions changed, mobs of "Chris'tians" throw down the statues and temples of the ancient gods. The Emperor Theodo'sius I. (379–395 A. D.) forbids by severe penalties the celebration of the old rites. Heathenism expelled from the cities lingers in the country districts (*pa'gi*), thus getting the name of "paganism." In remote valleys it exists two or three centuries more, and curious travelers tell us that traces of it remain to this day in the superstitions of Cala'brian peasants.

Under Valentin'ian I. (364–375 A. D.), Va'lens (364–378 A. D.), and their immediate successors, the redoubled pressure of the northern barbarians upon the frontier, required the attention of two emperors of equal rank and authority. Again for a single year (394 A. D.), the great soldier-emperor, Theodo'sius (379–395 A. D.), ruled without a colleague, but at his death the provinces were parcelled out to his two minor sons, Arca'dius, the elder, receiving the East, and Hono'rius the West. There was still in theory one undivided empire of Rome, but the barbarian flood submerged the West in the fifth century, while the eastern monarchs, ruling from Constantino′ple, continued for another thousand years until the advent of the savage Turk (1453 A. D.). When it is noticed that the division was along the well-marked line (pp. 200, 201) it will readily be understood why the eastern section, sometimes called Byzan′tine, from the ancient name of its capital, is best known as the Greek Empire.

Byzantine or Greek Empire. 395–1453 A. D.

By the advice of Augus′tus, the Rhine and the Dan′ube had been accepted as the northern limits of Ro′man conquest in Eu′rope, and as civic life and loyalty declined, it had taxed the entire energy of the State to keep these barriers closed. From the North and Bal′tic Seas to the Eu′xine, Central Eu′rope had been inhabited from time immemorial by tribes of Ger′mans, warlike people, of powerful frame, and unconquerable spirit. They practiced a rude agriculture but preferred the excitements of the chase and war to the dull round of toil. They seem to have been without permanent habitations, and their settlements were mere hamlets of wooden huts. They had no literature, indeed, no proper alphabet, and were strangers to the arts of civilization. All freemen of the tribe were equal, and their so-called kings were chieftains, supposed to be descended from the gods. They worshiped many gods, with mysterious rites and human sacrifices. Our names of the days of the week are memorials of some of their divinities,*—for it must be remembered that these Ger′man barbarians conquered Brit′ain and made it Eng′land. The barbarians were, moreover, distinguished for their chastity and for the respect in which women were held. Drunkenness was their notorious vice.

The barbarian world.

Religion and character.

History early discovers these Ger′man tribes occupying the

---

*Tuesday=Tiu's dag; Wednesday=Woden's dag; Thursday=Thor's dag; Friday=Freya's dag.

vast region of Central Eu′rope from the U′ral Mountains to the Atlan′tic. It soon finds them in commotion, one tribe encroaching upon its neighbor's lands, and the tribes adjacent to the empire indulging in raids into its inviting realm. The first formal invasion had reached the valley of the Po before it was stopped by Ma′rius (102-101 B. C.). The Ger′man invader, Ariovis′tus, was stopped in Gaul by Ju′lius Cæ′sar. The emperors of the second century had been kept busy in defending the frontiers. In the third century the attacks redoubled in frequency and fierceness. A new force began to act in the fourth century when the Huns, yellow-faced Mongo′lian nomads from the deserts of A′sia, crossed the Vol′ga and attacked the Ger′mans in the rear. Then began in earnest that tremendous migration of the nations in which the Ro′man defenses gave way and a flood of Ger′man barbarism overwhelmed the provinces of the West. It is in these mighty movements of population—which brought the rude and warlike Teu′ton from his native forests to conquer and dwell among the highly civilized Ro′mans—that the foundations of Mod′ern Eu′rope were laid.

Movement of barbarians.

The great migrations.

Before the dawn of the pivotal fourth century, the countless petty tribes of Ger′many had by some obscure process been brought together into a few powerful confederacies or nations. Of these the Goths were the first to effect a permanent entrance within the empire. As early as the reign of Aure′lian the West Goths had been permitted to settle in the Ro′man province of Da′cia, and before the death of Con′stantine thousands of them were serving in the imperial armies. It had long since become almost impossible to induce Ro′man citizens to bear arms, and the government eagerly enlisted the brawny

Barbarians in the imperial armies.

blue-eyed Ger′mans, taught them the use of civilized weapons, and drilled them in the tactics and discipline which had conquered and ruled the world. It is not long before we find the armies both manned and officered by men of Ger′man name.

In their devastating westward progress, the terrible Huns had subdued the East Goths, and their kinsmen, the West Goths, turned to the emperor for shelter. Va′lens, then ruling at Constantino′ple, let them enter and occupy the frontier province of Mœ′sia, just south of the Dan′ube (375 A. D.). They soon proved themselves troublesome tenants, and Va′lens, endeavoring to check their ravage, was defeated and killed in battle at Adriano′ple. His successor, Theodo′sius, purchased peace and took their fighting men into the pay of the empire. But they continued to harass their hosts, perceiving more and more clearly their own strength and the decay of the imperial system. Al′aric was the most famous of their kings. He terrified Arca′dius into appointing him to a high military command and stationing him at a point whence he could strike the outlying provinces of the West. In 400 A. D.—or perhaps 401 A. D.— he invaded It′aly. Stil′icho, himself a Ger′man, the general of Hono′rius, the boy emperor of the West, hastily gathered troops and blocked his path at Pollen′tia (403 A. D.), and the baffled Al′aric returned to his province to prepare for a fresh invasion. Six years later the armies of the West Goths re-entered the Ital′ian peninsula. Stil′icho had fallen a victim to the jealousy of the emperor whom he had saved and the Goths penetrated to the very gates of Rome. An enormous ransom postponed the capture of the city for a few months, but in the closing days of August, in the year of our Lord 410, the barbarian Al′-

aric entered the eternal city. Rome was no longer the capital even of the West, for Hono'rius had found and fortified a more defensible retreat at Raven'na on the western coast of It'aly, but its palaces and shops supplied abundant spoil. Al'aric and his men were Chris'tians, though of the A'rian creed, and, even in their pillaging, they reverenced the sanctity of the Christian churches—afterwards a subject of high boasting to the clergy, who challenged the heathen priests to show an instance where the old gods had saved their shrines from the spoiler. Al'aric was only a raider. Not tarrying to set his conquests in order he was soon off, marching toward the wealthy South, but death struck him unexpectedly before the year of his glory was old.

Death of Alaric. 410 A. D.

His proud followers buried the first barbarian conqueror of Rome in the bed of the river Busen'to, whose waters they turned aside until the work was accomplished.

Al'aric and his Goths had taken Rome, but, though the great disgrace was felt throughout the world, the fall of no single city or province could destroy the empire. Indeed the barbarians had no wish to destroy it, nor any thought that it was destructible. They were eager

The empire unshaken.

enough to sack its cities, and to enjoy its honors, but they viewed the imperial system with reverence and respect as a necessary institution. So At'aulf, Al'aric's brother-in-law and successor, was proud to marry the sister of Hono'rius, and confessed that he chose the glory of restoring and defending the old Ro'man institu-

Roman policy of Ataulf.

tions rather than to attempt to build up a Goth'ic state with savage and lawless men. Accordingly, as the general of the empire he led the West Goths out of It'aly into Gaul, which had lately been the scene of great events.

It may have been the report of Goth'ic success in the East, or wild rumors of the oncoming Huns, or the mere sight of the feebly defended cities of Gaul — something prompted the western barbarians to swoop down upon the empire in the time of Al'aric. A vast confederacy, chiefly Sueves, Burgun'dians, and Van'dals, barbarians whose ancestral customs and religion had not been softened, as had the Goths, by contact with Rome, advanced to the attack. They came on in two sections, the main body threatening Gaul from the Rhen'ish frontier, while Radagai'sus, with some 200,000 men of many nationalities, pushed on by the south and east across the Upper Dan'ube and over the Alps into It'aly (406 A. D.), still suffering from Al'aric's first incursion. With an army obtained by stripping the provinces of their garrisons, Stil'icho, the general of the empire, came up with the heathen as they were besieging the city of Flor'ence, defeated them with enormous slaughter, and cut off the head of their chief.

Western migrations.

Stilicho defeats Radagaisus 406 A. D.

Radagai'sus had failed in his dash at It'aly, but the national movement, of which his army had been a small part, went on unchecked. The barbarian swarms — Sueves, Burgun'dians, Al'ans and Van'dals — who had remained behind in Ger'many turned promptly to the west and on the last day of the year 406 crossed the icy Rhine into Gaul.

Invasion of Gaul 406 A. D.

From the Rhine to the Pyr'enees, Gaul was a country of fertile farms and thriving cities. Four centuries and a half of peaceful occupation had made it little less Ro'man in language, institutions, and laws, than It'aly itself. The Chris'tian faith especially had taken root among its people; the Gal'lic churches were wealthy, the Gal'lic bishops powerful. The Rhen'ish frontier, long guarded by the steady valor of the legions, had in more recent times been as faithfully defended by a tribe of the Franks, a well-

Gaul under the empire.

disposed Ger'man people who had lost some of their barbarism by long intercourse with the provincials, and had been settled along the lower course of the stream.

Into this smiling quarter of the West came the barbarian swarms, plundering the palaces, burning the churches, murdering the priest at the altar, and dragging citizen and matron into slavery. Stil'icho, twice the saviour of the West, was detained in It'aly, and Gaul, without a leader or an army, fell a helpless victim. The province was overrun without a battle. The Ger'mans who crossed the Ro'man boundary on that winter's day in 406 A. D. never retraced their steps. For two years they had free course in Gaul. The Burgun'dians settled permanently on the Rhone and the Sueves and Van'dals passed on to the southward to continue their devastating work in hitherto sequestered Spain (409 A. D.).

Barbarians ravage Gaul 407-9 A. D.

At this juncture when all Gaul was smarting from her recent ills, and the barbarians who had smitten her were busy at the same sad work in Spain, Al'aric's successor, At'aulf, holding an imperial commission from Hono'rius, led his Goths out of It'aly to relieve the Ro'man provincials of the suffering West. Here he began, and Wal'lia completed the foundation of a new kingdom within and nominally subject to the Ro'man Empire. From their capital, Tolo'sa, (Toulouse') the successors of Wal'lia governed a considerable region on both sides of the Pyr'enees for nearly a century (415-507 A. D.). In Gaul this Vis'igothic state was checked and limited by the growing power of the Franks, but in Spain the Goth'ic kings subdued the short-lived states founded by the Sueves and their companions and set up a Vis'igothic kingdom with its capital at Tole'do, which flourished until smitten by the storm of

The West Goths in Gaul 415-507 A. D.

The West Goths in Spain 507-711 A. D.

Moham'medan invasion in the eighth century (711 A. D.).

When Stil'icho and Hono'rius assembled the legions (400-410 A. D.) to intercept Al'aric, the remote Brit'ons were left to the mercy of their foes, the un-Ro'manized Celts of Ire'land and the Scot'tish highlands. After a generation of ceaseless struggle, the unwarlike provincials were fain to seek help from the barbarians—Ang'les, Sax'ons and Jutes—of the North Ger'man seacoast. The first ship load of the Jutes came in the middle of the fifth century (449 A. D.). They returned only to bring reinforcements, and for a century and a half the tide of pagans flowed in, submerging Ro'man, Brit'ain, and establishing a group of Ger'man or An'glo-Sax'on kingdoms, whose partial union under King Eg'bert (802-837 A. D.) may be reckoned as a starting point of An'gle-land or Eng'land.

<small>Britain occupied by the English.</small>

Of the Ger'man nations which crossed the Rhine in 406 A. D., the Van'dals remained long enough in Spain to give their name to one of its chief regions ([V] Andalu'sia) and then passed on to a fresh and terrible career. Separated from Spain by a few leagues of blue water, lay the happy and prosperous province of Af'rica, the "granary of the world." The wars which for a century had vexed the peace of the northern half of the empire, left it undisturbed. Under the Ro'man rule since the fall of Car'thage, Af'rica had become distinguished among the provinces for the purity of its institutions. Christian'ity had found a ready acceptance there. The Af'rican church gloried in its roll of martyrs, and its bishop, Au'gustine, is by many accounted the greatest of the Chris'tian fathers.

<small>The Van'dals in Spain.</small>

<small>The Roman province of Africa.</small>

While the Van'dals and Sueves were quarreling over the Spanish spoil, a change had taken place at Raven'na, the western capital. Hono'rius was dead and his sister Placid'ia was regent for Valentin'ian III. Two able but jealous generals, Aë'tius and Bon'iface, commanded her armies. While the latter was governor of Af'rica, his rival poisoned the empress' mind against him, and forced him into rebellion. To strengthen his position, in a moment of evil coun-sel Bon'iface sought an alliance with the Van'dals, just across the straits in Spain, offering them permanent abodes in return for their military support. The invitation was ac-cepted and in 429 A. D. the Van'dal Gen'seric crossed from Gibral'tar and landed 50,000 men on the Af'rican coast. Too late the governor and empress dis-covered the duplicity of Aë'tius, and the peril of Af'rica. But Gen'seric, one of the most able, am-bitious, and cruel of the barbarian conquerors, swept through the corn lands and orchards like a firebrand, putting noble cities to the torch and tender women to the sword. The A'rian Van'-dals showed slight respect even for the churches of these Cath'-olic Chris'tians of Af'rica. During the siege of Hip'po, its famous prelate, the aged "Saint" Au'gustine died (430 A. D.). Car'thage was taken by storm (439 A. D.), and the seacoast, whose natural advantages had enriched in turn the countrymen of Han'nibal and of Scip'io, now contributed to the prosperity of Gen'seric and his Ger'mans. Their kingdom, powerful by land and sea, existed for a century (429–533 A. D.) and its freebooting fleets, the forerunners of the Norse'men, held the ports and islands of the West in terror, and even made havoc of the commerce of the Eastern Empire.

Preparations were on foot throughout the Ro'man world to chastise the pestilent Van'dal when frightful tidings from the plains of Rus'sia aroused every energy to repel a fresh invasion.

The Huns, the terror of whose name had spurred the Ger'-

FALL OF THE EMPIRE IN THE WEST.

The Huns. man nations to their attack on the empire, had halted in Eastern Eu'rope for half a century. They had subjected many nations—Ger'man, Slave, and Mon'gol—from whom they exacted tribute and military service. About the year 433 the famous At'tila became their king. "His portrait," says Gibbon,

Attila. 463-453 A. D. "exhibits the genuine deformity of a modern Cal'-muck; a large head, a swarthy complexion, small deep-seated eyes, a flat nose, a few hairs in place of a beard, broad shoulders, and a short square body." By his own genius for war and government he subdued to his authority an immense congeries of barbarians, before he turned his keen vision on the empire which the repeated invasions of the Ger'mans seemed to leave his easy prey.

It seems to have been the Van'dal Gen'seric who instigated the attack of At'tila upon the empire, to save himself from the just penalty of his piracies. For ten years

Attila in the East. 441-450 A. D. (441-450) the Huns rode through the dominions of the eastern Cæ'sar (Theodo'sius II.) seeking ravage and ransom and destroying seventy cities; but with their rude appliances for siege work they failed to make an impression on Constantino'ple. Their devasta-

"The Scourge of God." tions won for their king the title of "the Scourge of God," and it was said that no blade of grass would grow in the track of his armies. Law and order, Christian'ity, and the complex machinery of civilized life, which so strongly impressed the Ger'man barbarians, had no power on At'tila and his hordes. He was of an utterly different race, and to his almond eye the empire was no more than a warehouse to be pillaged and burned, a preserve for hunting slaves. Upon the accession of Marcia'nus, a more energetic emperor at Constantino'ple, the restless Hun turned his horse's head to the West and passing rapidly through the forests of Ger'many, flung a bridge of boats across the Rhine and entered Gaul (451 A. D.). No force was prepared to oppose him, and city after city was laid in ruins, until the light cavalry for which the Huns were famous were stopped by the strong walls of Or'leans. Before At'tila could reduce this obstinate fortress he was confronted by the motley levies of the Western Empire. Aë'tius, himself of barbarian birth, commanded for the emperor, with the title of "patrician," and Theod'oric, the Chris'tian king of the South, had brought his Vis'igoths to arrest the progress of the heathen Hun.

Attila's invasion of Gaul. 451 A. D.

At'tila gave battle to the Ro'mans and Goths on the Catalau'nian Fields, a vast plain near the modern Châlons' in France. The engagement (451 A. D.) which decided the fate of the West was a confused tumult of countless warriors. The number of the slain is counted by tens of thousands. Thanks to the valor of the Vis'igoths rather than to the Ro'mans the Huns were repulsed, and after a few days retraced their steps toward the Rhine.

Defeat of Attila at Châlons. 451 A. D.

The so-called Battle of Châlons' was the last great victory achieved in the name of the Western Empire, but it merely diverted the course of At'tila. In the spring of the next year (452) he suddenly emerged from the fastnesses of Ger'many, and dashing into It'aly took and destroyed the city of Aquile'ia. Fugitives from this wealthy port, and from other cities, warned by the awful fate of their sister, retired to the low lying islands at the head of the Adriat'ic and founded the city and republic of Ven'ice. The great towns of the Po valley quickly surrendered to the conqueror of Aquile'ia, and he might have marched against Rome itself had not the Ro'man bishop Le'o, surnamed

Attila in Italy. 452 A. D.

Venice founded.

the Great, pleaded its cause so boldly and adroitly. For a rich ransom and the promise of an imperial princess to wife, At'tila spared the ancient city and returned for the winter to his city of huts on the Dan'ube, where he died suddenly (453 A. D.), to the immense relief of the barbarians and the civilized world. No hand but his could keep together the strangely assorted group of nations which he had ruled; his tributary Ger'mans and Slaves revolted from his successor, and the name of the Hun became only a terrible memory.

<small>Death of Attila. 453 A. D.</small>

Aë'tius, who had been the animating spirit of the resistance to At'tila, was put to death by the feeble and jealous Valentin'ian III., who had no one left to fight his battles. The emperor himself was murdered a few months afterward and his widow Eudox'ia begged Gen'seric the Van'dal, to avenge her upon his assassin and successor, Max'imus. Nothing could have been more pleasing to the pirate king. He entered the Ti'ber with his fleet, and paying slight regard to the aged Le'o who had pleaded Rome's cause so well with At'tila, hastened on to the city which Al'aric's visit forty-five years before (410 A. D.) had by no means impoverished. After two whole weeks of plundering and license the Van'dals and their allies, the Moors, sailed for Af'rica. Their ships were heavily laden with the spoil of public and private treasuries and even of churches. The golden candlestick which Ti'tus had brought from the temple at Jeru'salem, and the gilded tiles of Ju'piter's dismantled shrine on the capitol were among the trophies of Gen'seric, and the repentant Empress Eudox'ia was to be seen among the multitudes of captives.

<small>Death of Aëtius.</small>

<small>Rome sacked by the Vandals. 455 A. D.</small>

Pitiable indeed was the condition of It'aly after the Van'dals had set sail, satiated for once with plundering.

Gen'seric might reappear at any moment, the terror of the Huns had not yet abated, and the Ger'man wilderness teemed with unknown enemies. The family of Theodo'sius had perished with Valentin'ian and no Ro'man of noble blood or governing faculty aspired to the honors and dangers of the purple. Gaul, Spain, and Af'rica were the seats of Ger'man kingdoms, half-civilized and practically independent of the empire whose "guests" they called themselves. For the safeguard of It'aly a force of barbarian mercenaries selected out of the minor Ger'man tribes was maintained and the "patrician" or commander of these troops (called *fœdera'ti*) was the real center of authority. These federates were not slow in perceiving that the government was at their mercy. Yet they hesitated to put a barbarian in the chair of the Cæ'sars. Their commander Ri'cimer, however reluctant to take the scepter into his own barbarian hands, set up and deposed emperor after emperor as long as he lived. These later sovereigns of the West, the "phantom" or "shadow" emperors, were, for the most part, puppets in the hands of the master of the troops. In 475 A. D. Ores'tes, a man of the old Ro'man blood who had succeeded to Ric'imer's office, gave the crown to his own half-grown son Rom'ulus, whom, for some reason, the populace nicknamed August'ulus ("Augus'tus the Little"). But in 476 A. D. the ambitious Odoa'cer (or Odov'acer), an Heru'lian soldier, persuaded the foreign troops, dissatisfied with the Ro'man policy of Ores'tes, to make him their leader, promising to give them farm lands in It'aly. With their support Odoa'cer made himself ruler of It'aly. The young emperor, who bore the names of the first king and the first

Miserable state of Italy.

The fœderati and "patrician."

Ricimer, king-maker.

"Phantom" emperors.

Odoacer deposes the last emperor. 476 A. D.

Augus′tus, obediently abdicated the crown and the Senate sent the symbols of the imperial office to the Emperor Ze′no at Constantino′ple, declaring that one emperor was enough for the Ro′man world, and asking him to appoint Odoa′cer his regent in It′aly with the title of " patrician."

These, in brief, are the circumstances, and this year of our Lord 476 is the date of the event which is famous in history as the " Fall of Rome." It was in fact the end of the line of emperors which had ruled in the West since the days of Octa′vian, but in the belief of those times the empire had not fallen, its two sections had only been re-united under the monarch reigning at Constantino′ple. Yet the consequences of the event were of far reaching importance. The eastern emperors, save for a brief period, exercised only the slightest authority over the Ger′man kingdoms which had parted among themselves the empire of the West, and as the Cæ′sar was more and more excluded from western affairs the bishop of Rome became the most eminent personage in the West. The East, in turn, saved from barbarian conquest by natural conditions and by the cessation of the great migrations, fell more and more under Greek influences, and its national Church drifted away from the Ro′man.

<small>The " Fall of Rome." 476 A. D. A re-union.</small>

<small>The Pope the gainer.</small>

Odoa′cer, hailed as king by the soldiers and recognized as patrician by "his magnificence," the Emperor Ze′no, reigned in It′aly for a dozen years. His overthrow by Theod′oric the East Goth (Ost′rogoth) marks a new epoch in the course of events which was slowly shaping the chaos of Ro′man and barbarian into a new order, unlike the old but even more useful to the progress of the race.

<small>Odoacer king in Italy. 476–493 A. D.</small>

This Theod′oric is the most attractive figure of the earlier Middle Ages. His nation, the East Goths, the kinsmen of

Al'aric, and his West Goths, had been one of the many peoples whom At'tila had subjected in his devastating raid through the heart of Eu'rope. After his death they had broken away from the Huns and elbowed their way among the ill guarded provinces of the Eastern Empire. It was in these days that Theod'oric, then eight years old, a prince of the Goth'ic blood royal, the house of the Am'als, went to live at Constantino'ple as the hostage for the good conduct of his tribe. For ten of the most impressionable years of his life the young barbarian lived among the refinements and splendors of the world's capital, among a people obedient to law, worshiping the God of the Chris'tians in stately churches, with gorgeous ceremonials. The lessons of this sojourn in the heart of the old civilization were afterward turned to good account.

The East Goths.

Boyhood of Theodoric.

In his early manhood Theod'oric returned to his people and was accepted as their king. But the Goths were uncomfortable neighbors, and in 488 the eastern emperor, thinking perhaps to play off one enemy against another, commissioned Theod'oric to attack Odoa'cer, who seemed disposed to enlarge his domain at the expense of the emperor, whose dutiful servant he professed to be. Accordingly the Ost'rogoths migrated from their settlements in Macedo'nia overland with their wives and children, as was the barbarian custom, toward It'aly. They passed the frontier unopposed and after defeating Odoa'cer in two battles (489 A. D.) they besieged him in Raven'na until in the third year of the siege the city surrendered. With his own hand the king of the East Goths slew Odoa'cer, the ambitious soldier who had stripped the purple from the last of the western Cæ'sars.

Theodoric commissioned to invade Italy.

Defeat and death of Odoacer 493 A.D.

When Theod'oric's supremacy in It'aly was assured he dis-

played the real nobility of his mind. By justice and liberality
he endeavored to consolidate the rival elements of
his kingdom, the half-civilized Goths and the polished Ital′ians. At Raven′na, where he chiefly
resided, at Vero′na, where he had a palace, at
Rome, whose history he revered, and in other cities of the
peninsula, he fostered art, architecture, and literature, restoring the famous buildings and aqueducts and in
all ways encouraging trade, agriculture, and manufactures. Though, like Al′aric and Gen′seric, he
held to the A′rian creed, which was heresy to the
Ro′man Catholics, he was tolerant of all faiths and was zealous for the Church. His soldiers he chose from his own martial people, but his clerks and lawyers from the
old Ro′man race. At his court lived Cassiodo′rus,
the historian of his time; and the learned Boë′-
thius, whose books were among the few treasured writings of
the Middle Ages, stood high in his favor until he fell under
fatal suspicion.

Theodoric king of Goths and Romans. 493-526 A. D.

His admiration of civilization.

His Latin scholars.

The foreign policy of the great Ost′rogoth was as broad
as his domestic program. He added extensive territories
north and east to It′aly, formed marriage alliances
with the Van′dal power in Af′rica, the Frank′ish
and Burgun′dian kings in Gaul, and the Vis′i-
goths of Tolo′sa, and after the downfall of the last named
power before the rising Franks, governed Vis′igothic Spain as
guardian for his grandson Amal′aric. Bright, indeed, would
have been the fame of this "barbarian champion of civilization," had not his closing years been cankered with suspicions and marred with cruelty. It was probably fear of a
Cath′olic conspiracy against him and his A′rians that sent the
philosopher Boë′thius, and the orator Sym′machus, and Pope
John to prison and death. His own end came suddenly at the

His foreign connections.

last and he died in his bed (526 A. D.), on the very day—so say the priestly historians—when by his order all the Cath'olic churches in his dominions were to have been turned over by his order to the heretical A'rians. His tomb, a worthy monument of the art of the sixth century, may still be seen near the walls of Raven'na, and under his Ger'man name—Die'trich of Bern (Vero'na)—the mythical exploits of the hero Theod'oric were embalmed among the legends of the Nib'elungs.

Within a year of Theod'oric's death Justin'ian I. began at Constantino'ple the reign which revived once more the glories of old Rome. This most illustrious of the successors of Con'stantine, seconded by his able consort Theodo'ra, set on foot a group of magnificent enterprises. At his instance the jurist Tribo'nian, with other lawyers, edited and published that noble collection of authorities on Ro'man law—the *Cor'pus Ju'ris Civi'lis*—in which the fruits of the legal experience of six centuries of civilization were preserved, to enlighten and civilize the barbarian inheritors of the empire.

Justinian emperor. 527–565 A. D.

Corpus Juris Civilis.

Scarcely less glorious than the publication of the "Code of Justin'ian" were the wars of his generals. At the age of twenty-five, Belisa'rius, the greatest soldier of the Eastern Empire, had proved his prowess in defending his country against the Per'sian, and three years later he was commissioned to clear the West of its barbarian invaders and restore the shattered unity of the Ro'man world. Landing at Car'thage he destroyed the Van'dal kingdom which Gen'seric had planted in Af'rica and carried its king to Constantino'ple to grace his triumph.

Wars of Justinian.

Belisarius destroys the Vandal kingdom. 533 A. D.

When next the fleets of Belisa'rius left the Bos'phorus their goal was It'aly. Under Theod'oric's daughter and her son,

FALL OF THE EMPIRE IN THE WEST. 221

the boy king Athal'aric, the kingdom had been distracted by rival claimants to the throne, by the jealousies of Goth and Ro'man, by the old strife of A'rian and Cath'olic. This period of confusion was the emperor's opportunity. In his name Belisa'rius took Sic'ily, Na'ples, and Rome in rapid succession (534–536 A. D.). Then came a season of reverses in which he was himself sorely besieged in Rome for one full year (538–539) by the Goths under their new king Vit'iges. The next year the tables were turned; the Imperialists took Raven'na, the Goth'ic capital, and for the second time Belisa'rius presented a captive king to his sovereign at Constantino'ple. In his absence the Goths took heart again and rose in rebellion under the energetic To'tila. But Nar'ses, an old Arme'nian eunuch who had displaced Belisa'rius in Justin'ian's favor, suppressed the rising and blotted out the Ost'rogothic kingdom which Theod'oric had founded. Fixing his capital at Raven'na, Nar'ses ruled It'aly as the "exarch" or deputy of the Ro'man emperor of the East.

Belisarius in Italy.

Narses destroys the Ostrogothic kingdom. 555 A. D.

But It'aly was scarcely cleared of Goths and recovered to the Cæ'sars, when another barbarian flood poured over the Alps to shatter the exarchate and to make the name of Lom'bardy historic.

Foundation of the "Exarchate."

The Lom'bards (Lang'obards, perhaps "Long-beards"), another migrant Teuton'ic nation, came to It'aly by slow stages from Northern Ger'many by way of the Dan'ube and Hun'gary. Hewing his way through the intervening tribes and welcomed rather than opposed by the aged Nar'ses, who was out of favor at Constantino'ple, the young Lom'bard king, Al'boin, made easy conquest of the Po valley (568–570 A. D.) and fixed his residence at Pavi'a. Al'boin died the death of a savage. At a drunken feast he compelled his queen, Ros'amund, to

The Lombards enter Italy. 568–570.

drink from his favorite bowl, the skull of her father. Over the draught the queen vowed vengeance, and her husband paid for his brutality with his life. His successors subjected a large part of It′aly, confining the power of the eastern exarch to a few cities, Raven′na, Rome, Ven′ice, Na′ples, etc.

The Lombards and the Exarchate. For the second time It′aly became the seat of a barbarian kingdom, but Al′boin and his followers were not of the mind of Theod′oric. As A′rians they had little tolerance for the Cath′olic Ital′ians; as barbarians they had no fellowship with the law-abiding natives. They disregarded the example of the great Ost′rogoth, who had endeavored to unite both peoples into a stable nation, by transfusing the rich new blood of the Teu′ton into the system of old Rome. Though Roman civilization and religion made rapid progress amid the rude heretics, yet throughout their two centuries of power (568-774 A. D.) the Lom′bards were the foes of the Greek exarch and generally hostile to the Ro′man pope.

Of the barbarian nations whose settlements we have traced within the lands of the old empire, not one—save the Eng′lish— *Ephemerality of the barbarian kingdoms.* survived the eighth century, as an independent kingdom. The Van′dals in Af′rica and the East Goths in It′aly, succumbed to the Byzan′tine general Belisa′rius. The Spanish kingdom of the West Goths fell before the cyclone of Moham′medan conquest which, beginning in Ara′bia in the middle of the seventh century, had half circled the Mediterra′nean before the middle of the eighth. The nation that blocked the Ar′ab at the Pyr′enees, that brought all Gaul and half Ger′many under one scepter, and that finally gave the deathblow to the kingdom of the Lom′bards, the nation that in alliance with the pope revived the Roman Empire in the West, the most famous of all the barbarian invaders, was the Frank.

The Franks came into the empire by way of the Rhine. They first appear as a confederacy of many related tribes combining upon occasion to effect a common object. The leading group of this confederacy was composed of the Sal′ic Franks who early occupied the lands at the mouth of the Rhine—the modern Neth′erlands and Bel′gium. A chieftain of this branch commanded a division of his countrymen in the army of Aë′tius which shattered the "Scourge of God" in the battle of Châlons′. From his name (Mero′veus), or from the name of their country (*Meer′we*, Meer′-gau=sea-district), the Sa′lian Franks have been called the Merovin′gians. As the Ro′man power in Gaul decayed, or was demolished by Goths and Burgun′dians, these Franks moved southward, and under their king Clo′vis, became the dominant race from the Rhine to the Pyr′enees.

The Franks in the empire.

Clo′vis,* the Merovin′gian, was fifteen years of age when his tribe accepted him as chief, but the boy-king was no child. He at once launched his people upon a vigorous course of conquest. He found the Vis′igoths entrenched in southern Gaul, the Burgun′dians mingling with and ruling the Ro′man provincials of the Rhone and Saone′ valleys, and a Ro′man governor, Syä′grius, still asserting in isolation and peril the authority of the empire over a limited region upon the Seine and Loire.

Clovis, founder of Merovingian power in Gaul.

The decisive victory of Soissons′ (486 A. D.), terminated the power of Syä′grius and admitted Clo′vis to Par′is, Rheims, and the heart of France.

Defeat of Syagrius. 486 A. D.

Thus far the Franks had remained heathen. Unlike the other migrant nations, they had retained a living connec-

---

*This is the Lat′in form of the Frankish word Hlodovech or Chlod′wig, the same which survives in the Ger′man Lud′wig and the French Louis. In the case of this and other proper names of this period, we have selected the commoner form, which is usually the Lat′in or the anglicized Lat′in.

tion with their kinsmen in the Ger′man fatherland, and the Franks on both sides of the Rhine still sacrificed to Wo′den. But in the person of Clotil′da, his queen, Clo′vis was maintaining a Chris′tian missionary at his court. Moreover, by the conquest of Rheims, and the other Ro′man cities the heathen king had come in contact with Cath′olic bishops and numbered thousands of Cath′olic Chris′tians among his subjects. The old faith and the new were on trial before him. In 496 A. D., in doubtful battle with a Ger′man tribe, he vowed if victor to renounce his gods and accept Clotil′da's Christ. His arms prevailed, and, true to his pledge, the king of the Franks was baptized in the cathedral church at Rheims by the exultant Cath′olic bishop, Remig′ius, who exclaimed: "Bow down, Sicam′brian, bow down; worship what thou hast burned and burn what thou hast worshiped." So the pillager of altars became the right arm of the church.

Conversion of Clovis. 496 A. D.

Little enough did the conversion of the king and his warriors signify to the heart and life of these bloody minded men. Clo′vis and his Franks abated nothing of their fondness for violence and plunder. But few events in history have played a greater part in the making of Modern Eu′rope. Clotil′da and the bishop of Rheims were Cath′olics, adherents of that Athana′sian or Ni′cene creed put forth by Con′stantine's famous council. The pope, who as bishop of Rome was already a considerable figure in Chris′tendom, was the champion of the same party. On the other hand, the barbarian kingdoms were, with few exceptions, A′rian, the trophies of A′rian missionaries, the opponents and frequently the persecutors of the Cath′olics. The fortune which made Clo′vis a Cath′olic prepared a staff for the papacy to lean upon and a sword for it to wield in the mighty effort which it

The Franks the allies of the Catholic church.

was soon to put forth forth for the sovereignty of Eu′rope.

We may well believe that Clo′vis had the counsel and applause of the Cath′olic bishops in his future wars, which were directed against his A′rian neighbors, for as one of them said: "Henceforth your victories are ours." The league of A′rian kingdoms, which Theod′oric had endeavored to bind by royal intermarriages failed in this hour of stress. Clo′vis turned from the conquest and "conversion" of Bur′gundy (500 A. D.) to deal one crushing and sufficient blow at the Vis′igoths. Their defeat at Vouillé (507 A. D.) ended their kingdom in Gaul, and drove their remnant into Spain where Vis′igothic kings reigned at Tole′do until the advent of the Sar′acens (711 A. D.) introduced a new and strange civilization into Eu′rope.

<small>Clovis subdues Burgundy. 500 A. D.</small>

<small>End of Visigothic kingdom in Gaul. 507 A. D.</small>

In the forests beyond the Rhine, in the Ger′man land where even the Ro′man legions could count few victories to balance the catastrophe to the arms of Va′rus, Clo′vis led his Franks from victory to victory, and at his death in 511 his authority was established with more or less security, not only throughout all Gaul (save a narrow Vis′igothic strip on the Mediterra′nean) but over the nations on the east bank of the Rhine from the low countries to the Alps.

<small>Franks on both sides of the Rhine.</small>

The empire of Clo′vis was parted at his death, obedient to a pernicious Frank′ish custom, between his four sons, and these "Chris′tian" princes squandered its substance and influence in civil war. It would be difficult to select a chapter in the history of Chris′tendom more revolting than that of the sixth and seventh centuries, when, beneath the pall of the Dark Ages, the Franks were working out in blood and hate the problem of the future of the West. With the lapse of time and successive divisions of the conquests of Clo′vis, the Frank land

(Fran′cia, France) began to show a line of cleavage. On one side, chiefly east of the Rhine, were Frank′ish tribes which Rome had never ruled; they were strangers to the Lat′in language, and until more than a century after Clo′vis, Christian′ity had not been successfully preached among them. West of the great stream lay Gaul, its Roma′no-Celtic people clinging to the Lat′in language, religion, and law through generations despite barbarian raiders and rulers. Both these regions were now included in the Frank′ish monarchy, and it is not strange that the Eastern or Austra′sian Franks preserved their Teuton′ic language and institutions, while their brothers in the West (Neu′stria) were in the course of time amalgamated with the Ro′manized Celts, forming the "Romance′" people of modern France. But we have only reached the age in which these slowly working influences began to act. There are yet four hundred years before we can surely say that France and Ger′many are born into the family of nations.

Austrasia and Neustria.

Germany and France.

Never another of the Merovin′gian line of kings was the equal of their wide ruling ancestor. As the royal race decayed a noble family usurped its place. It was characteristic of a Frank′ish court to entrust extensive authority to the mayor of the palace (ma′jor do′mus). Among the Austra′sian Franks this office became hereditary among the family of the Ger′man Pip′in, who greatly increased its importance. The same family gained the ascendancy in Neu′stria and Pip′in of He′ristal (687 A. D.) assumed the title of duke and prince of the Franks, wielding the full authority of the sovereign while the spiritless Merovin′gian kings, of the degenerate blood of Clo′vis, amused themselves with the rude dissipations of the court (*les rois fainéants*, or "do nothing kings").

"Mayors of the palace."

Pipin of Heristal. 687 A. D.

The descendants of Pip′in (called the Karl′ings, Carolin′-gians, or Carlovin′gians) inherited and enlarged his authority.

The Carlovingian family. The feeble Merovin′gians wore their crowns in quietness a few years longer, but Pip′in's son Charles, the mayor of the palace, was the able man of the kingdom, when, in 732 A. D., the nations of the Chris′tian West called on the Frank to save them from the Moslem.

The Moham′medans reckon their calendar from the year 622 A. D., when their prophet Moham′med fled from Ara′bian *Mohammed and his successors.* Mec′ca to propagate his new religion in more favorable soil. Ten years later the Ar′ab enthusiast was dead (632 A. D.). In his latter days he had taught his followers that he too "came not to bring peace, but a sword," and he had sent them forth to fight for the faith, with real weapons as against flesh and blood. He had given the quarreling Ar′ab tribesmen a remarkable singleness of purpose; for a demoralizing religion of polytheism and idolatry, he had inspired them with a real faith in the one God and the Prophet whom He had sent. "Unbelievers were Allah's foes and theirs." Confident in their simple creed, imbued with a consuming zeal, and welcoming death as the gateway to the sensual delights of the Mos′lem paradise, the Caliphs—as Moham′med's successors, the chiefs of the new political and religious movement, were called—sallied forth from their desert peninsula, conquered and converted Per′sia, took Syr′ia and E′gypt and all the Mediterra′-nean coast of Af′rica from the Eastern Empire, lying almost helpless under Justin′ian's unworthy successors—all this in fifty years. Constantino′ple, though fiercely attacked and long beleaguered, was conquest-proof, but at the other end of Eu′rope the Ara′bian was victor. The Moham′medan invader Tar′ik landed at the hill which still bears his name

(Gibral′tar, *Gi′bel-el-Tar′ik*, the hill of Tar′ik), with a force of Moors and Ar′abs. Rod′eric, king of the degenerate Vis′igoths, staked all upon one battle and lost it in the seven days' fight at Xe′res de la Fronte′ra (711 A. D.). The victors overran the Spanish peninsula, leaving a feeble remnant of the Goth′ic kingdom among the northwestern mountains. They even passed the Pyr′enees, for they considered the conquest of Spain but the first step toward the conquest of Eu′rope. "The vineyards of Gas′cony and the city of Bordeaux′ were possessed by the sovereign of Damas′cus and Samarcand′; and the south of France from the mouth of the Garonne′ to that of the Rhone, assumed the manners and religion of Ara′bia."

<small>The Arabs in Spain. 711 A. D.</small>

<small>Fall of Visigothic kingdom in Spain. 711 A. D.</small>

The mainstay of Chris′tendom in that critical struggle with the Moham′medan was Charles, the son and successor of Pip′in of He′ristal as mayor of the palace to the lazy Merovin′gian monarch. The common peril united Gaul and Ger′man, and the Chris′tian princes of the West turned as their only hope to this valorous duke of the Franks. Gathering an army out of many tribes and nations, Charles reserved his attack until the invading Ar′abs had reached the center of Gaul. Then in the one long battle or series of stubborn battles fought near Tours (732 A. D.), he struck the foreigners a succession of annihilating blows. Chris′tendom came off victorious; the Cath′olic Frank had set bounds to the Ar′ab empire and had determined that the Bible and not the Koran should mold the civilization of Eu′rope.

<small>Arabs defeated at Tours (732 A. D.), by Charles "Martel."</small>

The Ar′abs retired behind the rampart of the Pyr′enees to reign and prosper there for five hundred years, and—even after their state had been shattered under the blows of the Chris′tian kingdoms in the peninsula—to cling to their noble seat at Grana′da until Fer′dinand and Isabel′la should complete the conquest of Spain (1492).

"Martel'"—the Hammer—was the name which Charles the Frank brought from the battlefield of Tours, given doubtless in honor of the blow which smote once and finally the deadliest peril which had menaced Eu′rope since the raids of At′tila, "the Scourge of God."

Martel.

Great was his honor, and great the honor and reputation of his Frank′ish warriors, even beyond the Alps in It′aly, where a conflict had arisen between the "robber kings" of the Lom′bards, and that papal power which had just now cut loose from the eastern emperors and was looking for a secular arm to uphold its independence.

As early as the second and third centuries after Christ, we find the bishop of the church at Rome asserting a claim—not always allowed, to be sure—to superior eminence among the churches of Chris′tendom. The assertion was based upon the evidence of the gospels that Christ had given the headship of His church on earth into the hands of Saint Peter the alleged founder and first bishop of the church at Rome. As the church of the capital city it enjoyed a borrowed dignity, quite apart from any Pe′trine origin, which was endangered in the fourth century, when Con′stantine transferred the seat of government to the East and became, himself, in a sense the head of Chris′tendom. But the Ro′man bishops — the title *pa′pa*, or pope, meaning "father," was at first applied with equal propriety to all bishops—clung tenaciously to their rights and even gained something by the transfer; for in the strife of the A′rian and Athana′sian creeds they chose the orthodox side which ultimately prevailed, and, moreover, from their safe distance they could display a judicious degree of independence of the

Early assertion of Romish precedence.

Rome gains by removal of the capital.

Cæ′sar, who, as pon′tifex max′imus, had his own theories of ecclesiastical supremacy.

The fifth century—the century of Al′aric, At′tila, Odoa′cer, and Theod′oric—brought fresh and momentous responsibilities upon the Ro′man see which, in the wreck of the empire, became the main dependence of civilization in It′aly. For most of the barbarians who broke into the empire, if they respected nothing else revered the shrines, ceremonials, and officials of the church. The Roman popes of this age, In′nocent I. and Le′o I. (the Great), were distinguished for their influence with the invaders and their bold disregard of personal peril in the service of their people. Theod′oric, though an A′rian, was remarkably tolerant of the Cath′olic hierarchy, but when the overthrow of his West Gothic kingdom by Belisa′rius and Nar′ses had re-established the authority of the eastern emperors in It′aly in the person of the exarchs or viceroy of Raven′na, the Ro′mans and their pope sank to the condition of subjects. Almost simultaneously the fierce Lom′bards poured into the Po valley and down the spine of It′aly, establishing their kingdom and duchies, hostile alike to Greek viceroy and Cath′olic bishop.

Pope Gregory I. Though Pope Greg′ory the Great (590–604 A. D.), who sent Au′gustine to convert the heathen Eng′lish (597 A. D.), began a similar work among the A′rian Lom′bards through their queen, the pious Cath′olic Theudalind′a, that contentious people still coveted and menaced the city of Rome. As the power of the Greek viceroys declined, the popes again became the natural defenders of the Cath′olic Ital′ians and especially of the old imperial city. In these same years their influence was gaining beyond the Alps; the Cath′olic Chris′tians of Eng′land were organized into a Ro′man church by a papal legate (664–670 A. D.), and under Popes Greg′ory II. (715–731 A. D.) and Greg′ory III. (731–

741 A. D.), Boni′face, an Eng′lish monk, labored and preached and founded monasteries in the heathen Frank′ish lands east of the Rhine, and established the authority of the Ro′man pope among the people of France and Southern Ger′many.

Boniface in Germany.

The "iconoclas′tic controversy" of the eighth century released the Ro′man bishops from their subjection to the eastern emperor and gave them free hand in the West. Le′o III. (718-741 A. D), emperor at Constantino′ple, forbade the worship of images in Chris′tian churches. For four centuries the holiest shrines had been filled with pictures and images of the Vir′gin and the saints, and the Moham′medans, vaunting their own pure faith in one spiritual God, taunted the Chris′tians with idolatry. Le′o's edict against images kindled the fiercest tumults, and the attempt to enforce it in the exarchate lost him the most of his feeble authority there. The pope espoused the cause of the images, dear to the hearts of the Ital′ian people, and defied the imperial power. To the pope's ban of excommunication the bluff soldier Le′o replied by absolving his subjects in It′aly from obedience to the bishop of Rome. The Lom′bards seized upon this movement of confusion to sweep both viceroy and pope out of It′aly. They conquered most of the imperial province, but before they could finish their work by the capture of Rome the pope had sought and found an ally among the Cath′olic princes of the West.

Iconoclastic controversy.

Lombard attacks on Ravenna and Rome.

The powerful barbarian to whom the head of the Lat′in churches turned in his extremity, was none other than Charles Martel′, the Hammer of the Franks. Charles died in 741 without rendering the desired service, but the alliance of his descendants with the pope was the most powerful factor in the subsequent

Pope appeals to the Franks.

history of the Middle Ages. Pip'in, called "the Short," who ruled in his father's stead as mayor of the palace and duke of the Franks, sought and obtained the sanction of the pope for the deposition of Chil'deric III., the last king of the Merovin'gian line. The Franks, after their national custom, had raised Pip'in on their shields and hailed him as their king, and now Bishop Bon'iface, the evangelist of Ger'many and the staff of the papacy beyond the Alps, solemnly crowned the Frank'ish king in the Cathedral at Soissons', having anointed his head with holy oil as Sam'uel annointed the He'brew kings.

Boniface crowns Pepin "the Short" king of the Franks. 752 A. D.

The coronation of Pip'in the Short, the first Carlovin'gian king of the Franks, in the year of grace 752, brings us to a turning point in the history of the making of Modern Eu'rope. All that comes after this event is in a certain sense different from all that precedes this coronation. For from this time onward we have to reckon with a new political factor, the Rom'ish church, sometimes acting in concert with the civil power, oftener in opposition, but scarcely ever to be neglected.

Turning point in European history. 752 A. D.

We have endeavored to set forth with the utmost brevity the leading features of the four centuries within which the Ro'man Empire in Western Eu'rope sank from sight. We have seen its lands occupied by several kingdoms, Goth'ic, Van'dal, Burgun'dian, Eng'lish, Lom'bard, and Frank, of which only the three last named survived to enter the critical eighth century. The Ger'man invaders, foreign in language and rude in law and custom and religion, have not displaced—save in Brit'ain—the older and highly civilized population, Lat'in in speech, polished in manners, but have settled beside them, taking the best of the lands for themselves, and living under their own laws. Gradually

Summary.

the two peoples after long contact coalesce. Some princes, like Theod′oric, the East Goth, encourage the union, some, like Al′boin, the Lom′bard, frown upon it. But it goes on without let or hindrance. In It′aly, in Gaul, in Spain (until the Ara′bian conquest), Lom′bards, Franks, and Vis′igoths accept Cath′olic Chris′tianity and fit their clumsy tongues to the language of Ci′cero, which after many generations of development will emerge in the Romance′ languages, Ital′ian, French, and Spanish. The Ro′man law, also, survives and has its effect on the political arrangements of the new kingdom.

Teuton and Latin coalesce.

The seeds of a new Eu′rope had been sown; but few looking over the continent in the middle of the eighth century could have looked forward with confidence to the harvest. For four centuries the world seemed to have gone backward. The Teutonic nations were, indeed, advancing towards civilization, but it was at the cost of dragging the old civilization of the Ro′man era through a terrible slough of barbarism. The Teuton′ic migrations unsettled the world. Art languished and died; letters and the love of them failed; the poets and orators of antiquity were forgotten; architecture, cherished by the church, alone put forth signs of life. Even the handicrafts lost their cunning, and all the operations of life were ruder than of old. Superstition usurped the place of learning except among the clergy. Force counted for far more than right. The Dark Ages—ages of violence and ignorance—were upon the race, and men looked back upon the glories of the past as to a golden day that had set forever. But we of to-day may discern even in that apparent chaos, the strength and freedom of the Teu′ton combining with the law of the Lat′in, to produce a civilization grander and richer for the human race than the Greeks and Ro′mans ever knew.

The Dark Ages.

ANALYSIS OF CHAPTER VIII.

Preliminary, 198, 199.

I. *The Despotism*, 199–204:
    Constantine the Great, 199–203:
        Reunites the empire, 199.
        The empire Græco-Roman, 200, 201.
        Founds New Rome in the East, 201.
        Adopts Christianity, 201–203:
            Rise of Christianity, 201.
            In hoc signo vinces, 202.
            Council of Nice, 203.
    Sons of Constantine, 203.
    Julian the Apostate, 203, 204.
    Decline of "paganism," 204.

II. *The Eastern and Western Empires*, 204–215:
    Theodosius divides the empire, 204.
    The barbarians, 205.
    The great migrations, 206.
    The West Goths in the empire, 206–208, 210–211:
        Alaric takes Rome, 207, 208.
        Ataulf the friend of Rome, 208.
        The West Goths in Gaul and Spain, 210, 211.
    The western migrations, 209–215:
        Stilicho defeats Radagaisus, 209.
        Gaul severed from the empire, 209, 210.
        The English occupy Britain, 211.
        The Vandals in Spain, 211.
        Genseric founds Vandal state in Africa, 212.
        Genseric summons the Huns, 212–215:
            Attila in the East, 213.
            Attila in Gaul, 214.
            Attila in Italy, 214, 215.
    Vandal sack of Rome, 215.

III. *The Fall of the Western Empire*, 215–217:
    Italy after Genseric and Attila, 216.
    Odoacer deposes the last "phantom" Cæsar, 216:
        Consequences of "fall of Rome," 216.

IV. *Barbarian Kingdoms in Italy*, 217–222:
    Odoacer king in Italy, 217, 218.
    Theodoric the East Goth, 218–220:
        Founds Ostrogothic kingdom in Italy, 218.
        Fosters Roman civilization, 219.

His foreign alliances, 219.
(Justinian emperor of the East, 220-221 :
   The Corpus Juris Civilis, 220.
   Belisarius; wars, 220, 221 :
     Destroys Vandal power, 220.
     Defeats East Goths, 221.
   Narses destroys East Gothic State, 221.
   Foundation of exarchate, 221.)
The Lombards in Italy, 221, 222.

V. *Rise of the Frank Kingdom*, 223-233 :
   Clovis the Merovingian, 223-225 :
     Defeats Syagrius at Soissons, 223.
     Is converted to Catholicism, 224.
     Subdues neighboring kingdoms, 225.
   Premonitions of Germany and France, 226.
   Mayors of the Palace, 226-232 :
     Pipin of Heristal, 226.
     The Mohammedans in Spain, 227, 228.
     Charles Martel's victory at Tours, 228.
     Rise of Roman Church, 229.
     Extension in Britain and Germany, 230.
     The Iconoclastic controversy, 231.
     Pipin the Short crowned king, 232.
     Significance of the coronation, 232.
Summary and state of civilization, 232, 233.

REVIEW EXERCISE.

Fourth Period. Fall of the Empire in the West. 323-752 A. D.

1. What belief was current concerning the permanence of the empire?
2. By what steps did Constantine become sole emperor?
3. How did Constantine's court differ from that of the early empire?
4. What two elements were present in the empire?
5. What and where was the new capital of Constantine?
6. What was Constantine's attitude toward Christianity?
7. What was accomplished at the council of Nice?
8. To what does Julian, "the Apostate," owe his name?
9. How did Theodosius the Great divide the empire?
10. By what names was the eastern division called?

11. Describe the character and condition of the northern barbarians.
12. What new force set the Teutonic peoples in motion in the fourth century?
13. Describe the career of Alaric the West Goth.
14. How could the empire survive the capture of its capital?
15. What great victories did Stilicho win?
16. What Teutonic tribes ravaged Gaul?
17. What kingdoms did the West Goths establish in Western Europe?
18. Describe the Teutonic conquest of Britain.
19. When and by whom was the Vandal kingdom founded in Africa?
20. Who were the contending parties in the battle of Châlons?
21. What famous city dates from the invasion of Attila?
22. What circumstances attended the second barbarian capture of Rome?
23. What was the condition of Italy after the withdrawal of the Huns and Vandals?
24. What was the significance of Odoacer's famous act?
25. How does Theodoric merit the title "the barbarian champion of civilization"?
26. For what is the reign of Justinian chiefly famed?
27. By whom and when were the Vandal and East Gothic kingdoms destroyed?
28. What is meant by the terms "exarch," "exarchate"?
29. What barbarian race succeeded the East Goths in Italy?
30. What kingdom did Clovis found?
31. What did the battle of Soissons determine?
32. What were the circumstances and consequences of Clovis' conversion?
33. To which of the two great Christian sects did the barbarians mostly belong?
34. What two elements in Frankland contributed to the rise of France and Germany?
35. What is meant by "Mayors of the Palace"?
36. What was the early history of Mohammedan conquest?
37. What battle made the Arabs masters of Spain?
38. What was the battle of Tours, and from what did it save Europe?
39. How did the Roman church gain the ascendancy in Christendom?
40. What English monk led in the Christianization of the Germans?

41. What was the substance and effect of the "Iconoclastic controversy"?
42. To what Catholic princes did the popes turn for support?
43. By what double sanction did Pipin the Short become king of the Franks?
44. What new factor does the coronation of Pipin bring into mediæval history?
45. Of what combination were the Romance nations and languages the fruit?
46. What was the state of civilization in the Dark Ages?

CHAPTER IX.

FIFTH PERIOD.

EUROPE IN THE MIDDLE AGES.

FROM THE CORONATION OF PIPIN TO THE FALL OF CONSTANTINOPLE. (701 YEARS.) 752 A. D.–1453 A. D.

THE alliance struck between the ruler of the Franks and the head of the Chris′tian Church in the middle of the eighth century, marks the beginning of a period which lasted for seven centuries. Its annals record some of the noblest achievements of mankind, and many of the greatest lives of Chris′tendom contributed to make these ages what they were. The Feud′al System—that strange link between the early world and ours—the so-called restoration of the Ro′man Empire, the influx of the Nor′mans, the political power of the papacy, the Crusades, the Great Charter of Eng′land, the new birth of learning, the Eng′lish Parliament,—all these great subjects and others of equal importance, belong to the Middle Ages. Connected with them are the names of the great Emperors Char′lemagne, Ot′to, and Barbaros′sa; the masterful Popes Hil′debrand, Alexan′der, and In′nocent III.; the French Kings Phil′ip Augus′tus and St. Louis; and the Nor′man-English William the Conqueror, the Plantag′enet Richard Lion-heart, and Edward I. This was the grand age of building—of Cologne′ and Rheims and West′minster;

Features of mediæval history.

Rulers.

then Pe′trarch, Boccac′cio, and the immortal Dan′te in
It′aly, and Chau′cer in Eng′land, lived and
wrote. The Cid in Spain, the Bruce in Scot′land,
and the Maid of Or′leans are among its heroic characters
who have fixed themselves forever in the imagination of
Chris′tendom.

Letters.

The mere chronology of events of these busy centuries
would exceed the limits set for this chapter; a volume
would not contain the simplest narrative which
should attempt to set forth their history in due
order and proportion. Our task must be rather to
point out a few commanding features of the vast landscape,
leaving to other works the consideration of the history in
detail. For these concluding chapters of our book are not
so much a history of Eu′rope as a summary account of the
agencies which have contributed to the making of Modern
Eu′rope, and the stages which mark the progress of their
development.

Only a general view possible.

Let us glance again at Eu′rope in the middle of the eighth
century. A Christian emperor, the successor of Augus′tus and
Con′stantine and Justin′ian, rules at Constanti-
no′ple, though the Moham′medan Ar′abs have
robbed him of Af′rica and most of A′sia, while
Slavon′ic people have encroached upon his
Europe′an domains. The West, after repeated ravagings, has
seen almost the end of the great migrations. The viceroy of
the eastern emperors governs the southern portion of It′aly;
the Lom′bards rule the north and menace the pope at Rome,
who has just thrown off the authority of Constantino′ple.
Spain, save the tiny Chris′tian kingdom of Astu′ria, is in the
hands of the Ar′ab "infidel." The Eng′lish kingdoms in
Brit′ain have been Christianized and are approaching unity.
All Gaul, from the frontiers of the Ara′bian state in Spain to

Review of Europe in eighth century.

the Eng′lish Channel, and among the forests beyond the Rhine and the Alps where the power of Rome never reached, is subject to a single barbarian chieftain, Pip′in the Short, the son of the duke Charles Martel′, who has deposed the feeble Merovin′gian sovereign and has been anointed and crowned sole king of the Franks with the approval of his people and the blessing of the pope.

For the substantial aid afforded by the Church in thus transferring the crown to his own head, Pip′in paid well. The Lom′bards were soon at their old tricks in It′aly threatening Rome and the independence of its bishop. In his distress Pope Ste′phen in person sought the support of the Franks. King Pip′in invaded It′aly and chastised the Lom′bards. Again they threatened Rome and again the king, summoned this time by a letter written in the name of St. Pe′ter himself, administered a second chastisement, and before quitting It′aly, made over to Pope Ste′phen (754 A. D.) the sovereignty of those lands of Northern It′aly (Raven′na, Bologn′a, etc.), which the Lom′bards had wrenched from the Eastern Empire. This is the famous "Donation of Pip′in," and marks the beginning of the temporal power of the pope.

Pipin the Short, first king of the Carlovingian line.

"Donation of Pipin." 754 A. D.

In 771 A. D., three years after the death of Pip′in, his son Charles became sole king of the Franks. Although his real name was Karl and he was Ger′man in language, blood, and sympathies, a curious fate has made him a national hero of the French, and on their roll of fame his name wears the Gal′lic guise of Char′lemagne (Latin, Car′olus Mag′nus= Charles the Great). In the magnitude of his designs and the success of his ambitious plans, in the many-sidedness and nobility of his nature, this prince not only eclipses all his

Charles the Great. (Charlemagne). 771-813.

kinsmen of the Carlovin′gian line, but he shines forth a luminary of the first magnitude among the heroes of the world—the first soldier and statesman whom Christendom produced to rank with Ju′lius Cæ′sar and the giants of the elder day.

Charles was a man of extraordinary physical strength, standing head and shoulders above his assembled chieftains, and he had no equal in feats of the chase and war. His tremendous energy was devoted to enlarging the Frank′ish kingdom upon every side and forcing his supremacy and Cath′olic Christianity upon the neighboring peoples. In Gaul he was soon supreme. He crossed the Pyr′enees into the Span′ish peninsula and drove the Ar′abs south of the E′bro. Beyond the Rhine he waged a long series of wars with the heathen Sax′ons, conquering, Christianizing, and building castles, churches, and towns through their lands along the north Ger′man rivers. Nearly all Ger′many acknowledged his authority, and the Hun′nish A′vars and Slaves of the eastern border bowed to the terror of his sword.

Personal characteristics.

His conquests.

It might well be supposed that the ambition of the popes, which had already profited by the loyalty of this powerful line, would seek new favors from the great Carlovin′gian. The Lom′bards, reckless of consequences, had renewed their attacks upon the lands of the Church, when the urgent appeal of Pope Ha′drian brought down an awful chastisement. Upon his invitation Charles crossed the Alps (773 A. D.), deposed the last Lom′bard monarch and added the crown and title to his own.

Charles in Italy.

Twenty-seven years later, at the height of his fame, Charles came again to It′aly. It was during this visit that on Christmas day of the year 800, before the high altar of the old church of St. Pe′ter at Rome, Pope Le′o III. placed the crown of the Cæ′sars upon his

Coronation of Charles. 800 A. D.

Ger′man brow. The head of the Chris′tian Church had allied itself with the world's most powerful prince to re-establish the world-empire of Rome, which, to the men of those times, was the only conceivable framework for that unity which alone could restore that peace which had vanished with the rise of the barbarian kingdoms.

To Charles and Le′o and the Ro′man citizens who shouted their approval on that renowned Christmas day it seemed as if the old empire was born again. Since the dethronement of Augus′tus the Little (476 A.D.), the Cæ′sar at Constantino′ple had been the nominal ruler of the world, though his authority was neither respected nor exerted in the western provinces in which the Teuton′ic kingdoms had sprung up. In the year 800 the eastern throne was occupied by a weak and wicked woman, a striking contrast to the kingly Charles, to whom the pope professed to transfer the headship of the world,—"professed," we say, for the empire established by that day's doings never brought, nor attempted to bring, the East under its sway, and Constantino′ple continued to obey Cæ′sars of its own until the end-all of 1453.

Charles' empire not universal.

Charles reigned for fourteen years as Ro′man emperor; all It′aly except the Greek provinces of the extreme south was subject to him; all Gaul was his, and the larger part of modern Ger′many. He devoted his unflagging energies to the organization of the realm. For its better government he divided it into districts under dukes and counts, who exercised a local authority while owing allegiance to the crown. Commissioners (*mis′si*) of the monarch traversed the empire representing the central power and fostering unity. More than once in the year the freemen were assembled, after the Teuton′ic custom, to listen to and accept or reject the proposals of the sovereign.

Organization of the Frank empire.

The pope was the spiritual head of the State, and the Church was highly favored, the bishoprics, especially in Ger′many, being endowed with princely gifts of land.

It will be remembered that in the sixth century Theod′oric, the Ost′rogothic conqueror of It′aly, had endeavored to preserve the fine old Ro′man civilization and utilize it in the erection of a Roman′o-Goth′ic kingdom. So Charles, though of barbarian race, was great enough to perceive that the hope of the world lay in the cultivation of what remained of Ro′man institutions. He gathered about him a group of scholars, among them the Eng′lish Al′cuin, and delighted in their association. He, too, first of the Ger′mans, encouraged the foundation of schools, under the care of priests and monks, and the dissemination of such poor culture as had survived the Dark Ages.

A greater than Theod-oric.

The emperor died in 814 A. D. at the age of seventy, and was buried in the church at Aach′en (Aix-la-Chapelle′), which he had built. As the Ger′man and Scandina′vian legends had made free with the deeds of Theod′o-ric, so the ballads and romances which were to mark the beginnings of Nor′man and Ital′ian literature took up the exploits of Charles the Great, and magnified them to more than human size. Yet his work was of no common magnitude. For his career, though the succeeding age sank back toward barbarism, had given the world proof of the possibility of a restored order; it had collected and saved the remnants of ancient civilization in the West; it had opened Ger′many to the influences that were to make it a nation; it had flung wide the door to the ambition of the Ro′man popes.

Death of Charles. 814 A. D.

Significance of his reign.

Under the old empire Rome had been able for many centuries to rule the most diverse peoples under a common system

of law. So protracted and so thorough was this *régime*, that
she had in effect abolished national distinctions,
and the Gaul, the Ital'ian, the Af'rican, and the
Greek were equally proud of the Ro'man name
and citizenship. No such leveling principle pervaded the Ro'man Empire as restored by Charles the
Great. In It'aly the Lom'bard and Goth and Lat'in
were not yet fused into the Ital'ian race; in Gaul were the
Ro'manized Celts, whom Ju'lius Cæ'sar had conquered, and
the Ger'man Franks, two elements which were still far
from losing their identity in the Frenchman; beyond the
Rhine were the Ger'mans, inhabiting a country which Rome
had never mastered. Charles might hold these
incongruous and semibarbarous elements together
by his almost superhuman abilities enforced by
the co-operation of the Church, but the unity could not
long survive his death. Moreover the Frank'ish custom of
dividing an inheritance instead of preservation in the line
of the eldest son, insured the rapid dissolution of the empire.

Charles' empire not homogeneous like the Roman.

Elements of disintegration.

For a few years Louis the Pious, the emperor's son and
successor, held the nations together. The pope crowned
him at Rheims and all went well; but his attempt to favor a younger son, Charles the Bald,
aroused the bitter jealousy of his children by a
former marriage. After his death (840 A. D.), his son, the
Emperor Lothar, endeavored to "freeze out" his own brothers
but they combined against him and defeated his partisans in a
pitched battle at Fontenay' (841 A. D.). Lothar
could make no head against their opposition,
and in 843 A. D. he consented to the famous
Treaty of Verdun' for the partition of the empire. By this
compact the princes cut their grandsire's empire into three
strips, each extending from sea to sea. Charles the Bald re-

Successors of Charles the Great.

Treaty of Verdun. 843 A. D.

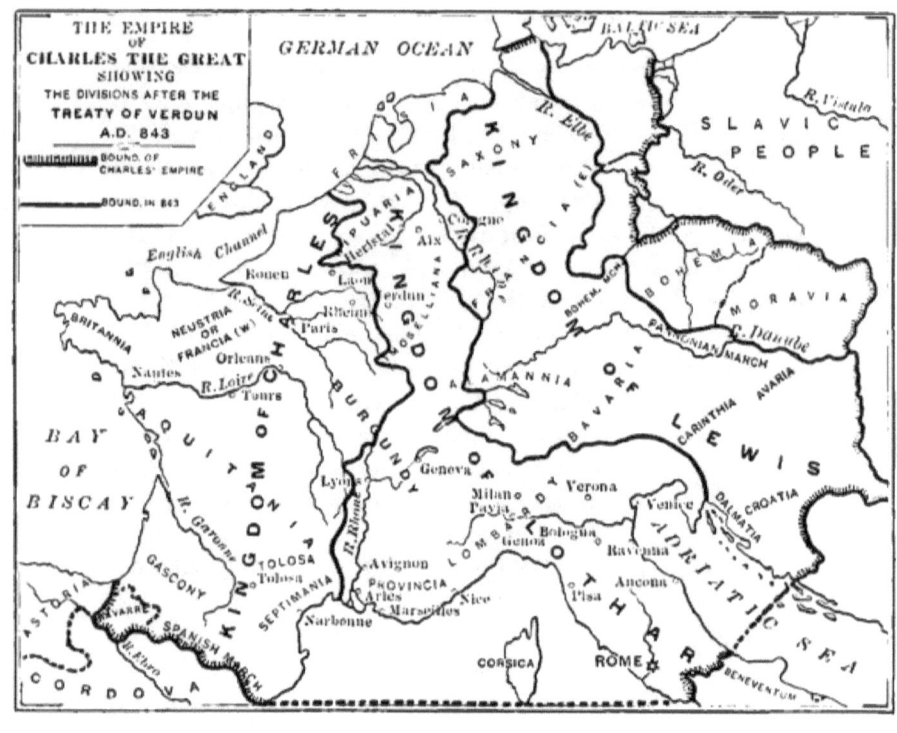

ceived the western lands from the Rhone to the Channel and Bis'cay—the country whose Frank'ish population was already Ro'manizing. Lew'is, "the Ger'man," took the eastern section, from the Rhine to the El'be and the Dan'ube, where the Lat'in language and customs were almost unknown. To Lothar, the emperor, was allotted the central division stretching from the mouth of the Rhine, along its west bank, southward over the Alps into It'aly, so as to comprise both the imperial capitals, Aach'en and Rome. It was called Lotharin'gia (Lothring'en, Lorraine') and, being peopled by many diverse races, went through many partitions and under many sovereigns in after years, while the portion of Charles was steadily developing into the kingdom of France, and the portion of Lewis was destined to endure as the core of Ger'many.

Three kingdoms: East Franks, West Franks, Lotharingia.

It would seem as if nature had concentrated in Charles the Great the qualities of mind and body that were denied to his descendants. For the Carlovin'gian stock after producing Charles the Hammer, Pip'in the Short, and the emperor, put forth no shoots so sturdy and soon ceased to bear. Lothar's line was extinguished by the death of Louis II. in 875. After a momentary reunion of the Frank Empire under Charles the Fat (884–887 A. D.), the family of Lew'is the Ger'man died out in 911, and the sovereignty of the East Franks passed to princes of other lineage. The descendants of Charles the Bald continued on the throne of the West Franks, though in lessened dignity and enfeebled power, until their great vassals the Capets, dukes of Paris, displaced the last of them and gained for themselves the throne of France (987 A. D.).

Decay of Carlovingian family.

Closely interwoven with the history of the later Carlovin'gians, and notably hastening their fall, are two great features of mediæval Eu'rope. The first is the development of the Feudal System, the second the advent of a new element of population, the heathen North′men or Nor′mans, from Scandina′via.

Feudalism was a novel institution. It had no counterpart in the old Ro′man state, none among its barbarian conquerors. Indeed, so far as we can gather where much is uncertain, it grew out of the conquest of Ro′man Gaul by the Ger′man Franks. Clo′vis and his descendants seem to have granted estates in Gaul to their under-chiefs and freemen, exacting a pledge of fidelity in return. This was the so-called system of *benefic′ia* (benefices). By its side developed the custom of vassalage, by which each freeman chose some more powerful man for his lord. This personal tie was called "commendation." "With head uncovered, belt ungirt, unarmed, the tenant knelt, and placing his hands between those of his lord, promised to become his man or vassal and took the oath of fealty." The union of beneficia and commendation completed the feudal plan. Then each tenant became the personal vassal of the lord of his land, pledging obedience and military service and receiving certain privileges and the assurance of his liege lord's protection.

Origin of feudal system.

Its essence.

On this basis of tenure and fealty grew up a complicated system. The king was in theory the landlord of the kingdom, and his great vassals (the dukes and counts) were his men and "held," as the phrase was, their duchies and counties directly from him. But the duke and count had their undertenants, the lesser lords and barons, who were at the same time their personal vassals and the lords of still inferior tenants. At the bottom of the scale, and outside the system, were the villeins, who were serfs, bound to the soil which they tilled for its feudal proprietors.

Place of the king in a feudal state.

Following close after the great Charles' attempt to create

a centralized Chris'tian state, feudalism seems like organized disunion. In the place of the emperor, whose power was supreme, though he might delegate it to governors and other officials, we have a monarch who is merely the landlord-in-chief—the capstone of a pyramid of land-tenants, each the vassal of the class above him, the peer of his fellow-tenants, and the lord of those who hold their lands immediately from him. The feudal army is no longer the mass of freemen, as in the days of the Frank conquest, nor a paid band of professional soldiers, as under the Cæ'sars. For the system has a military bearing, and in their several grades the armed tenants follow the banner of their lord who in turn follows his lord to the wars. The right of private war springs up and the barons fortify their houses against their neighbors. The jurisdiction of the lord of the land is admitted and the tenant must sue for justice at the castle of his lord. So we might follow it, did space allow, through the thousand ramifications by which it gained access to every department of life, social, governmental, military, even ecclesiastical, in the course of two centuries after the death of Charles the Great. His feeble descendants saw the powers which he had bequeathed melt away in a system which brought the dukes on a close rivalry with the crown. Feudalism came to its fullest development in the kingdom of the West Franks, but before we can consider its part in the establishment of the French kingdom, we must glance hastily at the North'men, whose migration played a grand part in the making of Modern Eu'rope.

In those centuries when Goth and Van'dal were looting the Ro'man Empire, another branch of the Teuton'ic stock made its way northward into the lands about the Bal'tic, comprised in the modern states of Nor'way, Swe'den, and Den'mark. Here, far removed from Rome and their Ro'manizing kinsmen who were spoiling the empire, they lived on in a state of barbarism until the eighth century, having little intercourse with the southern lands, and preserving their manners, language, free government, and religion of many gods. In the eighth century the dwellers on the coasts of Brit'ain, Ger'many, and the Frank lands began to suffer from the sudden forays of these "North'men," who, in their long black ships crowded with warriors, pounced down upon defenseless harbors for plunder or ransom.

The Scandinavians.

Charles the Great lived to see his people suffer from the early raids of these sea-rovers, and in the middle of the ninth century their depredations were redoubled. In the third quarter of that century (855–878 A. D.) the North'men, oftener in this connection called the Danes, had conquered for themselves and occupied the half of Eng'land. In these years also they seized the Scot'tish islands and planted a Norse colony in far-away Ice'land. Almost simultaneously (862–879 A. D.) Ru'rik, a Swede, entered the broad Slavonic lands east of the Bal'tic and became Grand Prince of Rus'sia, where his descendants ruled until the Mongol invasion.

The Northmen in England, Iceland, Russia.

The North'men penetrated every river of Western Eu'rope that promised booty, but their favorite was the Seine. They visited every coast from Sles'wick to Sic'ily, but only on the border of the Eng'lish Channel, on both sides of the Seine, have they left their name. A thousand years has not erased the name of Nor'mandy from the land where the viking Rolf or Rol'lo began his ravages about the year 876.

Normandy.

The capital of the West Franks was at Laon in the north,

but in 861 Charles the Bald, the feeble Carlovin'gian king, had designated Par'is, with its surrounding territory, as a frontier post or "march" against the Nor'mans. Rob'ert the Strong, as count of Par'is, was charged with its defense. This is the birthday of the importance of that historic city. Rol'lo tried in vain to capture the stronghold, and, though unsuccessful, he extorted from King Charles the Simple the famous treaty of Clair-sur-Epte (912 A. D.) by which the district since called Nor'mandy was given over to Rol'lo and his vikings. Rol'lo became the vassal of the West Frank'ish king, fixing his capital at Rouen and founding that line of dukes which a century and a half later produced William the Conqueror of Eng'land.

Paris, a march against the Normans. 861 A. D.

Treaty of Clair-sur-Epte. 912 A. D. Rollo, first duke of Normandy.

It was characteristic of the Nor'man genius that the men of Duke Rol'lo soon exchanged their religion, language, and customs for the Chris'tian rites and Lat'inized tongue of the surrounding population. Political changes in Scandina'via and the organization of the three kingdoms of Nor'way, Swe'den, and Den'mark put an end to the migrations, and the flow of new Norse blood into the southern settlement soon ceased; Nor'mandy lost its foreign air and became an integral part of the kingdom, sometimes even throwing its influence on the side of the Frank'ish king, whose authority, however strenuously asserted, was gradually retreating before the rise of great feudal nobles, the dukes and counts of Bur'gundy, Flan'ders, Vermandois', and Par'is.

The Normans adopt Gallic civilization.

The change which had been preparing through many generations was about to be consummated. From the day of Sya'grius' defeat (486 A. D.), the Ger'man kings of the West Franks had ruled in Gaul. The kings were Ger'man still, but their subjects—the original Celts Lat'inized by the long dominion of Rome,

Triumph of the old Romano-Celtic element in West Frank kingdom.

the Ger′man Franks of Clo′vis and the Scandina′vians of Rol′lo—had coalesced into a Roman′ic or "Romance′" people, hostile to Teuton′ic influences and speaking the transformed Lat′in tongue which has since gained the name of French. It was but natural that the Carlovin′gians—Ger′man in all their ties—should lose their hold on such a people. They struggled well against an adverse fate, but the power of the feudal king at this time was weak at best, and when the Nor′man dukes joined with the dukes of Par′is, resistance was futile. In 987 A. D., at the death of the Carlovin′gian Louis the Fifth, the nobles chose Hugh Ca′pet, duke of Par′is, for their king. The crown, thus transferred from the Ger′man line of Charles the Great to a French speaking noble, continued in the family of the Ca′pets until Louis XVI. perished in the first frenzy of the French Revolution (1793). Thus out of confusion and anarchy the French kingdom was launched. Endowed with Ro′man culture, the vivacity of the Celt, the political aptitude, steadiness, and energy of the Nor′man, liberated at last and forever from Frank′ish and Ger′man control, the new nation entered upon its separate history. But the kingdom of the first Ca′pet had far to go to reach stability. His people were half-barbarous, with small consciousness of their unity and no dream of their destiny; his dukes were his natural foes and nearly his equals in power and revenue; yet all the factors were present in the tenth century, which eventuated in the "grand monarch" of the eighteenth century, who could say with truth, "The French State, it is I."

Great as was the part of the Nor′mans in the establishment of the French kingdom, they had still a grand rôle to play. The roving spirit which had brought Rol′lo out of the North led his Nor′man-French descendants abroad on many a valorous enterprise. They attacked the Ar′abs in Spain but found no lodgment. Early in the eleventh century they planted colonies in It′aly, adding another to the motley of races that shared that sunny land.

<small>Normans in Italy.</small>

They wrested his Ital′ian province from the Greek emperor and, doing homage to the pope, founded in Sic′ily and the south of the peninsula a prosperous kingdom which flourished until conquered by the Ger′man emperors at the close of the twelfth century (1194-5). But of all the Nor′man names the greatest is that of Duke William, and the exploit which the world will longest remember is his conquest of Eng′land.

The states which the various Ger′man tribes had formed in Brit′ain were reduced to a sort of unity by the Sax′on King Eg′bert, a contemporary of Charles the Great. This Eng′lish kingdom was long exposed to the ravages of the Norse vikings. The Danes had first harried the coast, then brought their families and occupied large districts, and finally the Dan′ish Canute′ (1016-1035), had wrested the scepter from the Eng′lish kings. It was regained a generation later, but not for long. The Eng′lish Earl Har′old, who was elected king in 1066, had to meet two terrible foes in a single year. He defeated the Norwe′gian King Har′ald Hardra′da but fell in battle with the Nor′man duke.

<small>Saxon and Dane in England.</small>

Duke William of Nor′mandy claimed the Eng′lish throne (1) by right of his wife Matilda, who was of the Eng′lish blood royal, (2) by the alleged bequest of the late king, his cousin, Ed′ward the Confes′sor, and (3) by the alleged sworn promise of Earl Har′old himself. With the blessing of the pope, whose authority in the island Church he pledged himself to increase, he crossed the Channel with a small but well-armed

<small>William the Norman's claim to England.</small>

and determined force, defeated Harold in the single battle of Sen'lac (1066), and added the crown of a kingdom to his ducal coronet. His followers were rewarded with great estates, and thus the Eng'lish landed aristocracy, which boasts that "it came in with the Conqueror," was established.

Conquest of England. 1066 A. D.

As in France, so in Eng'land, the Nor'mans, though an energizing and directing power, could not maintain their distinct nationality. In course of time the language of the Eng'lish yeomen drove out the Nor'man-French of the court, and many of the old Teuton'ic popular institutions survived the pressure of Nor'man feudalism. Instead of being an outlying possession of the Nor'man dukes, as seemed its probable fate, Eng'land developed in her own way. Eventually the two states broke apart, the duchy remaining subject to the French monarchs, and the kingdom, energized and invigorated by its dash of foreign blood, became the mighty and independent nation which we know.

England profits by the conquests.

France and Eng'land were conspicuous rivals throughout the later Middle Ages and were the first of the kingdoms to develop a strong spirit of nationality, but during a portion of this period the commanding figure in the world was the "Holy Ro'man Empire," which had been restored by the kings of Ger'many.

The Holy Roman Empire.

The East Frank'ish kingdom was not only the frontier of Europe'an civilization, exposed to savagery of Slaves, Huns, or whatever heathen tribe might spring out of the plains and forests of the East, but it had itself no substratum of Ro'man culture, such as underlay and gradually permeated and assimilated the West Frank power in Gaul. While the German'ic tribes who settled west of the Rhine, within the bounds of the old empire in Gaul,

No Roman substratum in Germany.

Spain, It′aly lost their identity and became Roman′ic (Romance′), those of kindred stock in Brit′ain, Scandina′via, and Ger′many, although eventually adopting the religion and much of the civilization of Rome, have retained their own Teuton′ic speech and to a less considerable extent their peculiar political institutions.

<small>Latin and Teutonic kingdoms.</small>

By the partition treaty of Verdun′ (843 A. D.) the Frank′ish lands east of the Rhine fell to Lew′is or Lud′wig, called "the Ger′man," the grandson of Charles the Great. Between the North′men, who penetrated the country by its rivers, and the Slaves, who harassed its eastern border, the kingdom was in great distress. As the Carlovin′gian kings grew feebler, the attacks from the East redoubled, and the Mag′yars or Huns ravaged the Ger′man lands almost unchecked. These were dark years for Ger′many; with order and peace gone, morality, religion, and learning at low ebb, the kingdom seemed on the point of disappearing, when, as in France and Eng′land, a new line of able rulers refounded the monarchy and raised it to its highest pitch of power.

<small>The kingdom of the East Franks.</small>

<small>Its decline and revival.</small>

The rehabilitation of Ger′many began under Henry "the Fowler," duke of the Saxons, who in 919 was chosen "king of the East Franks" (as the Ger′man monarchy was still called). He infused new vigor into the conduct of the State, the frontiers on the north and east were strengthened by fortresses and towns, the Hunga′rians (Magyars) were defied, and the Sax′ons, Franks, Bava′rians, Swa′bians, Thurin′gians, and Lorrain′ers felt the stirrings of a common pride in the feudal lord of their dukes. This germinant national feeling mounted higher under Ot′to, Henry's greater son (936-973 A. D.), who built up the royal

<small>Henry "the Fowler." 919 A. D.</small>

power at the expense of his great vassals, the dukes, and by defeating the Mag′yars on the Lech′feld (955 A. D.) confined these heathen tormentors of the West to their own place, where they eventually formed the Chris′tian kingdom of Hungary (St. Stephen their first king was crowned 1000 A. D.). At last the hand had been raised in Ger′many stronger to guard and govern than any since Charles the Great, and like Charles', so Ot′to's hand was to lift again the scepter of the Cæ′sars.

<small>Otto the Great. 936-973 A. D.</small>

The high hopes with which Pope Le′o and the Frank′ish conqueror had revived the Ro′man Empire in the year 800 had been bitterly disappointed. Instead of the universal State as broad as Chris′tendom, subject to a Ger′man Cæ′sar and a Ro′man pope, which had been the substance of their splendid dreams, there had come division and war between the emperor's children, and in the hands of the later Carlovin′gians the name of Cæ′sar had become a mockery. After the death of Charles the Fat (888 A. D.) even this vain title passed from them, being borne now by a Ger′man, now by a prince of Bur′gundy, now by the leader of one of the factions which distracted the feeble kingdom of It′aly.

<small>Decline of the empire under the successors of Charles.</small>

<small>Burgundian and Italian emperors. 891-962 A. D.</small>

The papacy had sunk lower than the empire. The rise of local independence which encouraged dukes and counts to defy their feudal overlord showed itself in the Church. Bishops beyond the Alps ceased to obey the bishop on the Ti′ber, and the papal authority in It′aly scarcely extended beyond the gates of Rome. The sacred office was conferred upon men of shameless life and for a time the elections were controlled by still more shameless women.

<small>Degradation of the papacy.</small>

It was John XII., one of the most profligate of the popes,

who summoned the German king to It′aly. The chivalrous Ot′to had already come in 951 to befriend the widowed and persecuted Queen Ad′elheid, and in 962, with the glory of the Lech′feld fresh upon him, he came to the rescue of the pope. On the second of February John crowned him emperor.

Otto the Great crowned at Rome, 962 A. D.

The empire, as restored by Ot′to the Great in 962 and handed down to his successors, until the beginning of the nineteenth century (1806) is known in history as the "Holy Ro′man Empire." Its emperors were, in the theory of the time, at least, the successors of the sovereigns of the early empire. The imagination of mankind still kindled at the tale of past glories and pictured to itself a Chris′tian State which should be universal like that of old Rome, whose monarch should be liege lord of all Chris′tian kings and potentates, and throughout whose length and breadth the Church and State, emperor and pope, should go hand in hand. Although this ideal was never realized, it was ever in men's minds and strongly affected the life of the Middle Ages. The emperor was in some sort recognized as above and apart from the merely national kings, and though he seldom, if ever, fixed his residence at Rome, he continued to enjoy throughout this period and far down almost to our own day the title and insignia of Cæ′sar.

The Holy Roman Empire. 962-1806 A. D.

Theory of Church and State.

The epithet "Holy" was applied to the empire as being the kingdom of God on earth in its secular aspect. From the churchman's point of view, the same realm was the domain of the pope as the spiritual head of Chris′tendom. Unless pope and emperor were in strictest accord, this duality was sure to lead to a conflict of authority. In fact the pope was almost invariably an Ital′ian, the emperor even more frequently a Ger′man.

Irrepressible conflict of emperor and pope.

Both were ambitious, both strenuous for their own prerogative, and the two were soon plunged in a tremendous struggle.

For the first hundred years, however, the masterful emperors of the Sax′on and Franco′nian houses carried everything before them. In Ger′many they ruled their vassals with sternness and success, maintained and extended their borders, compelling homage from the rulers of Den′mark, Hun′gary, Po′land, Bohe′mia, and Bur′gundy. Once at least in each reign they entered It′aly to be crowned in the imperial city; but the Ital′ians had no love for their alien lords and rendered little more than nominal obedience. Three Ot′tos—father, son, and grandson—St. Henry, Con′rad II., and Henry III., were the emperors who raised the empire to its pitch of pride, but their very efforts toward good government wrought their own undoing. The stench from the foul papal court had overpassed the Al′pine barrier and offended the nostrils of the Teuton′ic monks and bishops. Burgun′dians and Ger′mans protested against these "monsters." The emperors assumed the power of selecting the popes. Otto III., "the wonder of the world," bestowed the pontificate upon his tutor Gerbert (Sylvester II.), an austere and learned monk (1000 A. D.). In the next century the papacy again declined. At one time there were three rival claimants to the chair of Peter, and again the emperor (this time Henry III.) interfered for the good of Chris′tendom, and setting aside the unseemly quarrel, appointed a Ger′man to the holy office. A succession of Ger′mans raised the tone and temper of the popedom and gave it a new ambition. Under Le′o IX. and his shrewd adviser Hil′debrand (a Tus′can carpenter's son), the Church itself took up the work of reform within and ag-

Saxon and Franconian emperors.

Great period of the empire. 962–1056 A. D.

The German popes. Reform of the papacy.

Hildebrand, bishop and pope.

gression without, and when in 1073 A. D. Le′o's adviser became pope himself, with the name of Greg′ory VII., the Church had found its champion, and the battle of the empire and the papacy was on.

From the fourth century when Con′stantine adopted Chris′tian′ity until the question of images in the churches began to divide the East from the West, the Church Cath′olic acknowledged the supremacy of the emperor.

The history of papal submission.

Weak and dependent, the popes of the eighth century struck the alliance with the barbarians which culminated in the coronation of Charles as Ro′man emperor (800 A. D.). The earlier Frank emperors and their more energetic successors of the Sax′on line of Ot′to exercised high authority in ecclesiastical matters, bestowing bishoprics with free hand and even making and unmaking popes in their desire to lift the papacy out of the slough of immorality and worldliness in which it had wallowed during the imperial decadence. They succeeded too well for their own advantage.

New ideals.

In the minds of the enlightened Ger′man popes of the eleventh century sprang up a new conception of the prerogatives of the spiritual head of Chris′tendom. The method of election was now reconstituted and removed from imperial interference. The forged Donation* of the eighth century and the False Decre′tals of the ninth supplied the popes with a basis of authority and a system of ecclesiastical law and courts. The election of Greg′ory VII. placed in the chair of Peter a remarkable man, who was to do more for the Church than Charles had done for the empire. Austere of life, inflexible of purpose, he devoted himself unreservedly to the task of

Character of Gregory VII. His policy. 1073-1085.

---

* The so-called "Donation of Con′stantine" (now an admitted forgery, but accepted as genuine in the Middle Ages) was probably put forth in the eighth century. By its terms the Emperor Con′stantine on removing the capital of the world to Constantino′ple donated to the Bishop of Rome, Sylves′ter II., the sovereignty of It′aly and the western dominions of Rome.

elevating the Church to the supremacy of the world. His first endeavor was to purge the priesthood of immorality by enforcing the monastic regimen and the celibacy of the clergy. He attacked the practice of simony—the purchase and sale of church livings—which had corrupted the priesthood. His second and supreme endeavor was to carry out his theory that the Church as representing the heavenly was the highest earthly power, and that earthly monarchs could rule only as servants of the vicar of God.

Fully one half of Ger'many was subject to the Church. The feudal customs, now in full flower, required that the ecclesiastical lords of this land, the bishops, abbots, and priors, should do homage to the sovereign for these holdings. The emperors claimed and exercised the right of investiture, by which each ecclesiastic upon his election to high churchly office was "invested" with or put in feudal possession of the temporal sovereignty of the lands belonging to his see or abbey. Before investiture the new bishop was only a priest, after the solemn ceremony he was a feudal prince with a court, an army, and large revenues. By virtue of his authority in this matter, the emperor practically controlled the selection of the Ger'man bishops.

Church holdings in Germany.

Investiture.

The dauntless Greg'ory struck at this prerogative and precipitated the tremendous struggle of the investitures. Early in his pontificate he forbade, on pain of deposition, any clergyman to accept investiture at the hands of a layman, and followed up the edict by threatening all who disobeyed its provisions—whether priest or layman—with excommunication. The passionate emperor, Henry IV., saw his authority menaced throughout the ecclesiastical lands—half his entire domains—and at once defied the pope. But Greg'ory put the curse of

Henry IV. and Gregory VII.

the Church upon him, annulled the feudal bond, and absolved his subjects from obedience, until the monarch begged for quarter. That was, indeed, the most notable sight of the age when Henry, the heir of the Cæ′sars, stood for three days and nights, coarsely clad, and shivering with cold, in the courtyard at Canos′sa, awaiting the pleasure of the stern high priest who lodged within those towers (1077). Fortune wavered a few years later, it is true, and Greg′ory died in exile, though unhumbled. But his principle survived and gained a substantial though incomplete victory, when the Emperor Henry V. and the Pope Calix′tus II. came to terms by the Concor′dat (or treaty) of Worms (1122).

Henry humbled at Canossa.

Although the direct outcome of the struggle between the empire and the papacy was in the nature of a compromise, its indirect results were various and important. It had been a war to the knife between a Ger′man prince and a Ro′man prelate. It humiliated the emperor in the eyes of his Ger′man subjects, and slackened his hold upon his great vassals. On the other hand, there was pride enough in the Ger′man breast to resent the disgrace of Canos′sa. The Ital′ian cities seized upon the period of strife to assert and maintain a species of independence, calling the pope to their aid against the sovereignty of the empire. But perhaps the most notable result of the strife was that the theory of a universal Chris′tian State, for whose wise and righteous government the emperor and pope should work in harmony, was rudely shattered at the very time when Chris′tendom was gathering itself for a blow at the Moham′medan. When the popes summoned the nations to enlist for the Crusades′ the emperor who should have led the way held aloof.

Results of struggle of pope and emperor.

Papal influence superior in the crusades.

The Crusades', or wars of the cross, engaged the energies of Western Eu'rope from 1094 to 1291, a period of two centuries. Their purpose was the recovery of Pal'estine, and especially the Holy Sep'ulchre from its Moham'medan captors. For nearly a thousand years it had been the custom of western Chris'tians to make pilgrimages to the land which they believed to be sanctified by the life of Je'sus. No mere motives of interest or curiosity lured them over the weary leagues of sea and dangerous miles of land; they were taught that heaven was nearer to that country and that the pilgrimage, even should it end in death, would hide a multitude of sins. The earlier Moham'medan conquerors had not molested these western pilgrims to whom the name of Frank, still common in the East, was universally applied. But in the early years of the eleventh century persecution began, and before its close the Turks of the Sel'juk horde, fresh from the high deserts of Central A'sia, invaded A'sia Minor, plucking away from the Eastern Empire a handful of its choicest provinces and laying their bloody hands upon Jeru'salem (1076 A. D.). Soon the West rang with tales of barbarous cruelty, of the vile Moham'medan defiling the sacred places, of Chris'tian pilgrims of gentle and even noble blood, foully robbed, beaten, and done to death.

The Crusades.
Pilgrims to Palestine.
The Seljuk-ian Turks.

The emperor at Constantino'ple, who saw his inheritance crumbling and dropping piecemeal into the whirlpool of Turk'ish barbarism, and the returning pilgrims burning with righteous rage over their insults and torments, appealed together to the chivalry and the religion of Western Chris'tendom. The monarch of the Holy Ro'man Empire, the fit agent for the chastisement of the infidel, was at enmity with the head of the Church.

Appeal to the West.

The appeal came therefore to the pope. Greg′ory VII. could do little in his lifetime, but Ur′ban II. (1088-1099) took up the cause with vigor. Pe′ter the Hermit, a French fanatic, who had seen with his own eyes the sufferings of the pilgrims, went up and down through the West with the pope's approval, calling the people to take arms for the recovery of the Holy Sepulchre. At a great church council, held at Clermont′ in France in 1095, Ur′ban himself being present, the First Crusade was proclaimed amid fiery enthusiasm. "It is the will of God," shouted the multitude when the pope had closed an impassioned speech in which he promised paradise to all who took the vow. "It is indeed His will," said Ur′ban, "and let these words be your battle-cry. You are soldiers of the cross; wear, then, on your breasts or on your shoulders the blood-red sign of him who died for your salvation. Wear it as a token that his help will never fail you; wear it as the pledge of a vow which can never be recalled."

Urban II. and Peter the Hermit.

Council of Clermont. "It is the will of God."

Chris′tian Spain had business at home with her own Moham′medan kingdoms; Ger′many was at odds with the pope; in England the conqueror's son, "the Red" William, was occupied in upholding Nor′man rule; Northern It′aly had distractions of its own. No nation—if the word nation can properly be used of these feudal states—therefore joined in the First Crusade. But many feudal nobles, chiefly from the Nor′man lands in Southern It′aly and the French kingdom took the cross. These dukes and counts and lesser barons the pope released, for the time, from their allegiance to their feudal superiors. The Truce of God was confirmed, which suspended private wars (so common in those times) from Wednesday night to Monday morning, the days of Our

Condition of Europe.

French and Norman crusades.

Lord's passion and death. The Church further undertook the care of estates and the guardianship of wives and minors, and acquired much gain thereby.

Months before the feudal array could arm and equip itself for the long march around the Mediterra′nean, an enormous swarm of improvident and poorly armed fanatics set off for the Holy Land under the Hermit Pe′ter and one Walter, well called "the Penniless." But those who did not fall by the wayside in Eu′rope were massacred by the Turks before they reached their destination. In their track followed the gallant troops of the great French and Nor′man nobles. They journeyed by land to Constantino′ple, fought their way through A′sia Minor, took An′tioch after a struggle, whose horrors are not all to be laid to the charge of the Mos′lem, and in July of 1099 A. D., three years after their departure from France, they took Jerusalem amid scenes of sickening butchery.

Peter and Walter.

Fall of Jerusalem. 1099 A. D.

Perhaps the most important result of the First Crusade was that it saved the Eastern Empire from the ever encroaching Turks and postponed its extinction for 350 years, but its immediate effect was the establishment by the crusaders of the Chris′tian kingdom of Jeru′salem, organized upon the feudal pattern, its first king being the crusading Duke God′frey of Bouillon and its nobles the leaders of the Crusade. This kingdom, composed of conquerors and conquered, Chris′tian and Moham′medan, isolated from Eu′rope by long roads and stormy seas, and surrounded by hostile Moham′medan empires, was in a state of continual ferment within and constant menace from without. Many a Crusade was yet to be fought for its defense or recovery.

Latin kingdom of Jerusalem. 1099-1187 A. D.

Godfrey king of Jerusalem.

The Second Crusade (1147-1148) had a famous preacher, St.

Bernard′, Abbot of Clairvaux′, a monk of infinite earnestness and burning eloquence, who persuaded even kings to take the vow. His word-pictures of the terrors of the last day overcame the better judgment of the Ger′man Emperor Con′rad III. and he marched with the French king, Louis VII. They reached the Holy Land after terrible losses, but through discord and treachery accomplished nothing at all.

<small>Second Crusade. Bernard of Clairvaux.</small>

Eighty-eight years after the capture of Jeru′salem by the crusaders it again fell into Sar′acen hands (1187 A. D.) and the pope summoned Chris′tian Eu′rope to the rescue. The Ger′man Emperor Frederick (I.) Barbaros′sa (Red Beard) lost his life on the way to the East. Two powerful kings, Phil′ip Augus′tus of France and Rich′ard of England ("the lion-hearted"), led their armies to Pal′estine, but the Third Crusade (1190-1192) ended in a truce which left Jeru′salem unreclaimed.

<small>Fall of Jerusalem. 1187 A. D.</small>

<small>Third Crusade. Philip and Richard I.</small>

The Fourth Crusade (1196-1197) a Ger′man undertaking, was worse than useless, but the Fifth * (1202-1204), though it never reached Pal′estine, was eventful. The French barons who composed it struck a bargain with the rich republic of Venice by which the Vene′tians not only furnished naval transportation for the crusaders, but joined the expedition with a contingent of vessels and armed men under their aged doge, Hen′ry Dan′dolo. Instead of proceeding to Pal′estine they paused in the Adriat′ic to conquer certain coveted territory for the Vene′tians, then sailing to Constantino′ple they first intermeddled in the affairs of the Eastern Empire and then (1204 A. D.) besieged and took its capital, treating the Greek Chris′tians with the same barbarity of insult and cruelty which the captors of Jeru′salem had inflicted upon the Moham′medans.

<small>Fifth crusade. 1202-4.</small>

---

* Some writers omit the Crusade of 1196 and count this as the fourth.

The crusa′ders attempted to build up a Lat′in empire at Constantino′ple after the feudal model. Bald′win, count of Flan′ders, was its first emperor. The pope's authority was proclaimed in the East, the Lat′in ritual displaced the Greek in the eastern churches and it was hoped—perhaps believed—that the great schism in Chris′tendom was healed.* But it was not to be so. The crusading baron had none of the gentleness of the Christ whom he proposed to serve and his harshness produced rebellion instead of reunion. The old Greek Empire revived in many provinces. The West withheld its hand and in 1261 Mi′chael Paleol′ogos recovered Constantino′ple and started the Empire of Con′stantine and Justin′ian once more upon its path to the grave.

Latin empire of Constantinople.

Restoration of Greek Empire. 1261.

The Lat′in empire was brief, but it served more than one end. It opened a new field of trade to the Vene′tians in the Levant′ which made their city the world's commercial metropolis; and it gave the members of the Greek Church such cause for lasting hatred of the Lat′ins, that the reunion of the churches of the East and the West has ever since seemed impossible. More than this, the men of the West who visited Constantino′ple while it was under Lat′in rule, saw much that was new and strange. Con′stantine's capital had never known barbarian conquest and the Lat′ins found it stored with products of ancient art and literature of whose existence they had never dreamed. Indeed they showed the appreciation of savages for this treasure-trove, but some new sense of the beauty of order and of law, of form and of color, filtered into the western mind and first in It′aly and then beyond the Alps

Results of Latin occupation of Constantinople.

---
* Since 1054 the Ro′man and Greek churches which had been growing apart for centuries were definitely separated. Each accused the other of holding heretical doctrines.

the first faint premonitions might be noticed of the new intellectual birth by which the Mod′ern Eu′rope was to rival that "golden prime" of Rome and Ath′ens.

The era of the Crusades closed with the close of the thirteenth century. Some count seven in all, some nine, some even more, so numerous were the minor expeditions from the West to the thirsty East, whose soil drank up the blood of many thousand Chris′tian warriors in those days. There were famous figures among the later crusaders: the Emperor Fred′erick II., who had none of the old rage for "infidel" blood; Louis IX. of France, a king with the spirit of a monk and an exalted piety which—rare enough in monarchs of that age—earned for him the honors of a saint; and Prince Edward of England, afterward one of the best of her kings. But the kingdom which God′frey and his associates had founded was lost forever. In 1291, almost exactly two centuries after Pe′ter the Hermit had kindled the zeal of the West, the last of the crusaders retired from Pal′estine and the Moham′medan was left in undisturbed possession.

Later Crusades.

Although the Crusades failed of their purpose to clear the Holy Land of the infidel, they wrought momentous changes in Eu′rope. In the first place they had postponed the term of the Eastern Empire which with all its weakness was a barrier against Turkish invasion. The Church, assuming to inspire and direct them and to collect funds for them in all Chris′tian states, had intruded its authority upon new territory and the pope had greatly increased his authority over merely secular lords. The feudal system broke down under the new conditions; the greater vassals pledged or sold their estates to crown or Church for funds to equip their private armies. In the general financial stress many cities purchased privileges and immunities from their overlords and became

Effect of Crusades on Europe.

Weakening of feudal system.

practically self-governing. Contact with the luxury and learning of the East awakened slumbering desires in the western heart. The blank ignorance of the tenth century never returned after Eu′rope had laid eyes upon the literature and art of Constantino′ple. Commerce throve in the Levant′ as it had not since the old Ro′man Empire, and the Ital′ian city states, Pi′sa, Gen′oa, and above all Ven′ice, which controlled this trade, were filled with the palaces of merchant princes. Out of the half spiritual, half military spirit of the Crusades′ developed the orders of knighthood—the Knights Templar, the Hos′pitallers, and the Teuton′ic Knights, who added to the monastic vows the oath of eternal hostility to the infidel.

Chivalry. Three crusading orders.

The thirteenth century was the dawn of a better era for Eu′rope. Since the light of the old Græco-Ro′man civilization had been dimmed and well-nigh quenched by the barbarian flood, there had been but fitful gleams through the earlier Middle Ages, but from the latter years of the twelfth century to the end of the thirteenth the flame increased with unprecedented steadiness and power, the old shadows began to fade, and men of hope might now for the first time in almost a thousand years hazard the prophecy of a future that should outshine the brilliancy of antiquity. The Lat′in and Teuton′ic kingdoms entered upon their course of separate national development and at the same time art, science, letters, and religion took on new life. We may now review rapidly the progress of the several Europe′an states from the thirteenth century to the end of this period.

The thirteenth century.

In 1138 the crown of the Ger′man kingdom and with it the sovereignty of It′aly and the right to be crowned Ro′man emperor came to the family of Ho′henstauf′en. The great emperors of this house, Frederick (I.) Barbaros′sa, Henry

VI., and Frederick II. were involved in fresh difficulties with the papacy, growing out of their claims to the sovereignty of the cities of Northern It′aly in which the spirit of independence was vigorously at work. Barbaros′sa, strong and beloved in Ger′many, was baffled and beaten in his contests with the Lom′bard cities and their ally the pope. His son, Henry VI., (1190-1197) was snatched away by death in the midst of magnificent designs for the aggrandizement of the Ger′man monarchy. The minority of Frederick II. (1212-1250) gave the popes an opportunity to crown and discrown emperors as the earlier emperors had made and unmade popes. The second Frederick was not so easily handled. Of indomitable spirit, the flower of chivalry, a scholar, a poet, and a lover of the fine arts, he cared little for the papal excommunications. But the Church stirred up a swarm of enemies against him, deposed him, and set up two rival emperors in Ger′many.

The empire under the Hohenstaufen. 1138-1254.

The pope triumphed over the empire; the Ho′henstauf′en family was extinguished and the power— but not the name—of the Holy Ro′man Empire came to an end. Southern It′aly passed to French (An′gevin) and afterward to Span′ish (Aragonese′) princes, and the cities of Northern It′aly acquired substantial freedom. The Great Interreg′num (1254-1273), which left the Ger′man throne unoccupied or scrambled for by several claimants, gave a staggering blow to Ger′man unity. The feudal states, which Barbaros′sa had inspired with some sense of pride in a common Ger′man fatherland, drifted apart again in the absence of their feudal head. The Ger′man portion of the empire dissolved into a great number of states— dukedoms, counties, principalities, lordships, and free cities. In 1273 Ru′dolf of Haps′burg was elected emperor, rather to supply a visible point of union for the Ger′man states than

Italy divided.

The Great Interregnum. 1254-1273.

to wield the power of his predecessors. The right of choosing the emperor became vested in an electoral college of seven great lords (three archbishops and four laymen) and the imperial office was gradually shorn of its power. From the election of Albert II. in 1438 to the dissolution of the Holy Ro'man Empire in 1806 the dukes of Aust'ria were, with but two exceptions (in 1742 and 1745), elected emperors, making use of the office to increase the personal possessions of their own family of Haps'burg, now the imperial and royal house of Aust'ria-Hun'gary.

The Hapsburg emperors.

The thirteenth century which witnessed the fall of the Ho'henstauf'en, saw the papacy at the culmination of its power. The popes, as the promoters of the Crusades', were more than ever the spiritual directors of Chris'tendom, the estates of the Church in It'aly and abroad were enormously increased by gifts and unredeemed pledges of crusading tenants, and the right of the pope to excommunicate temporal sovereigns for neglect of their crusading vow was exercised against emperors and kings. Innocent III. (1198-1216), perhaps the ablest of the entire papal line, realized in his own person Hil'debrand's dream of papal supremacy. It was in these years (1208-1229) that the heretical sect of the Albigen'ses in Southern France was harried out of existence by a religious war under the papal orders. The Inquisi'tion was established in 1229 to crush out the remnants of this heresy. The same era saw the rise of the two mendicant or begging orders, the black-friars of St. Do'minic (1216) and the greyfriars of St. Fran'cis (1223), who sought by preaching and by incessant clerical labors to establish the ascendancy of the Church over the common people as the pontiff' had established it over their rulers. The missionary zeal and self-

The papacy in the thirteenth century.

Innocent III.

Albigenses. Inquisition. Friars.

sacrifice of these consecrated men carried them everywhere and won back to the Church the masses who had become disgusted with the immoralities of parish priests and the wealth and worldliness of the monks and prelates.

Although relieved to a great degree from their ancient rival, the emperor, the popes found the French kings quite as dangerous. The haughty Bon'iface VIII., attempting to oppose the laws of Phil'ip IV. of France, found himself openly defied. The king, determined to be master of his own kingdom, was powerful enough to secure the election of his own candidate for the pontificate, and in 1309 the French Pope Clem'ent V. abandoned Rome and fixed his court at Avignon' on the French border, where it remained under French influence until 1376, this sojourn being afterwards termed the "Babylo'nish Captivity." The return to Rome was followed almost immediately by a contested election which divided the West in the support of rival popes. This "Great Schism" which was not healed until 1417—following the period of subserviency to France—shook the hold of the Ro'mish Church upon the nations of Chris'tendom and prepared the way for the Prot'estant Reformation whose pioneers, the Eng'lish Wyc'lif (1324-1384) and the Bohe'mian Huss (1373-1415), had already lived out their noble lives. The general councils (at Pi'sa, Con'stance, and Ba'sel) which were convened in the hope of reuniting and reviving the Church, failed to effect its real reform. The old abuses continued and the popes, gradually losing their super-national position, found their temporal authority limited to the "States of the Church"—the Ital'ian lands donated to them by Pip'in and his imitators.

Boniface VIII. and Philip IV.

The Babylonish Captivity.

Decline of the papacy.

The French and Eng'lish monarchies, of which we witnessed the beginnings in the tenth and eleventh centuries, were greatly strengthened in the thirteenth century and entered upon a protracted rivalry, frequently involving them in bloody warfare but crystallizing their national spirit. The conquest of Eng'land by a feudal vassal of the French king brought the two kingdoms into close and often delicate relations. By inheritance and by marriage Henry II. (1154-1189)—the first Plantag'enet king of Eng'land—was feudal lord of more than half of France. Had his descendants been of the same acquisitive turn, and had the French monarchs of the thirteenth century been as weak as their predecessors, Eng'land and France might have become a single state. But such was not the case. Henry's son Richard (1189-1199) neglected his patrimony for crusading honors, and John (1199-1216) was a knave who could not command the obedience of even his own Eng'lish, to say nothing of his continental possessions. At the same time Phil'ip Augus'tus (1180-1223), one of the most sagacious of her monarchs, occupied the throne of France, and won back four-fifths of the Eng'lish domain. While the English barons, bishops, and common people were compelling John to sign the Great Charter (Mag'na Char'ta), which guaranteed their liberties against despotic rule (1215), Phil'ip Augus'tus was getting the mastery of the French nobles and laying the foundations of an absolute monarchy. In the long reign of Louis IX. (1226-1270), called "Saint Louis," the monarchy became popular among the French people for its justice and public spirit, the authority of the crown was increased, and the feudal rights of the nobles further curtailed. By a gradual revolution the king was becoming the national sovereign of France, instead of the chief lord of a feudal aristocracy.

Rivalry of France and England.

English fiefs in France.

Philip Augustus.

Magna Charta. 1215.

Louis IX.

While the tendency in France was toward an absolute monarchy, the people of Eng'land were gaining fresh liberties. In the weak reign of John's son, Henry III., Earl Si'mon de Mont'fort summoned the representatives of the towns to a national council or parliament. The sagacious Edward I. (1272-1307) accepted the innovation and after 1292 the commons were regularly represented in parliament.

<small>The House of Commons.</small>

From 1285 to 1314 Phil'ip the Fair carried the French monarchy to fresh triumphs. Fortified by quotations from the ancient Ro'man law codes which taught the absolute supremacy of the monarch, he trampled upon feudal usages and the privileges of the Church. This was the king who dared defy Pope Bon'iface VIII. and burn his bulls, and he it was who made the papacy his tool and brought about the Babylo'nish Captivity.

<small>Philip the Fair.</small>

Edward the Third (1327-1377), the grandson of Edward the First, claimed the throne of France by descent from his mother, the daughter of Phil'ip the Fair. The war which broke out in 1339 lasted, with brief breathing spells, for more than a century. In the first period of the war (1339-1360) Eng'land conquered a large section of France. This soon slipped away, but Henry V. (1413-1422) was even more successful; taking advantage of a civil war, he invaded France and became its master, governing most of the country as regent. Again it seemed as if France and Eng'land would obey a single monarch, but Jeanne Darc ("Joan of Arc"), a poor French peasant girl, put new courage into fainting hearts and changed defeat to victory. The Eng'lish were driven out of one province after another, until in 1453 their

<small>Edward III. claims the French crown.</small>

<small>The Hundred Years' war. 1339-1453.</small>

<small>Jeanne Darc.</small>

possessions in France had shrunken to a few seaports and the Channel Islands.

The Hundred Years' war impoverished France and made such havoc among the nobles that the kings of the succeeding century were able to shake off the remaining trammels of feudalism. The war taught Eng'land to depend upon herself. Her monarchs forgot their French blood in their wars with France and became more thoroughly Eng'lish. The corrupted French tongue, which had prevailed among the upper classes since the Nor'man conquest, gave way to the Eng'lish language, which had been kept alive by the common people. Trade was brisk with the towns of the Low Countries, the Hansa cities of Ger'many and the merchants of Flor'ence, Gen'oa, and Ven'ice.

Results of the war.

Our period closes with the empire reduced to a name, Ger'many and It'aly disunited, France on the high-road to absolutism, Eng'land arrived already at a government of comparative freedom. It remains only to take a broad and hasty view of the minor Europe'an states, and of the general state of civilization.

The minor kingdoms.

While the Eng'lish, French, and Ger'mans were doing battle in the East for the recovery of the Holy Sepulchre, the Christian peoples of the Span'ish peninsula were prosecuting a crusade against their Moham'medan neighbors. Prowess in these wars made Ruy Diaz, called the Cid, (died 1099) the hero of his nation.

Spain recovered from the Moors.

The expansion of the Chris'tian power made room for the kingdoms of Castile' and Ar'agon, and in 1139 Port'ugal, recently recovered from the Moors, began its separate national existence. Reduced at last to the kingdom of Grana'da the Moham'medans held out with wonderful tenacity. It was not until late in the fifteenth century that the Span'ish monarchy was united

Castile. Aragon. Portugal.

by the marriage of Ferdinand of Ar′agon with Isabel′la of Castile′ and not until the year of Colum′bus' momentous voyage that Grana′da yielded and the Moham′medans retired from Spain forever. They left their mark, not merely in the graceful architecture of Alham′bra and Alcazar′, but even more deeply in the sternness, cruelty, and religious zeal, which seven centuries of unremitting warfare with an alien and infidel race had burned into the Span′ish heart.

The Spanish brand.

The three Scandina′vian countries, from which the North′men had gone out to colonize or conquer Southern Eu′rope and to invigorate the southern races, received Christian′ity from the Ger′mans near the beginning of the eleventh century. They went their own way, taking small part at this time in the affairs of Western Eu′rope. In 1397 the three crowns of Nor′way, Swe′den, and Den′mark were united by the Union of Cal′mar, which outlasted the fifteenth century.

Scandinavia.

East and south of Ger′many lay Po′land, Bohe′mia, Hun′gary, Switz′erland, and Bur′gundy. Po′land, a Slavon′ic state, once tributary to the emperors, became independent during the Great Interreg′num and remained a separate kingdom until its partition between Rus′sia, Aust′ria, and Prus′sia a century ago (1795). Bohe′mia, a kingdom after 1198, remained within the empire but was joined in the fifteenth century to the motley dominions of the Haps′burg family to whom it still belongs. Hun′gary, the kingdom of the Magyars, had to bear the brunt of the invasion of the Mon′gols in the thirteenth century, and later of the Ot′toman Turks. In the fifteenth century its crown was acquired by the Haps′burgs of Aust′ria, to whom, after some interruptions and changes of tenure, it still belongs.

Fragments of the empire.

Poland.

Bohemia. Hungary.

Switz′erland was the one land which even the greedy Haps′burgs could not hold. The liberty-loving mountaineers of the "forest cantons," U′ri, Schweiz, and Un′terwald′en, took up arms to resist the Aust′rian dukes in 1307. Their victory at Morgar′ten (1315) brought other cantons into the confederacy and later triumphs (1386-8) over the Aust′rians gave them the freedom which they maintained until the French Revolution.

Switzerland.

The unimportant kingdom of Bur′gundy (or Arles), lying between the Rhone and the crest of the Alps, which since 1032 had been a dependency of the empire, was in the years of imperial decrepitude gradually absorbed by France.

Kingdom of Burgundy.

Prus′sia, with which we are familiar as a powerful monarchy, was scarcely known in the Middle Ages. Its original Slavon′ic inhabitants were conquered and converted by the Teuton′ic knights, returned crusaders, in the thirteenth century. The lands were colonized by Ger′mans and became part of the Margraviate of Bran′denburg which was acquired in 1411 by a nobleman, Frederick of Ho′henzol′lern, the twenty-fifth lineal ancestor of the present Prus′sian sovereign.

Prussia.

Under the princes of the Scandina′vian house of Ru′rik the Slavon′ic Rus′sians came in contact with the Greek emperors at Constantino′ple, and in the eleventh century adopted Chris′tianity according to the Greek Church. The development of a united nation was checked in the thirteenth century by a Mon′gol invasion as ruthless as that of At′tila. The national forces rallied at length about Mos′cow and in the fourteenth century entered upon the arduous task of conquering and expelling the Asiat′ic hordes that had occupied the Rus′sian steppes. The work was finished in the

Russia adopts Greek Christianity.

Mongol occupation.

last quarter of the fifteenth century, but it had so absorbed the energies of the people that the nations of the West had far outstripped them in the march of civilization.

Rus'sia was not the only sufferer from Asiat'ic invasion. In the thirteenth century the Mon'gol chieftain, Gen'ghis Khan, and his descendants swept like a consuming pestilence from Eastern As'ia to Central Eu'rope. Ar'ab and Chris'tian alike went down before their swarms of Tar'tar horsemen. In their track the Ot'toman Turks from Central A'sia moved westward in the fourteenth century, making prey of the outlying provinces of the Greek emperors on both sides of the Bos'phorus. The territory of the Eastern Empire was reduced to a narrow strip around its ancient capital; its rulers were weak, its people few and dispirited. Ruin seemed inevitable, when suddenly the Turks under their sultan Baj'azet were confronted and beaten by the Tar'tar conqueror Tam'erlane (1402). The destruction had merely been postponed. The Turks resumed the aggressive; western Chris'tendom withheld her succors; in 1453 Con'stantino'ple fell, and with it the last of the Cæ'sars, Con'stantine XII., and the last visible vestige of the empire of old Rome. The city which Con'stantine the Great had built for a Chris'tian capital became the seat of the Ot'toman Empire, and the historic church of Saint Sophi'a was transformed into a Moham'medan mosque. From the Dan'ube to the three seas the entire Balkan' peninsula became Turk'ish soil.

Asiatic invasions. Genghis Khan.
Ottoman Turks.
Fall of Constantinople. 1453.

In traversing the history of this period we have had scarcely a word for any events beyond those of politics or war. But momentous changes were taking place in the heart of these nations whose external growth we have been reviewing. The establishment of peace

Internal changes.

and order was encouraging industry and commerce, on the fruits of which the common people, for whom the Feudal System made no adequate provision, were rising to wealth and claiming recognition in the State. The universities—Par′is, Bologn′a, Ox′ford, and others—were thronged with eager students, whose minds the writings of the Greek poets and philosophers awakened to a new sense of the truths and beauties of creation, and a new confidence in the dignity and power of humanity. Literature blossomed afresh in the poetry of the Proven′cial Trou′badours, the Nor′man Trouvères′, the Ger′man Min′nesing′ers, in Bocca′ccio, the story teller, in Pe′trach, and Dan′te, the masters of Ital′ian song, and in our Eng′lish Chau′cer. In the universal re-awakening of human powers the fine arts had their share. Cimabu′e of Flor′ence in the thirteenth century, and the other North Ital′ians who carried on his work, began to paint from nature as they saw it, ceasing to copy the conventional designs and colorings handed down through the Dark Ages. Sculpture joined in the movement. Architecture achieved its greatest triumphs. For eleven centuries the church-builders of Chris′tendom had played their variations upon the Ro′man style—the Roman′esque combinations of round arch and vault and column. In the twelfth century a new style, the distinguishing feature of which is the pointed arch, made its appearance, possibly copied from Oriental buildings by returned crusaders. France brought this so-called "Goth′ic" style to its perfection, but it is seen in most of the Europe′an cathedrals of this golden age of church-architecture — structures which no modern builders have surpassed.

Revival of learning.

The golden age of architecture.

In 1453 the distinctive marks of the Middle Ages were disappearing one by one. The Crusades′, the rise of the burger-class, the concentration of power in royal hands, the revo-

lution in warfare occasioned by the invention of gunpowder—
all these were death-dealing blows to the Feudal
System. The repeated failures of the Holy Ro'-
man Empire had exposed the difficulty of re-
alizing the mediæval theory of a universal Chris'-
tian state; and the rise of individual kingdoms, distinct in
language and in interests, had disposed of that tempting dream. Physical force, the ruling principle of this
period, might read its sentence in the stirrings of a new intellectual life; and the spiritual authority of the Ro'mish
church was doomed when men learned to prove all things by
the test of reason. The time had come for the assertion of
the rights of the individual—his rights of body, of mind, and
of spirit—and their assertion is the distinguishing feature of
the epoch which may be said to open in the fifteenth century,
the modern epoch in which we have our lives.

The passing of the Middle Ages.

ANALYSIS OF CHAPTER IX.

Preliminary: Features of mediæval history, 238, 239.
Europe in the eighth century, 239.

I. *The Frankish restoration of the Roman Empire*, 240-247:
Alliance of Pipin and the papacy, 240.
" The Donation of Pipin," 240.
Charles the Great (Charlemagne), 240-244:
Character and career, 241.
Coronation as Roman emperor, 241.
Extent and organization of Charles' empire, 242.
Significance of his reign, 243.
Disruptive tendencies in the empire, 244.
Descendants of Charles the Great, 244, 245:
Partition treaty of Verdun, 244, 245.
Decay of the Carlovingian family, 245.
The Feudal System, 245-247:
Its origin and essence, 246.
Weakness of the feudal king, 246, 247.
Feudal army and law courts, 247.

II. *The Normans in Europe*, 247-252:
    The Northmen in Scandinavia, 247, 248.
    The Northmen in England, Iceland, Russia, 248.
    The Northmen in France, 248-250:
        Duke Rollo of Normandy, 248, 249.
        "The Birthday of Paris," 249.
        Assimilation of the Normans, 249, 250.
        Overthrow of Carlovingians, 250.
        Starting point of French history, 250.
    The Normans in Italy, 251.
    Saxon and Dane in England, 251.
    The Norman Conquest of England, 252.

III. *The Holy Roman Empire*, 252-259:
    The kingdom of the East Franks, 252:
        Its Teutonic character, 253.
        Decadence under the Carlovingians, 253.
        Revival by "Henry the Fowler," 253.
        Otto the Great restores the empire, 253-255:
            Decline of Carlovingian empire, 254.
            Degradation of the papacy, 254.
            Otto crowned at Rome, 255.
        Theory of the restored empire, 255.
        Conflict of secular and ecclesiastical authority, 255-259:
            Saxon and Franconian emperors, 256.
            Reform of the papacy, 256.
            Gregory VII. (Hildebrand), 257.
                The right of investiture, 258, 259.
                Henry IV. at Canossa, 259.
                The Concordat of Worms, 259.
                Results of the struggle, 259.

IV. *The Crusades*, 260-266:
    Their object, 260.
    The appeal of emperor and pilgrims, 260, 261.
    The First Crusade, 261-262:
        The hermit Peter and Pope Urban, 261.
        The Council of Clermont, 261.
        Composition of the crusading army, 261.
        Capture of Jerusalem, 262.
        The Latin Kingdom of Jerusalem, 262.
    The Second Crusade, 262, 263:
        Saint Bernard, 263.
    The Third Crusade, 263.
    The Fourth Crusade, 263.

Capture of Constantinople, 263.
The Latin Empire of Constantinople, 264.
Results of Latin empire, 264, 265.
Later Crusades, 265.
Influence of the Crusades upon Europe, 265, 266:
Strengthening of the church and monarchy, 265.
Weakening of feudalism, 265.
Intellectual and commercial stimulus, 266.
The age of chivalry.

V. *The Individual Kingdoms,* 266-277:
The eventful thirteenth century, 266.
The Holy Roman Empire, 267-268:
    The Hohenstaufen emperors, 267.
    The Great Interregnum, 267.
    Decline of imperial authority, 267.
    The Hapsburg emperors, 268.
The papacy, 268-269:
    Culmination under Innocent III., 268.
    The Albigenses and the Inquisition, 268.
    The Dominicans and Franciscans, 268.
    Babylonish Captivity, 269.
    The Great Schism, 269.
    Decline of the papal power, 269.
Rivalry of France and England. 269-272:
    Intimate relations under Normans and Plantagenets, 270.
    Philip Augustus saves France, 270.
    Saint Louis strengthens the French monarchy, 270.
    Magna Charta and the English Parliament, 270, 271.
    Philip IV. and the popes, 271.
    The Hundred Years' War, 271, 272.
The minor kingdoms, 272, 274:
    Spain and Portugal, 272.
    The Scandinavian kingdoms, 273.
    Poland, Bohemia, and Hungary, 273.
    Switzerland and Burgundy, 274.
    Prussia, 274.
    Russia, 274.
Invasions from Central Asia, 275-277:
    The Mongols of Genghis Khan, 275.
    The Ottoman Turks, 275.
    The Tartars of Tamerlane, 275.
    The end of the Eastern Empire, 275.
    Progress in the arts of civilization, 276, 277.

REVIEW EXERCISE.

Fifth Period. Europe in the Middle Ages. 752-1453 A. D.

1. Mention eight leading subjects of mediæval history.
2. Mention ten famous persons of the Middle Ages—four kings, four poets, and two national heroes.
3. State briefly the political condition of Europe in 750 A. D.
4. How did Pipin pay the pope for his crown?
5. Who was Charles the Great?
6. When, where, and by whom was Charles crowned emperor?
7. What was the extent of Charles' empire and how was it organized?
8. What were the lasting results of Charles' reign?
9. What caused the Frank empire to break up?
10. What partition of the empire took place in 843 A. D. ?
11. What two modern nations were foreshadowed by the treaty of Verdun?
12. What was the character of Charles' descendants?
13. What two causes hastened the breaking up of the Frank empire?
14. What is the probable origin of the Feudal System?
15. What was the essence of feudalism?
16. What was the position of a feudal king?
17. What is said of the feudal army and law courts?
18. When did the Northmen enter Europe?
19. What were some of the achievments of Northmen in the ninth century?
20. Where is Normandy?
21. What gave Paris its earliest prominence?
22. What was settled by the treaty of Clair-sur-Epte?
23. What transformation took place in the West Frankish kingdom?
24. What may be termed the starting point of French history?
25. What state did the Normans found in Southern Europe?
26. What was the condition of England in the tenth and eleventh centuries?
27. On what grounds did William the Norman claim England?
28. How did England profit by the Norman conquest?
29. In what respect did the East Frankish kingdom differ from the other barbarian kingdoms of Western Europe?
30. What difficulties beset the East Frankish kingdom?
31. What monarchs (father and son) revived the East Frank (or German) kingdom?

32. What became of the empire under Charles' successors?
33. To what degradation had the papacy sunk?
34. What was the theory of Otto's "Holy Roman Empire"?
35. Why was a conflict of emperor and pope inevitable?
36. What emperors raised the imperial authority to its highest pitch?
37. What pope undertook the reform of the church?
38. How did the quarrel in regard to "Investitures" originate?
39. What was the famous incident of Canossa?
40. What was the Concordat of Worms?
41. What were the results of the struggle of the popes and the emperors?
42. What were the Crusades?
43. What preacher and pope were connected with the First Crusade?
44. What did the First Crusade accomplish?
45. What is the history of the "Latin Empire of Constantinople"?
46. What did the Crusades do for Europe?
47. What were the three orders of crusading knights?
48. What century gave most brilliant promises of the future?
49. Name the leading emperors of the Hohenstaufen line.
50. What was the condition of the empire after the Great Interregnum?
51. Under whom did the papacy reach its prime?
52. What events and causes contributed to the decline of the papacy?
53. What opposite characters did monarchy assume in France and England?
54. What circumstances formed the Spanish character?
55. When did Switzerland achieve its freedom?
56. What is the place of Prussia in this period?
57. With what difficulties had Russia to contend?
58. Describe the fall of Constantinople.
59. What is said of the progress of civilization in and after the thirteenth century?

CHAPTER X.

CONCLUSION.

MODERN EUROPE. FROM THE FALL OF CONSTANTINOPLE (1453 A. D.) TO THE PRESENT TIME.

IT IS impossible to point to any single event in the history of Eu′rope and say, "At this point modern history begins; all that precedes is old and dead." For the current of history is one, and though its flood is swollen by frequent and powerful affluents, it undergoes no sudden transformation. Forces are active in this closing decade of the nineteenth century, whose germs the historical student can trace to the Ath′ens of Per′icles and the Gal′ilee of Her′od. The year 1453 is selected as the starting point of modern history, because the fifteenth century was really an epoch-making century, and because the capture of Constantino′ple by the Turks marks the disappearance of the Eastern Empire of Rome, one of the landmarks of ancient history.

Gradual development of history.

We have attempted in the preceding chapters to sketch the progress of events which mark the transition from the empire of Rome to the states of modern Eu′rope. It is the purpose of these concluding pages to touch lightly upon the salient characteristics of this modern period. These characteristics may be roughly grouped under three heads: (1) Liberation of the human mind; (2) The admission of the common people to

Characteristics of the modern period.

political rights; and (3) The development of the "national idea." We will look at each in turn.

The wonderful thirteenth century, of which mention has already been made, saw the stirrings of the spirit which was to emancipate the human mind from the bonds of authority; to enable the painter to come face to face with nature, untrammeled by the canons of art; the architect to consult the needs of his time and his own sense of beauty, to the neglect of antique models; and the Chris'tian to worship God according to the light of the Bible and his own conscience, without fear of excommunication, pope, or ecclesiastical council. The fresh, free thought of the great Greek philosophers, the grace and beauty of their poets, were brought to the western kingdoms, driven thither, one might say, by the Turk'ish conquest of Constantino'ple, where Greek scholars had cherished through all these ages the precious heritage of their race. There sprang up in the universities of It'aly and Ger'many and France and Eng'land an ardent zeal for the Greek studies, and the students of the new learning, the "humanists," as they were called, were inspired with something of the old Greek ardor for all things human, and the old belief in the race and its capabilities. It'aly was the first to profit by the new impulse. Mi'chael An'gelo (1475-1564) and Raph'ael (1483-1520), and a score of their country-men, of slightly inferior genius, were contemporaneously busy with brush or chisel producing works worthy of Praxit'eles or Phid'ias. From It'aly the revival of art spread over all the West.

Liberation of the human mind.

The revival of learning.

The Renaissance.

The invention of printing by means of movable types—which is variously ascribed to Dutch and Ger'man* artisans

---

* The best accredited candidates for the honor of the invention are John Koster of Haarlem, 1438; John Fust of Mentz, 1442; and John Gutenberg of Strasburg, 1450-56. William Caxton set up a press in London in 1470.

Invention of printing. of the middle of the fifteenth century — contributed enormously to the rapid diffusion of learning by manifolding copies of the Bible and the precious manuscripts of the classical authors, and placing literature within reach of men of limited means.

The revival of learning received more hearty encouragement from princes than from the Church, for among its first results was to lift the attention of reading and thinking men out of the narrow ecclesiastical and theological channels in which mediæval thought had been confined, and fix it upon secular matters—upon the facts of nature and speculative questions concerning the deepest problems of existence. Men ventured to test the Church itself, its doctrines, its organization, the conduct of its priests and pontiffs by the Bible and the enlightened conscience. The Protestant Reformation was the outcome of this revolt against authority.

Effect upon the Church.

The Middle Ages had had their reformers—men who had striven to restore the Church to its primitive simplicity and to substitute personal religion for the ritualism of the Ro′mish system. The Eng′lish Wyc′lif in the middle of the fourteenth century, and Huss, the Bohe′mian, in the first years of the fifteenth, had preached a purer faith ; but ecclesiastical persecution had restricted their influence to a narrow circle. A century, almost to a year, from the burning of Huss (1415), the young Sax′on monk, Mar′tin Lu′ther, nailed his ninety-five theses against "indulgences" to the door of Wit′tenberg Church (1517), and thus set in motion a new Reformation. Originally a loyal but discriminating Cath′olic, Lu′ther's opinions led him step by step into an attitude of opposition to the pope. The emperor—the powerful Charles V.—pronounced against him, but he had the support of

Mediæval protesters.

Martin Luther.

some of the leading nobles of the empire, and gained a strong hold upon the popular heart. In an imperial diet or convention of representatives of the states of the empire, held at Spei′er in 1529, the followers of Lu′ther protested against the imperial order prohibiting the new doctrines—hence the name "Protestants," which now attaches to millions in Eu′rope. Meantime Zwing′li had preached the reformed doctrines in Zu′rich and, soon after, Cal′vin introduced them at Gene′va. From Gene′va the new doctrines entered France, where the powerful sect of Hu′guenots sprang up, and Scot′land, where John Knox impressed them upon the people. Thanks to an opportune personal quarrel of Henry VIII. and the pope, Eng′land joined the reforming tide. By the close of the sixteenth century the Scandina′vian kingdoms, the northern states of Ger′many, and the island of Great Brit′ain had renounced the authority of the pope and reorganized their churches without monks or nuns, with a married priesthood, with vernacular preaching, and with the free circulation of the Scriptures—together with many other departures from the old order in government, rite, and doctrine.

"Protestants."

Spread of Reformation.

In Ger′many the two religions failed to dwell together in harmony. The earlier wars settled the right (1555) of each prince and free city to choose the form of worship which should obtain in their dominions. But the bitter feeling resulted in fresh outbreaks, one of which, the Thirty Years' War (1618-1648), embroiled all Northern Eu′rope and further destroyed the crumbling fabric of the old empire and impoverished its members. By the peace of Westphalia (1648), however, Cath′olic and Prot′estant were placed on an equality in the affairs of the empire.

Religious wars in Germany.

The Reformation did not sweep over Eu′rope, although its earlier years promised complete and rapid conquest. In the

Council of Trent (1545-1563), the Cath′olic Church pulled itself together, and, retracting nothing of the offensive dogmas, undertook to carry out certain necessary reforms in the character and training of its priesthood. But before the ponderous machinery of the church could be started, one man of enormous energy and foresight, Igna′tius de Loyo′la (1491-1556), had organized the Order of Jes′uits, which held the Lat′in nations to their loyalty to Rome and carried the Ro′mish faith to the remotest corners of the widening world. More than anything else it was the labors of the Jes′uits that fixed the bounds to the revolt from the old Church.

The anti-reformation.

The Society of Jesus.

From Alexan′der to Cæ′sar, from Cæ′sar to Char′lemagne, from Char′lemagne to the fall of Constantino′ple, the Mediterra′nean Sea had been the world's highway and the surrounding countries had comprised practically all that was known of the inhabited world. We have seen Scandina′via, Ger′many, and Rus′sia emerge late enough from the outer darkness, and had we looked closer we might have heard an occasional adventurer, like Mar′co Po′lo, the Vene′tian, tell of a land of astonishing wealth and a strange civilization lying beyond the deserts of A′sia. But it was reserved for the last decade of the fifteenth century for the Por′tuguese and Span′ish navigators, trusting in the newly utilized magnetic compass, to make discoveries which should revolutionize geographical knowledge, and materially alter the course of Europe′an history. In 1492 Colum′bus, searching for the golden East, gave to Spain a new world in the western sea. In 1498 Vas′co de Ga′ma, sailing eastward around Af′rica, discovered a water-route to In′dia and opened to Por′tugal the commerce of that wealthy land. These voyages were but two out of the

The Œcumene or "Inhabited World."

Modern geographical discovery.

Spanish and Portuguese navigators.

hundreds that were undertaken in that age when Eu′rope entered upon the career of expansion which has peopled the western hemisphere and colonized a considerable portion of the older continents and the islands of the sea.

The first result of the new discoveries was to remove the commercial center of Eu′rope from the Mediterra′nean cities to those of the Atlantic. Ven′ice and her sisters lost their eminence and the wealth of the Indies fell to the Span′ish and Por′tuguese markets, to Lon′don and the merchants of Hol′land. At the same time the series of wars between the Emperor Charles V. and Fran′cis I. of France for the possession of It′aly dissipated the accumulated resources of the Lom′bard cities and left them weak or enslaved.

Change of trade routes.

Italy impoverished.

The modern spirit working against old forms gave us the Protestant Reformation, elevated the grade and extended the benefits of education, cast off the restraints of ignorance and superstition and gave us modern science, quickened the spirit of invention and gave us the present age of industrial development when the subjection of steam and electricity and the use of machinery have given mankind a mastery over the material world surpassing the dreams of the ancients.

The Emancipation of the Modern Mind. Summary.

A second feature of the modern period has been the rise of the common people, the free citizen, or "burgher," class. Feudalism bound the landless man to the soil to live a sunless life as a serf—little better than a slave. In the Middle Ages the dwellers in cities acquired a degree of freedom, which grew apace in the trading towns of It′aly and North Ger′many, and in the manufacturing towns of France, and the Low Countries. In Eng′land the Great Charter and the Commons' House of Parliament from the thirteenth

The Rise of the Commons. Democracy.

The Commons in the Feudal Age.

century further protected the middle class in the state. But between the government of the feudal nobility and the era of democracy the kingdoms of Western Eu′rope had in most cases to pass through a period of despotism, when the monarch, having beaten down the feudal nobles, gathered their powers into his single hand and exercised untrammeled authority until the people wrested it from his grasp.

Through Despotism to Democracy.

In Eng′land the Wars of the Roses (1455-1485), between the rival princes of York and Lan′caster, embroiled the kingdom in a civil war which extinguished many a noble family, destroyed the castles (which from Nor′man times had been so many fortresses against the sovereign), and left the field free for Hen′ry Tu′dor and his strong willed progeny to establish a tyranny. Their successors, the Stuart kings, lacking the Tu′dor tact and popularity, overstrained the loyalty of their subjects, and by their tyrannous rule brought on the Civil War. Under Crom′well the people of Eng′land abolished the monarchy, and after the brief restoration of the Stuarts (1660-1688) the Revolution of 1688 firmly established the authority of Parliament. Subsequent events have only served to admit the Eng′lish freemen in increasing numbers to the fullest political rights.

England: The Tudor Tyranny.

The Stuarts. Cromwell. Revolution of 1688.

In France the struggle was fiercer and more protracted. By degrees the tenacious family of Ca′pet made themselves masters of the kingdom which, in the first Hugh's time (987), had been but a weakly tied cluster of powerful dukedoms. Louis XI. (1461-1483), Louis XII. (1498-1515), and Fran′cis I. (1515-1547) were sovereigns in fact as well as in name, and kept down the nobility as well as the middle class. The remnant of the century is filled with the religious wars, Cath′olic against Prot′estant.

Rise of monarchical power in France.

From them the monarchy emerged stronger than ever, and before the close of his seventy-two years' reign (1643–1715), the "grand monarch" Louis XIV. could point to himself and say,

Louis XIV. "I am the state." "*L'etat c'est moi!*" The despotism which his genius had maintained became intolerable oppression under his successor (Louis XV. 1715–1774), and in 1774 Louis XVI. found France on the brink of insurrection. Of good intentions but lacking in resolution, the young king

The French Revolution. failed to meet the demand for reform and at last (1789–1792) the French Revolution swept all before it—monarchy, nobility, privilege of every sort. The new ideas of "liberty," "equality," and "fraternity," the watchwords of the Revolution, were caught up all over Eu′rope, and there was a mighty trembling of thrones and gathering of soldiers in the Ger′man and Aus′trian dominions to protect the ancient order. But out of the revo-

Napoleon Bonaparte. lutionary army came a citizen-soldier, Napo′leon Bo′naparte, who made himself master of France, and France the virtual arbiter of Eu′rope. The united powers of Eu′rope crushed him at Waterloo′ and in

Reaction. Congress of Vienna. the Congress of Vien′na rearranged the disturbed map of Eu′rope. Blind to the profound meaning of recent events, the kings attempted to restore unaltered the despotism of the anti-revolutionary epoch. But

The years of Revolution. 1830–1848. the tidal-wave could not be quenched; 1830, the "year of revolution," saw risings in the name of more liberal government in France, Bel′gium, Po′land, and elsewhere. The conflagration spread; in 1848 France again cast out her king and became a republic; the Ger′man and Ital′ian states thrilled with new hopes of liberty, and Kos′suth raised the Hunga′rians against Aus′tria. But President Louis Napo′leon subverted the French Republic and erected the second empire; while

Aus'tria, backed by the Rus'sian Czar, roughly repressed the popular aspirations of Ger'many, It'aly, and Hun'gary—repressed, but not destroyed, for in France the second empire has given place to the third republic, while Aus'tria herself with Hun'gary, Prus'sia with her sister states of the new Ger'man Empire, and even It'aly, free and united, within the past fifty years all have placed substantial limitations upon the power of the monarch, and secured to the masses of free citizens a considerable share in the enactment of the law. In the last decade of the nineteenth century the Czar remains the only autocrat in Eu'rope.

Triumph of Liberal ideas.

The Czar the only despot in Europe.

Modern Eu'rope then has witnessed the abolition of slavery and serfdom, the decline of aristocratic privilege, the disuse of private war and justice. The home of the private citizen is his castle, which the law of the land defends as valiantly as mailed men at arms defended the keep of their feudal lord. Dukes and counts and marquises still exist as titles of honor, but like the humblest laborer, they must obey the law. Liberty and legal equality have dawned and men scan the eastern sky for signs of a brighter social day.

The rise of the common people. Summary.

A third characteristic of the modern period has been the awakening of the several nations to a sense of their unity and necessary independence. Rome succeeded in bringing the civilized world into one universal state and the greatest minds of the Middle Ages —always looking backward out of the chaotic present—strove to realize the same design. Char'lemagne and Ot'to had this before them when they obtained the sanction of the popes to their "Holy Ro'man Empire," which in its best estate fell short of its ideal, a universal Chris'tian state. The great mediæval popes, from Hil'debrand

The growth of the national spirit.

Unity; the mediæval idea.

to Bon′iface VIII., proclaimed the same doctrine, though in the condition which they saw prefigured in the Word of God, the successor of Pe′ter was to be above all emperors and kings. The tendency of modern times has been toward independent statehood and the encouragement of national churches.

The Middle Ages had their separate states and kingdoms, but the sense of national loyalty pervading all grades of society was scarcely known until modern times.

Class feeling instead of national loyalty. In the earlier epoch the aristocracy of the several kingdoms had more in common with each other than with the lower classes in their own state. But the growth of trade and the persistence of long feuds, like the Hundred Years' War between the kings of France and Eng′land, bound upper and lower classes together

Beginnings of patriotism. by a sense of common interest, and begot a pride in the national language, customs, and institutions. Under the modern conditions of warfare, consequent upon the introduction of firearms, a national army of foot-soldiers took the place of the mailed horsemen who formerly followed the flag of their feudal chief; here again loyalty to a national king supplanted the feudal allegiance to a lord who might wage war with his neighbor or even with his own sovereign.

Spain consolidated its nationality through a duel with the Moham′medan power, which was not ended until the conquest of Grana′da in 1492. For another century

Spain. under Charles I. (1516-1556) and Phil′ip II. (1556-1598), Spain lavished the wealth of the Indies upon an attempt to build up a comprehensive Cath′olic state, and then sank back into the exhaustion, ignorance, and superstition from which it has not yet recovered. From 1580 to 1640, "the sixty years' captivity," Por′tugal was included in the Span′ish monarchy.

The national fortunes of France and Eng′land we have

already followed in reviewing the progress of modern constitutional liberty. Of the Scandina′vian countries it is enough to say that Swe′den broke away (1523) from the Union of Cal′mar, and has remained independent, its king receiving Nor′way, also, at the hands of the Congress of Vien′na in 1815. The three kingdoms early embraced the Lu′theran reforms and the Swe′dish king Gusta′vus Adol′phus was the Protestant hero of the Thirty Years' War.

<small>Scandinavia.</small>

Under Pe′ter the Great, (1689-1725), Rus′sia was awakened rudely enough from the slumber of ages, and brought into the circle of western civilization and western politics, where its ambition, coupled with diversities of government, race, and creed, have made its influence as alarming as it has been important.

<small>Russia.</small>

Strangely enough, the Ger′mans were among the last to awake to a consciousness of their own unity, and the Ger′man Empire is the creation of a generation which has not yet quite disappeared. The influences which perpetuated the divisions in Ger′many may be traced directly to the Holy Ro′man Empire. The Ger′man kings of the Middle Ages were great and powerful and bore their part in the making of Eu′rope, but the very extent of their authority was gained by neglecting the affairs of their Ger′man kingdom. While they were beyond the Alps seeking the crown of the Ro′man Cae′sars and fighting their unwilling subjects in Northern and Southern It′aly, the dukes and counts were making themselves the real rulers of Ger′many, and after papal opposition, feudal insubordination, and Ital′ian revolt had overthrown the Ho′henstauf′en, the Ger′man prince-electors and petty nobles became virtually independent. The Haps′burg dukes of Aus′tria, who in time attached Bohe′mia, Hun′-

<small>Germany.</small>

<small>Unity sacrificed to the imperial idea.</small>

<small>Aggrandizement of the Hapsburg princes.</small>

gary, the Neth'erlands, and other states to their family possessions, were, one after another, elected emperors, but their authority—save in the hands of a few sovereigns abler than their kinsmen—was merely nominal. In the eighteenth century in the place of a united Ger'man nation there were more than three hundred Ger'man states, from Aus'tria with its millions of subjects to some petty principality with an army of a corporal's guard. When Napo'leon began smashing the old boundaries and overturning the crusty forms of Ger'man mediævalism, these little states collapsed by the score. It was time to drop the curtain upon the farce of the Holy Ro'man Empire—" no longer holy, nor Ro'man, nor an empire," said the wit of the age. On the 6th of August, 1806, Fran'cis II. resigned the old imperial dignity and, assuming the new title of hereditary emperor of Aus'tria, retired to the government of the Haps'burg dominions. "One thousand and six years after Le'o the Pope had crowned the Frank'ish king, eighteen hundred and fifty-eight years after Cæ'sar had conquered at Pharsa'lia, the Holy Ro'man Empire came to its end,"* to quote its most acute historian.

Francis II. becomes emperor of Austria.

End of the Holy Roman Empire. 1806.

After the Napoleon'ic cyclone had swept by, the Vien'na Congress of the Powers (1814-1815) tried to set the empire on its feet again, re-uniting the Ger'man states—now shrunken in number to thirty-nine—into a "Ger'man Confederation", a loose league of kingdoms and states overshadowed by the strength of Aus'tria and distracted by the rivalry of Prus'sia.

The German Confederation. 1815-1866.

Of Prus'sia there is a word to say before completing our tale of the unification of Ger'many. While the Haps'burgs, with the prestige of the imperial crown, were building up their

---

*Bryce: *Holy Roman Empire.*

motley monarchy in the southeast, the family of Ho′henzol′-
lern was winning a patrimony in the northeast.
The Rise of Prussia. The first of them was Margrave of Brand′enburg
in 1415. From the seventeenth century they were
electors of the empire. In 1701 the Elector Frederick took the
title of King of Prus′sia. The political and military genius of
his grandson Frederick (II.) the Great made Prus′sia a first-rate
military power—the natural rival of Aus′tria.

The Ger′man Confederation brought the two powers face to
face. The liberal ideas disseminated by the French Revolution,
Rivalry of Prussia and Austria. the spirit of Ger′man nationality kindled by poets
and statesmen, and by Ger′mans fighting shoulder
to shoulder for a common fatherland in the war
which drove Napo′leon beyond the Rhine (1813-1815), had borne
fruit and the despots of Ho′henzol′lern and Haps′burg could
not repress it. For a moment during the revolutions of 1848,
when Aus′tria was beset by rebellions, the Prus′sian king
might have become the head of a new Ger′man Empire; but
he faltered; Aus′tria recovered herself, and the old disunion
was restored. But new men came to the front in Prus′sia, the
next king, William I., called Bis′marck and Molt′ke and
Von Roon about him. They perfected the army and in the
Triumph of Prussia. 1866. brief campaign of 1866 drove Aus′tria out of the
confederacy. By maneuvers as skillful, Prus′sia
gathered the Ger′man states about her in the war
with France (1870–1871), and in the burst of patriotic feeling
engendered in that year of Ger′man victory, the
The German Empire. 1871. princes and people enthusiastically united to form
a Ger′man federal empire with the king of Prus′-
sia for its hereditary sovereign.

Side by side with the Ger′man Empire, but independent of
it, stands Aus′tria-Hun′gary, a union of Aus′trian kaiser and
Mag′yar king in the person of the Haps′burg Fran′cis Jo′seph.

Besides these states, three other independent kingdoms have arisen out of the ruins of mediaeval empire. The Low Countries, or Neth'erlands, lying about the mouths of the Rhine, inhabited by a thrifty and liberty-loving people, passed in the sixteenth century, soon after their conversion to Protestantism, into the hands of intolerant Catholic Spain. After forty years of stubborn resistance the independence of the Dutch Republic was recognized. From this, by a series of internal changes, has come the modern kingdom of the Neth'erlands. The Catholic provinces of the Neth'erlands were constituted a separate kingdom (Bel'gium) in 1830-31.

The Rise of the Dutch Republic.

Netherlands and Belgium.

Our history closes where it began—with It'aly. From the time of Al'aric the Goth until yesterday the most beautiful region of Eu'rope was the prey of the foreigner. Goth and Van'dal, Lom'bard and Frank, Nor'man and Sar'acen, Ger'man, French'man, Span'iard, and Aus'trian, have in their turn wrangled over its soil and made spoil of its cities. The kings of the Ger'mans, in their character of Ro'man emperors, were ever interfering in Ital'ian affairs, but never bringing the whole peninsula under a stable government or evoking a thought of a common nationality. After the thirteenth century the emperors seldom visited It'aly. This was the era of the Renaissance in the Lom'bard cities, the flowering-time of literature and art and architecture. The discovery of Amer'ica, with the innovations in trade, blighted the prospects of the Ital'ian cities and left them to be fought for and parted among the sovereigns of France, Spain, and Aus'tria. Again the advent of Napo'leon, before whom the foreign princes fled from their thrones in It'aly, set the spark of national spirit aglow in the Ital'ian breast, and although the

Foreign Rulers of Italy.

The German Emperors.

Italy in the Renaissance.

Foreign Domination.

reactionary Vienna Congress (1814–1815) restored the tyrants, the spark was unquenched. It flamed up fitfully in the "Young It′aly" movement of 1831–33. It blazed out threateningly in 1848 but was trampled down by the armed heel of Aus′tria. Vic′tor Emman′uel, the faithful King of Sardin′ia, guided by the statesman Cavour′ and spurred on by Mazzi′ni and Garibal′di, took up the cause of united It′aly and after years of diplomacy and war established the kingdom of It′aly (1861) which since 1871 has extended from the Alps to the sea. Even the states of the Church, the ancient "donation of Pip′in," joined the youthful kingdom, and left the pope, the self-styled "prisoner of the Vat′ican," to bewail the loss of his temporal power.

Birth of National Spirit.

United under Victor Emmanuel.

"The prisoner of the Vatican."

The Turks, who at the dawn of this period were entering Eu′rope in the full vigor of conquest, were repeatedly checked on the upper Dan′ube and in the Adriat′ic, and after the seventeenth century ceased to be aggressive. In the eighteenth century the Chris′tians took on the offensive. Rus′sia extended her power to the Black Sea. Aus′tria pushed down toward the Bos′phorus. The Turk′ish state became more enfeebled. Greece broke away from it (1829). Turkey was "the sick man of Europe," and the great powers began to be anxious concerning the disposition of his property. The western nations suspected Rus′sia of designs on Constantino′ple and to prevent their execution France, Eng′land, and Sardin′ia helped Tur′key to beat off a Rus′sian attack in the Crime′an War (1854–1856), and Eng′land interfered in 1877 in time to save Constantino′ple from the Czar. The disappearance of the decaying Turk′ish power from Eu′rope is only a question of time, and the fate of the capital on

Turkey in Europe.

"The sick man of Europe."

Russo-Turkish wars.

The Eastern Question.

the Bos′phorus is one of the unsolved problems of modern history.

Our task is done. Turning back for a moment from our survey of Modern Eu′rope, we may see in the remote past the little band of La′tian settlers fixing their precarious hill-fortress upon the banks of the Ti′ber.

<small>Concluding summary.</small>

We see them fighting under their local chieftains for the supremacy of the surrounding villages, then under consuls and Senate setting out to conquer It′aly and the world. Their genius for government brings all the Mediterra′nean nations to live in peace and happiness under a universal law. Military revolution places a single sovereign—the emperor—in the place of the Senate, but the unity is undisturbed, "the empire is peace," but peace too long continued, and prosperity unbounded, beget luxury and sloth. The stern fiber of the conquerors grows flaccid. The population diminishes in numbers and vitality. In these degenerate days millions of warlike Ger′mans quit their homes in the northern forests and dash against the imperial defenses. All devices to stay the onset are exhausted. The flood breaks through and from the Black Sea to the ocean the barbarian mingles with the old population. Christian′ity, which has prevailed in the last days of the empire, is a force strong enough to subdue the newcomers and the Ro′man law commands their respect. Out of the association spring the Lat′in nations of the West—French, Span′ish, Ital′ian; the northern nations—Eng′lish, Ger′man, Scandina′vian—preserve their language but adopt the religion and civilization of the South. The Moham′medan Arabs throw themselves against

<small>Rome.</small>

<small>The decline and fall.</small>

<small>Christianity and law.</small>

<small>The Latin and Teutonic Kingdoms.</small>

these nascent kingdoms, but are checked at the Pyr'enees and finally driven back to Af'rica. The empire in the West has fallen before the inrush of barbarians, but the Frank, Charles the Great, revives it, and with the coöperation of the bishop of Rome will reassert its universal sway. In the incompetence of his descendants and the influx of new hordes of barbarians, the North'men or Nor'mans, it goes down. But Ot'to, the Ger'man, lifts it from the dust and makes it great. In a great awakening impulse western Chris'tendom takes the Cross and hurls itself against the Sar'acens, bringing East and West into contact after long separation, making the popes supreme above temporal rulers and undermining the feudal system which had prevailed in Eu'rope since the barbarian conquest. In a duel for the mastery—emperor against pope—the empire falls. Ger'many splits into a hundred petty states not to be brought together until our own day. It'aly is parcelled among the nations to remain a "mere geographical expression" until in the nineteenth century. Eng'land and France rise by friction upon each other. Turks from A'sia plunder the east of Eu'rope, and capturing Constantin'ople wipe out the Ro'man Empire of the East. But the West takes up the old Greek learning that the East has cherished. The human mind shakes off the trammels of a thousand years, and the world swings into the path of progress. A new world rewards Colum'bus's search for a short road to the back of the old. Religion revives and the Protestant Reformation lets the light of liberty and education into the darkened mind. Science comes with invention and industry. The modern era has dawned—the era of revolt against the old

The Mohammedan Invasion.

Charles the Great.

The Holy Roman Empire.

The Crusades.

Pope vs. Emperor.

The Turks in Europe.

The Renaissance.

CONCLUSION. 299

forms, the era of the reign of reason, the era of the free man in a free state.

<small>The Future.</small> Wonderful has been the progress of the world in these modern times. For many generations after the fall of the Ro′man Empire men were accustomed to look back upon the system and civilization of Rome as the acme of human attainment and sighed for the return of the " good old times " which seemed forever gone. As the year 1000 A. D. approached a great dread came over Chris′tendom that the times were accomplished and the end of the world was at hand. With what opposite feelings do we approach the dawn of the twentieth century! The past has been fruitful, the present abounds in human achievements not matched in any previous epoch, but our gaze is turned toward the future with high hope, with firm faith.

> " Not in vain the distance beacons. Forward, forward, let us range,
> Let the great world spin forever down the ringing grooves of change.
>
> " Through the shadow of the globe we sweep into the younger day;
> Better fifty years of Europe than a cycle of Cathay! "

ANALYSIS OF CHAPTER X.

Preliminary: Gradual Development of History, 282.
Characteristics of Modern History, 282.

I. *Liberation of the Mind*, 283-287:
  The Revival of Learning, 283.
    The Renaissance, 283.
  The Protestant Reformation, 284-286:
    The anti-reformation, 286.
    The Society of Jesus, 286.
  Geographical Discoveries, 286-287:
    New trade routes, 287.
  Summary of Progress, 287.

II. *Rise of the Common People (Democracy)*, 287-290.
  The Commons in the feudal age, 287.

300 ROME AND THE MAKING OF MODERN EUROPE.

  Through Despotism to Democracy, 288-290:
   England, 288:
    Tudors and Stuarts, 288.
    Cromwell, and the Revolution of 1688, 288.
   France, 288-290:
    The kings crush the nobility, 288, 289.
    The French Revolution, 289.
    Napoleon I., 289.
    From the restoration to the third republic, 289, 290.
  Constitutional liberty in the nineteenth century, 290.
  Summary of democratic progress, 290.
III. *Growth of National Spirit*, 290-297:
  The mediæval idea of a universal state, 290, 291.
  The beginnings of patriotic feeling, 291.
  Spain and Portugal, 291.
  Scandinavia, 292.
  Russia, 292.
  Germany, 292-294:
   Unity sacrificed to imperial idea, 292.
   Aggrandizement of the Hapsburgs, 292, 293.
   The Austrian Empire, 293.
   End of Holy Roman Empire, 293.
   The German Confederation, 293, 294.
   Rise of Prussian kingdom, 293, 294.
   Triumph of Prussia over Austria, 294.
   The German Empire, 295.
  Austria-Hungary, 294, 295.
  Holland and Belgium, 295.
  Italy, 295, 296:
   Under the empire, 295.
   Foreign domination, 295.
   United under Victor Emmanuel, 296.
  Disintegration of Turkey, 296.
   The Eastern question, 296.

  Concluding summary, 297-299.

REVIEW EXERCISE.

Conclusion. Modern Europe. From the Fall of Constantinople to the present time. 1453-1893 A. D.

1. Why is 1453 taken as the beginning of the modern period?
2. Under what three heads may the characteristics of this period be grouped?

3. To what source may we trace the revival of learning?
4. What spirit marked the Renaissance?
5. What German invention aided the spread of the new learning?
6. How did the new mental attitude affect the Romish church?
7. When and where did Martin Luther live?
8. Whence is the name "Protestant" derived?
9. To what countries did the Reformation spread?
10. What commotions did Protestantism cause in central Europe?
11. By what agencies was the Reformation circumscribed and checked?
12. How was the geographical knowledge of the world extended in this period?
13. Mention some results of the new discoveries.
14. Summarize briefly (see p. 287) the intellectual development of Europe in this period.
15. What was the condition of the common people under feudalism?
16. How did the English Tudors establish their despotism?
17. When did the English citizen class reassert its constitutional rights?
18. What shattered the French despotism?
19. To what extent has constitutional liberty triumphed in the past fifty years?
20. What was the mediæval ideal of political organization of Europe?
21. In what did national loyalty begin?
22. What has been the national career of Spain?
23. What is said of the Scandinavian kingdoms?
24. What monarch brought Russia into the affairs of western Europe?
25. What causes left Germany divided while England and France became great nations?
26. When did the Holy Roman Empire cease and the Austrian Empire begin?
27. What rival had Austria in the German Confederation?
28. Describe the course of events which led to the founding of the German Empire.
29. What circumstances postponed the union of Italy?
30. By whose efforts was Italy "redeemed?"
31. How did the union of Italy affect the temporal power of the pope?
32. What state is called "the sick man," and why?
33. Contrast the attitude of the nineteenth century with that of the tenth.

INDEX.

Aachen, 243, 245.
Actium, battle of, 151, 157.
Ædiles, 57.
Ægusan Islands, battle of, 77.
Aëtius, 212, 214.
Africa, Punic settlements in, 73; Roman province of, 92; Cæsar in, 141, 142; Vandal kingdom in, 211, 212; recovered by Belisarius, 220; conquered by Arabs, 227.
Agrarian law, 58.
Agricola, 177.
Agrippa, 147, 151; at Actium, 152, 157; builds Pantheon, 161.
Agrippina, 169.
Aix, 243.
Alaric, 207, 208.
Alans, 209.
Albigenses, 268.
Alboin, 221, 222.
Alexander Severus, 190.
Allemanni, 191.
Allies (socii), 70.
Allobroges, 127.
Ancyra, monument at, 165.
Antioch, 87.
Antiochus, 87, 88, 90.
Antoninus Pius, 182, 183.
Antony (Marcus Antonius), 137; Cæsar's friend, 138, 140; funeral oration, 146; joins Octavianus, 147; triumvir, 148; in Egypt, 149-151; defeat and death, 152, Apennines, 10.
Aquæ Sextiæ, battle of, 112.

Arabs, conquest of, 227-229; driven from Spain, 272, 273.
Arcadius, 204, 207.
Arian heresy, 208, 220, 224.
Arminius, 164.
Asculum, battle of, 69.
Ataulf, 208, 210.
Attila, 213-215.
Augusti, 192.
Augustus, as a title, 158.
Augustus (see also Octavianus), 158; preserves republican forms, 159; provinces under, 159, 160; buildings, 160, 161; literature, 162; his wars, 162-164; death and deification, 165.
Aurelian, 191.
Austrian Empire, 293.
Austria-Hungary, 294.
Avignon, popes at, 269.
Babylonish captivity, 269.
Bajazet, 275.
Barbarians menace the empire, 184, 185; character, 205; migration of, 206; in imperial armies, 206, 207; overrun the empire, 207-230.
Baths, Roman, 161.
Belisarius, 220, 221.
Beneventum, battle of, 70.
Bernard of Clairvaux, 263.
Boëthius, 219.
Bohemia, 273.
Boniface, Count, 212.
Boniface, Pope, 269.
Boniface, Saint, 231.
Brennus, 62.

Britain, Cæsar in, 135; Roman conquest resumed, 170; Agricola in, 177; Hadrian in, 181; conquered by Anglo-Saxons, 211.
Brutus, M. J., 145, 146, 148, 149.
Burgundians, 209, 223.
Burrhus, 170.
Byzantium, 201.
Byzantine Empire, 205.
Cæsar, Julius, 119; in democratic plot, 126; votes "No," 128; his early career, 133; in First Triumvirate, 134; in Gaul, 135; breach with Senate, 136; crosses Rubicon, 137; the civil war, 137-143; dictator, 139; settling the State, 142; assassinated, 145.
Caligula, 168.
Camillus, 62.
Cannae, battle of, 83.
Canossa, scene at, 259.
Canuleian law, 61.
Capet, Hugh, 250.
Capri, Tiberius at, 167.
Capua, joins Hannibal, 84.
Caracalla, 189.
Carlovingian Franks, 227, 232, 250.
Carrhae, battle of, 136.
Carthage, empire of, 73, 74; wars with Rome, 73-92; state in Spain, 78, 79; destroyed, 92.
Cassiodorus, 219.
Cassius, C., 145, 148; defeat and death, 149.
Cassius, Spurius, 58.
Catilina, L. S. (Catiline), 126.
Cato, M. P. ("The Censor") 91, 95.
Cato, the Younger, 128, 134, 135, 141, 142.
Catulus, Q. L., 77.
Caudine Forks, battle of, 67.
Celtiberians, 93.
Censors, 61.
Chæronæa, battle of, 117.
Châlons, battle of, 214.
Charlemagne, see Charles the Great.
Charles Martel, 227, 229, 231.
Charles the Great, 240-243.
Christianity, progress of, 201, under Constantine, 202, 203.

Christians, persecuted by Nero, 171; by Domitian, 176; by the good emperors, 186.
Cicero, M. T. 126; consulship of, 127, 128; a trimmer, 141; relation to assassins of Cæsar, 144; against Antony, 147; death, 148, 149.
Cimbri, invasion of, 111.
Cinna, L. C., 118-120.
Cisalpine Gauls, enfranchised, 148.
Citizenship, restrictions removed from Roman, 189.
Clair-sur-Epte, treaty of, 249.
Claudina II., 191.
Claudius, Appius, 60.
Claudius, Cæsar, emperor, 169, 170.
Cleopatra and Cæsar, 140, and Antony, 149, 151, 152, and Octavianus, 152, 153; death, 153.
Clermont, council of, 261.
Clodius, Publius, 135.
Clovis, 223, 224.
Colonies, Roman, 67; character of, 68; in Cisalpine Gaul, 78.
Colosseum, 175.
Comitia Centuriata, 55; changes in, 102; under Augustus, 159.
Comitia Curiata, 54, 55.
Comitia Tributa, 56, 59, 64.
Commodus, 186, 187.
Conspiracy of Catiline, 126-128.
Constantine the Great, 193, 194, 199-203.
Constantinople, founded, 201; baffles the Huns, 213; baffles the Arabs, 227; taken by Crusaders, 264; fall of, 275, 296.
Consuls, 54.
Corpus Juris Civilis, 220.
Corinth destroyed, 92.
Coriolanus, 58.
Crassus, M. L., consul, 123, his position, 131; Triumvir, 134; death, 136.
Crusades, 260-266.
Curio, 137.
Cynoscephalae, battle of, 88.
Dacia, 206.
Dacians, defeat Domitian, 177; conquered by Trajan, 179.

INDEX.   305

Darc, Jeanne, 271.
Dark Ages, 233.
Decebalus, 179.
Decemvirs, 60.
Decius, 190.
Deification of emperors, 165.
Delenda est Carthago, 91.
Denmark, 248.
Dictator, 54.
Didius Julianus, 188.
Dietrich of Bern, 220.
Diocletian, 192, 198.
Discoveries, 286.
Division of empire, 204.
Doles of food, in republic, 107; under empire, 162.
Domitian, 174, 176.
Donation of Pipin, 240, 296.
Drusus, M. L., 108, 113.
Drusus, Nero, 163.
Duilius, C., 75.
East, conquest of, 86-91.
Eastern Empire, 204, 205.
East Goths, 217; in Italy, 218-221.
Elagabalus, 189.
Empire (Roman), established by Augustus, 157-166; remodeled by Diocletian, 192, 198, 199; reformed by Constantine, 199-202; divided by Theodosius, 204; "end" of western section, 216, 217; revived by Charles the Great, 241, 242; revived by Otto, 255; fall of eastern section, 275; end of revived empire, 293.
England conquered by Normans, 251, 252, 270; reformation in, 285; Wars of Roses, 288; rise of people, 288.
English conquest of Britain, 211.
Equites, 103.
Etruria, final submission of, 66.
Euphrates, boundary of empire, 180.
Exarchate, 221.
Fabii, destruction of, 59.
Fabius, Q., dictator, 82; called "cunctator," 83.
Faineants, les rois, 226.
Feudal System, 246-247.

Feudalism, common people under, 287.
Flaccus, Fulvius, 106, 107.
Flamininus, T. Q., 88.
Flavian emperors, 174-177.
Fleet, first Roman, 75.
Florence, 209.
Fœderati, 216.
Forum of Trajan, 179.
France, premonitions of, 225, 226; coalescence of Franks, Latins, and Normans, 250; Capetian kings, 250; in Crusades, 261; and the popes, 269; rivalry with England, 270-272; rise of common people, 288-290.
Franks, 199, 223-228, 231, 232, 240-246, 253.
Friars, 268.
Gabinian law, 125.
Galba, 172, 173.
Gallic wars, 135, 136.
Gaul, Cæsar in, 135, 136; invaded by Germans, 209, 210; Franks in, 223-225.
Gaul, Cisalpine, colonized, 78; conquered by Hannibal, 81; reconquered by Rome, 86.
Gauls, sack Rome, 62; settled in Po valley, 78.
Genghis Khan, 275.
Genseric, 212, 215.
German Confederation, 294.
Germanicus, Cæsar, 166, 167.
Germans threaten Italy, 111, 112; Augustus' wars with, 163, 164; character of, 205; overrun the West, 211.
Germany, invaded by Julius Cæsar, 135; resists Roman conquest, 163, 164; Attila in, 214; missions in, 231; Charles the Great in, 241; beginnings of nation, 245; un-Romanized, 252; East Frank kingdom, 253; under Henry the Fowler, 253; merged in Holy Roman Empire, 254; under Saxon and Franconian emperors, 254-259; under the Hohenstaufen, 267; under the Hapsburgs, 268; causes

of disunion, 292; the German Confederation, 294; the German Empire, 294.
Gibraltar, 228.
Glaucia and Saturninus, 112, 113.
Golden House, 171.
Gothic architecture, 276.
Goths, see East Goths, and West Goths.
Gracchi, the, 103, 106-108.
Greece, compared with Italy, 16, 17; Rome conquers, 87-89; Hadrian in, 181; independence of, 296.
Greek Empire, 205; see Eastern Empire.
Greeks in Italy, 20.
Greek language and ideas in Rome, 94; in the empire, 200, 201, in the Renaissance, 276.
Gregory the Great, 230.
Gregory VII. (Hildebrand), 257-259.
Gustavus Adolphus, 292.
Hadrian, 178; emperor, 180-182.
Hamilcar Barca, 75, 77; in Spain, 78.
Hannibal, 79; invades Italy, 80-85; after Zama, 89, 90.
Hapsburg family, 267, 268, 273, 292.
Henry IV. of Germany, 258, 259.
Henry the Fowler, 253.
Heraclea, battle of, 69.
Herculaneum, 176.
Hiero, 74, 75,
Hildebrand, 256-259.
Hohenstaufen, 267.
Hohenzollern, 274.
Holy Roman Empire, 255; end of, 293.
Honorius, 204, 207, 208.
Hortensian law, 64, 101.
Huguenots, 285.
Hundred Years' War, 271.
Hungary, 273.
Huns, 206, 207; Attila, 212-215.
Iconoclasm, 231.
Illyrian emperors, 192.
Imperator, as a title, 158.
Informers, 166.
In hoc signo vinces, 202.
Inquisition, 268.

Interregnum, Great, 267.
Investitures, 258.
Italica, 114.
Italians, 17; Roman campaigns against, 66.
Italy, 9; geography, etc., 10-17; Ethnology, 17-19; Roman conquest of, 65-70; invaded by West Goths, 207, 208; invaded by Radagaisus, 209; invaded by Huns, 214; after Vandal invasion, 216; Odoacer, King, 217; East Gothic kingdom in, 218-221; exarchate in, 221; Lombards in, 221, 231; early popes in, 230; Charlemagne in, 241, 242; included in Lotharingia, 245; Normans in, 251; in tenth century, 254; German king in, 255-259; commercial cities, 266; divided among foreign princes, 267; Renaissance in, 276; united under Victor Emmanuel, 295.
Janus, Temple of, 157.
Jerusalem, taken by Pompey, 126; taken by Pompey, 174; in Mohammedan hands, 260; taken by Crusaders, 262; kingdom of, 262; retaken by Saracens, 263.
Jesuits, 286.
Jesus Christ, born, 165; crucified, 168.
Jews, Titus conquers, 174, 175; revolt of, 182.
Jugurtha, war with, 108-111.
Julian emperors, 157-172.
Julian, the Apostate, 203.
Justinian, 220, 221.
Knighthood, 266.
Labarum, 202.
Latin nations, 253.
Latin war, 67.
Legion, 66.
Legionary emperors, 172-174.
Lepidus, 122, 146; triumvir, 148; deposed, 151.
Leo the Great, 214, 215.
Leo III., 241.
Leucopetra, battle of, 92.

INDEX. 307

Licinian laws, 63, 64.
Licinius, Augustus, 199.
Literature, Augustan age of, 162; decline of, 232; revival of, 266, 276.
Livia, Augusta, 163, 167.
Lombards, 221, 222; threaten Rome, 231; chastised by Pipin, 240; monarchy destroyed, 241.
Lorraine, origin of, 245.
Louis XIV., 289.
Louis XVI., 289.
Loyola, 286.
Lucullus, 124.
Lusitanians, 92.
Luther, Martin, 284.
Macedonia, condition of, 86, 87; conquered by Rome, 90-92.
Mæcenas, 151, 157.
Magister Equitum, 54.
Magna Charta, 270.
Magnesia, battle of, 90.
Mamertines, 74.
Manilian law, 125.
Manlius, 63.
Marcus Aurelius, 183-186.
Marius, in Africa, 110; defeats Germans, 112; tool of Senate, 113; in social war, 114; in exile, 115; returns, 118; death, 119.
"Martel," Charles, 227, 229, 231.
Masinissa, 86, 91, 108-111.
Maximian, 192.
Mayors of the Palace, 226.
Merovingians, 223-227.
Memmius, 109.
Messalina, 169.
Metaurus, battle of, 85.
Metellus, 76, 110.
Middle Ages, 238-277.
Migrations, 206.
Milan, 192; edict of, 202.
Millenial celebration, 190.
Milo, 135.
Mithridatic wars, 114-117, 124-126.
Mohammed, 227.
Mongols in Russia, 274.
Munda, battle of, 143.
Municipia, 70.

Mutiny of the Tenth Legion, 141.
Mylæ, battle of, 75.
Napoleon I., 289.
Narses, 221.
National spirit, rise of, 290.
Nero, 170-172.
Nerva, 177.
Netherlands, 295.
New Rome, 201.
Nibelungen Lied, 220.
Nicæa, council of, 203.
Nicomedia, 192.
Normandy, 248, 249.
Northmen in Europe, 247-252.
Norway, 248.
Novus homo, 202.
Numantine war, 93.
Numidia, 86, 91, 92.
Octavianus, Cæsar, 143; at Cæsar's death, 147; consul, 147; triumvir, 148; in the West, 151; conquers Antony, 152; master of Roman world, 153 (see Augustus).
Odoacer, 216, 218.
Optimates, 102.
Orchomenus, battle of, 117.
Ostrogoths, see East Goths.
Otho, emperor, 173.
Otto the Great, 254, 255.
Pagans, why so called, 204.
Palmyra, 191.
Pannonia, 163, 164.
Papacy, origin of, 229, 230; degradation of, 254; German reform, 256; struggle with empire, 257-259, 267; French domination, 269; loses temporal power, 296.
Paris, outpost against Normans, 249.
Parliament, English, 271.
Parthians, defeat Crassus, 136; Cæsar's plans against, 144; peace with Augustus, 163.
Parties, Roman, 102, 103.
Patres conscripti, 54.
Paulus, L. Æ., 83, 90.
Perpetual Edict, The, 182.
Perseus, 90.
Persians, 190.
Pertinax, 188.

Peter the Hermit, 261.
"Phantom emperors," 216.
Pharnaces, 140, 141.
Pharsalus, battle of, 140.
Philip (emperor), 190.
Philip V., of Macedon, 88.
Philip Augustus, 270.
Philippi, battle of, 149,
Philippics, Cicero's, 147.
Phœnicians found Carthage, 73.
Pipin of Heristal, 226.
Pipin the Short, 232, 240.
Pirates, Illyrian, 77, 78; Pompey exterminates, 125.
Pistoria, battle of, 128.
Plebeians, rise of, 53-65.
Plotina, 178.
Poland, 273.
Pollentia, battle of, 207.
Polycarp, St., 186.
Pompeii, 176.
Pompey the Great, in Sulla's army, 120; in Spain, 123; in Servile War, 123; in the East, 125, 126; character, 132; triumvir, 134; champion of Senate, 136-140; death, 140.
Pompey (Sextus), 141-143, 150.
Popes (see also Papacy). Leo the Great, 214, 215, 230; John, 219; Gregory the Great, 230; Leo III., 231, 241; Stephen, 240; John XII., 254, 255; Sylvester II., 256; Leo IX., 256; Gregory VII., 256-259; Calixtus II., 259; Urban II., 261; Innocent III., 268; Boniface VIII., 269; Clement V., 269.
Populares, 102.
Portugal, 92, 291.
Prætorian Guard, 166, 167; disbanded, 199.
Praetorship, 64.
Prefectures, of Constantine, 199.
Printing, invention of, 284.
Probus, 192.
Protestants, 285.
Provinces, first Roman, 77; governmental reforms, 159, 160.
Prussia, 293, 294.

Publicans, 94.
Public land, 56, 59.
Publilian law, 59.
Punic Wars, First, 75-77; Second, 79-85; Third, 92.
Pydna, battle of, 90,
Pyrrhus, 69, 70.
Quaestorship, 54; open to the Plebs, 61.
Radagaisus, 209.
Ravenna, imperial residence, 208; taken by East Goths, 218; Theodoric's capital, 219; taken by Imperialists, 221.
Reformation, 284, 286.
Regulus, M. A., 76.
Religion, old Roman, 24, 25.
Renaissance, 283.
Republic, the Roman, 52-154.
Revival of learning, 276.
Rex sacrorum, 54.
Richard, Coeur de Lion, 263.
Ricimer, 216.
Roads, Roman, 68.
Rollo, Duke of Normandy, 248, 249.
Romance nations, 226, 249, 250.
Roman Empire, revived by Charles, 242.
Rome (the city), 10, 13; topography, 21-23; legends of founding, 31-33; head of Latin league, 37; earliest history, 39-41; revolution, 51; taken by Gauls, 62; conquers Italy, 65-70; humbles Carthage, 74-86; conquers the East, 86-92; taken by Sulla, 115; taken by Marius, 118; retaken by Sulla, 121; building era in, 160, 161; burning of, 171; capital removed from, 201; taken by Alaric, 208; sacked by Vandals, 215; Charles the Great in, 241.
Romulus Augustulus, 216.
Roses, Wars of, 288.
Ruric, 248.
Russia, adopts Greek Christianity, 274; under Peter the Great, 292.
Sacred law, 57.
Sacred mount, 58, 60.

Saguntum, 79.
Samnite wars, 67-69.
Scandinavia, 247, 248, 273, 292.
Schism, The Great, 269.
Scipio, Africanus major, 84, 85; conquers Hannibal, 85; in Asia, 90; career of, 96.
Scipio, Africanus minor, 91; at Numantia, 93; character, 97; senatorial leader, 104; death, 106.
Secession of Plebs, first, 57; second, 60; third, 69.
Sejanus, 167, 168.
Seljuks, 260.
Sempronian law, 105.
Senate, republican, 54; corruptions of, 101; under Sulla, 115, 121, 122; under Cæsar, 142, 143; under empire, 159;
Seneca, 170.
Septimius Severus, 188.
Sertorius, 118, 121; in Spain, 122, 123.
Servile war, 123.
Sicily, in First Punic war, 74; a province, 77.
Slavery, 43, 94, 95.
Social war, 114.
Soissons, battle of, 223.
Spain, Carthaginians in, 78; Scipio in, 85; a Roman province, 86; Cæsar in, 143; barbarians in, 210, 211, 225; Mohammedan conquest, 227, 228; recovered, 272, 291.
Spartacus, 123.
St. Augustine, 211, 212.
St. Louis, 270.
Stilicho, 207, 209.
Statesmen emperors, 178.
Sueves, 209.
Sulla, in Africa, 110; in Social War, 114; against Mithridates, 115; takes Rome, 115; in Asia, 117; returns, 120; triumph, 121; death, 122.
Sulpicius, 115.
Sweden, 248, 292.
Switzerland, 274.
Syagrius, 223.
Syracuse, 74, 84.

Syria, 87.
Tamerlane, 275.
Tarentum, 69, 70.
Telamon, battle of, 78.
Teutoberger Forest, battle of, 164.
Thapsus, battle of, 142.
Theodoric (East Goth), 217-220.
Theodoric (West Goth), 214.
Theodosius, 204, 207.
Thirty Tyrants, 191.
Thirty Years' War, 285.
Tiberius, Cæsar, 163, 164; emperor, 166-168.
Ticinus, battle of, 81.
Tigranes, 124-126.
Tigranocerta, battle of, 124.
Titus, 174; emperor, 175, 176.
Tolosa, 210.
Tours, battle of, 228.
Trajan, 177-180.
Trasimenus Lake, battle of, 82.
Trebia, battle of, 81.
Trent, council of, 286.
Tribunes, military, 61.
Tribunes of the people, 57; altered position, 104.
Triumvirate, first, 134-136; second, 148-153.
Turks in Europe, 296.
Twelve Tables, 60.
Ulpian, 190.
Vadimonian Lake, battle of, 68.
Valens, 204, 207.
Valentinian III., 212, 215.
Valerian, 190.
Valerio-Horatian laws, 60.
Vandals, 209; in Spain, 211; in Africa, 212; sack Rome, 215; and Belisarius, 220.
Varro, 83.
Varus, defeat of, 164.
Veii, war with, 62.
Venice, founded, 214; in the Crusades, 263; prosperity of, 266; decline of, 287.
Veni, vidi, vici, 141.
Vercellae, battle of, 112.
Verdun, treaty of, 244.
Verus, L., 183, 184.

Vespasian, 174, 175.
Vesuvius, 176.
Veto, tribunician, 57.
Victor Emmanuel, 295.
Vienna, Congress of, 289, 293, 296.
Vindex, revolt of, 172.
Virginia, 60.
Veriathus, 92, 93.
Visigoths, 207; see West Goths.
Vitellius, 173.

Wallia, 209.
Western Empire, fall of, 216, 217.
West Goths, in Dacia, 206; in Mœsia, 207; Alaric, 207, 208; in Gaul, 210; in Spain, 210, 211; at Châlons, 214.
William, the Conqueror, 251, 252.
Xanthippus, 76.
Xeres, battle of, 228.
Zenobia, 192.

www.ingramcontent.com/pod-product-compliance
Lightning Source LLC
Chambersburg PA
CBHW030810230426
43667CB00008B/1149